Communicating and Organizing

Communicating and Organizing

RICHARD V. FARACE
Michigan State University

PETER R. MONGE
California State University
San Jose

HAMISH M. RUSSELL
Department of Agriculture
Melbourne, Australia

 ADDISON-WESLEY PUBLISHING COMPANY
Reading, Massachusetts • Menlo Park, California
London • Amsterdam • Don Mills, Ontario • Sydney

Copyright © 1977 by Addison-Wesley Publishing Company, Inc. Philippines copyright 1977 by Addison-Wesley Publishing Company, Inc.

All rights reserved. No part of this publication may be reproduced, stored in a retrieval system, or transmitted, in any form or by any means, electronic, mechanical, photocopying, recording, or otherwise, without the prior written permission of the publisher. Printed in the United States of America. Published simultaneously in Canada. Library of Congress Catalog Card No. 76-12794.

ISBN 0-201-01980-9
BCDEFGHIJ-HA-7987

Preface

Communicating and Organizing arises from a set of beliefs shared by the authors and by many others in the field of communication. First, given the widespread view of communication as a process involving change over time, the book should deal more with processes than with static descriptions. Hence, the use of "ing" in the title, and the attention to such communication processes as "load," "rules," "networks," etc.

Second, and perhaps more fundamental, the book should give its primary attention to communication processes in organizations, rather than review the common organizational processes that already appear and reappear in most organizational texts. After all, only insofar as communication processes become more uniquely defined and better understood in organizational contexts will they be seen as something other than "ancillary" or "intervening" factors, or some better form of the classical "poor relative" among the social science aspects of organizational behavior.

Third, to the extent possible, the book should provide a theoretic framework that will guide the student in the analysis of specific organizational communication processes. Since we lack a theory of organizational communication, we present a higher-level systems theory, structural-functionalism, which provides a step-by-step *"map"* for dealing with communication processes.

Fourth, the book should sensitize the student to some of the different types of communication processes operating at different "levels" within the organization. What are key processes involving individuals alone...manager-subordinate dyads...communication groups...or entire organizational networks? These are discussed in detail in the book.

Fifth, the book should provide sufficient realistic examples so that the student can translate the concepts presented into tangible analogies in the context of ongoing organizational experience. There are numerous such examples in the book, and, in addition, a separate Instructor's Manual contains a simulation of an entire hierarchical organization that can be used to give students highly specific organizational experiences *in common*. Taken together, the examples and the separate organizational simulation provide numerous opportunities to reify the concepts discussed in the book.

Finally, the book should present information on how organizational managers can begin outlining strategies for systematically monitoring and diagnosing the performance of their organization's communication "system"—its collective practices and procedures for handling the flow of messages into, through, and out of the organization. This topic is dealt with in the earlier parts of the book by providing the necessary conceptual base, and then given specific attention in the final three chapters.

Communicating and Organizing is divided into three parts. The first, an introductory/theoretical section, is given in the first four chapters. The second part, which includes Chapters 5 through 8, shows the applications of the conceptual framework developed in Part I to four organizational communication problems. The final section of the book (Chapters 9-11) describes the tools and procedures needed to analyze the communication processes described in Parts I and II.

In the first chapter, we do three things. We describe the kinds of communication processes which are highly important, if not unique, to the functioning of organizations. Then we describe our behavioral origins, focusing on (1) its basis in systems theory, (2) its emphasis on dyadic (often managerial) relationships, (3) its concern with the analysis and management of large-scale communication networks, and (4) its practical applications to a variety of communication situations faced by communication managers. The chapter ends with examples of communication problems which people typically encounter in large organizations.

Chapter 2 presents the three primary theoretical concepts in the work: *organization, information,* and *communication*. The focus in this discussion is not on an organization as a static entity, but rather on the *process* of organizing which people go through in creating a productive set of relationships. A distinction is made between absolute and distributed communication, and between environmental, motivational, and instructional communication. Extended examples and illustrations of these different kinds of messages are provided.

Chapter 3 provides the theoretical framework for the rest of the book. It does so by providing the reader with a set of terms from systems theory, such as system, subsystem, boundary, and inputs. The last section of the chapter is devoted to structural-functional analysis; this section suggests that we can understand complex systems, particularly organizations and their communication patterns, if we are able to identify certain key aspects of those systems.

Chapter 4 shows how the theory articulated in the first three chapters is similar to or different from *other* organizational theories. Specifically, this chapter compares several major organizational theories in terms of selected dimensions of communication. The focus throughout this chapter is on the implications of these various organizational theories for understanding the kind of communication that would occur if those theories were truly in effect.

Chapter 5 opens the second part of the book; it is devoted to the applications of the conceptual framework from Part I to specific problems in an organization. Chapter 5 considers the topic of communication load. We attempt to identify the problems that are associated with both overload and underload. Another section reviews the major research in the field regarding the causes of overload in organizational contexts. Perhaps the most important applied section of this particular chapter is the material entitled "Coping with Overload," where 16 alternative recommendations for how managers may deal with the problem of overload are presented.

Chapter 6 deals with communication rules in the organizational hierarchy. The focus is clearly on the manager/supervisor-subordinate relationship. In this chapter we introduce the notion of communication rules, which represent specific expectations regarding proper communication behavior in the organization. We also cover the notion of coorientation, a term which describes similarity in views held by two people about some topic, and the extent to which they can accurately predict the other person's view.

Chapter 7 discusses the topic of communication in the small groups located within organizations. We take the structural-functional theoretical perspective presented earlier in the book and apply it specifically to the functioning of small groups. We describe the communication structure of small groups (micro-networks) and the power and leadership structures. The key traits of small groups identified for this analysis are adaptation, control, management of feelings, and integration. It is argued that if these traits are maintained within the necessary ranges, then the group will be able to fulfill its assigned functions. The mechanism for doing so is defined as communicative interaction, which makes the structures work effectively to perform their various functions.

Chapter 8 deals with communication patterns in large organizations, or as we call them, macro-networks. In this chapter we identify communication-network members and their links. We also identify important network roles. The first of these is network members, or people who participate in the network. They are either group members or group linkers. People who do not participate are identified as isolates. An example of a network analysis of a group of 19 people is provided. We also provide examples of how these concepts may be used to analyze information flow and communication structure in large organizations.

Chapter 9, the first of three in Part III of the book, is entitled " 'Tools' for Diagnosing Communication Problems." These tools are directed primarily toward the same concepts discussed earlier in the book. We show different procedures for gathering the data for the various concepts—e.g., we describe alternative procedures for gathering network information. In another section, we describe the procedures for analyzing communication rules in large organizations.

Chapter 10 is used to outline different ways to analyze macro-networks; that is, large-scale networks. While in previous chapters we discussed what network analysis was, here we show how persons may actually undertake that kind of analysis. Some interesting differences and organizational implications can be seen quite easily from this analysis. The chapter concludes with a discussion of the implications of this type of network analysis for the health, functioning, and well-being of organizations.

The final chapter, "Managing Communication," addresses the questions of what a communication manager needs to do and know in order to manage a communication system in an organization. In a sense, it's an attempt to tell people who have chosen this kind of occupation how to utilize and apply the concepts and techniques described previously in the book. Here we talk about the need to analyze and understand communication flow within the organization, how to interact with other people in the company in order to be able to make adequate kinds of analysis, how to include communication as an important part of the job-performance appraisal, and how to help the company to develop flexible communication policies that can be modified as the changes and needs of the company are modified.

September 1976   R.V.F.
P.R.M.
H.M.R.

Acknowledgements

The preparation of this book absorbed our time and energy in what, from our perspective, was a classical example of communicating and organizing processes. As we became committed to the task of writing, it was clear we would be subject to the same processes of organizational creation, maintenance, and, ultimately, dissolution, that we had often read about or seen firsthand. It became necessary for us to develop specialized functions, to coordinate our contributions, and to adhere to rudimentary control procedures. Implementing feedback mechanisms between East Lansing, San Jose, and Melbourne renewed our beliefs in the role spatial separation plays in hindering rapid and efficient interaction. On the other hand, this same condition opened informational resources to us that would have otherwise gone unused. We have tried to be sensitive to the information richness in the environment for many of the ideas expressed in the book.

Following the time-line from the inception of the book, we would like to recognize the useful comments, criticisms, suggestions, and assistance of the following individuals:

- Our reviewers, Len Hawes, Ted Benedict, and Bob Wendlinger, who made the types of remarks that not only pointed out inadequacies but took the crucial further step of suggesting viable solutions.
- Our associates, Jim Danowski, Georg Lindsey, Don MacDonald, Mike Pacanowsky, and Bill Richards, who developed innovative, substantive conceptual inputs, unique to each person.
- Our associates, Janie Edwards, Jennifer Shelby, and Teri Albrecht, who provided important reviews and critiques of the text, and who also supplied thorough and detailed editorial services. The diagrams and figures were redrawn and improved for us by Kathy Clyde.
- Our partners in the production process at Addison-Wesley, who were competent and gracious—and gracious and competent. Rather than break company policy and name them, we will be most happy to provide references on request.

Consequently, it is clear that a dynamic, highly interactive goal-oriented organization arose from the collective actions of the individuals we have mentioned. We would like them to receive much of the credit which may accrue to the book. However, in front of us sits one of those tacky but accurate plastic signs, "The Buck Stops Here." Thus, for whatever errors there are in our thinking or presentation, we assume final responsibility. The mechanism operating amongst the three of us for dealing with errors is our own trade secret and cannot be divulged.

The authors also wish to acknowledge the Office of Naval Research Organizational Effectiveness Research Programs. Chapter Eight, "Communication Patterns in Organizations," was supported by the Office of Naval Research Organizational Research Programs, contract no. N0014-75-C-0445; Peter R. Monge, principal investigator.

There is one other acknowledgement we are pleased to make; it is of sufficient added importance to place it separately on the following page.

To Rebecca Archey, for conceiving, designing, and executing the artwork that appears on the cover and throughout the book. She combined her extensive organizational experience and artistic talent to express many of the key ideas that we pursue in the text.

Contents

Part I The Conceptual Framework

Chapter 1	Introduction.. 3	

Communication in the organizational context 3
Approach of the book 7
Analyzing "communication": specific examples 9
Plan of the book.. 13

Chapter 2   Organization, Information, and Communication............ 15
Organization 15
Information: a basic discussion 21
The concept of communication: some further distinctions 41
Summary... 45

Chapter 3   A Structural-Functional Framework for
Organizational Communication........................ 47
Systems terminology 48
Communication: by level, function, and structure 50
Structural-functional analysis 60
Summary... 68

Chapter 4   Some Communication Implications of Major
Organizational Theories............................... 71
Organizational communication: concepts 75
Selection of organizational theories 77
Analysis of organizational theories...................... 79
Systems theory—contingency theory 90
Conclusion.. 93

Part II Applications of the Conceptual Framework

Chapter 5 *Communication "Load"* 97
What is load? 100
How can load be measured? 103
Comments on the determinants of load 105
Consequences of underload and overload 108
Coping with overload 115
Summary 124

Chapter 6 *Communication "Rules" in the Organizational Hierarchy* 127
The concept of communication rules 129
The inevitability of different rule expectations 133
Communication rules: content rules and procedural rules 135
Communication rules: some specific examples 138
"Coorientation" on communication rules 141
Beyond agreement and accuracy: "realization" 147
Some empirical findings 147
Comments on applications 152
Summary 153

Chapter 7 *Communication in Organizational "Groups"* 155
What constitutes a group? 156
The structure of small groups 157
Small-group traits 168
The mechanism: communicative interaction 172
How the mechanism operates 175
Summary 175

Chapter 8	Communication Patterns in Organizations—	
	"Macro-Networks"................................	177
	Communication networks: basic concepts	180
	Summary	203

Part III Diagnosing and Managing Communication

Chapter 9	"Tools" for Diagnosing Communication Problems............	205
	Studying communication networks and flow	207
	The analysis of communication "rules"....................	214
	Other diagnostic communication tools....................	223
	Summary	224
Chapter 10	Macro-Network Analysis—Procedures and Uses	227
	Assessing the work network	227
	Assessing the innovation network	231
	Comparison between networks	234
	Some descriptors for company X: group and individual	236
	Further comments on applications of network analysis........	245
	Summary	246
Chapter 11	Managing Communication..............................	248
	What does a communication manager do?	252
	Communication management: some specific examples	253
	Summary	258
	Bibliography	261
	Author Index	273
	Subject Index	277

The Conceptual Framework

I

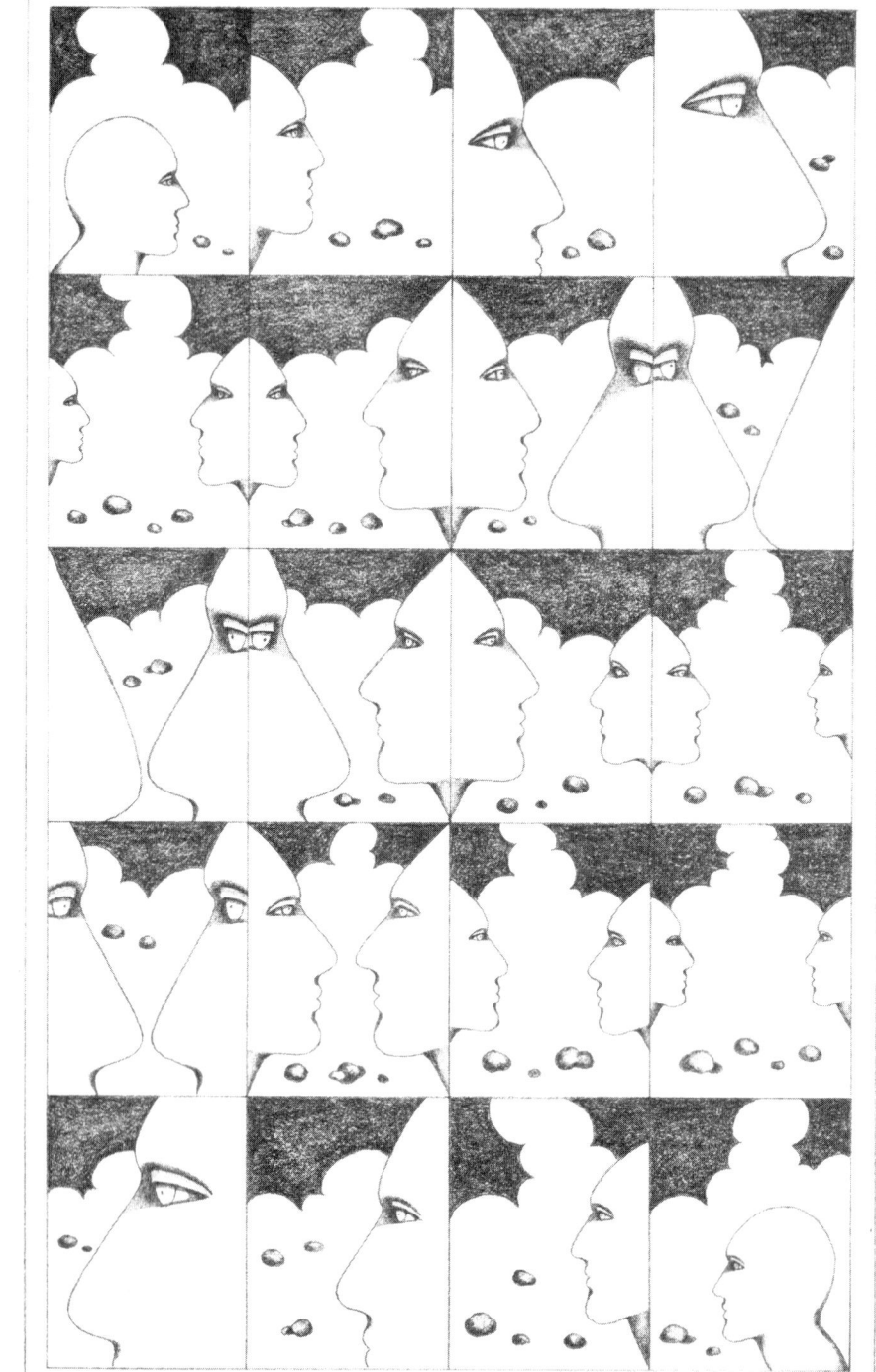

Introduction 1

COMMUNICATION IN THE ORGANIZATIONAL CONTEXT

It is a commonplace observation in contemporary society that organizations continually affect—if not control—most of our life's activities from birth to death. We usually enter the world with the assistance of services from a health care organization, returning to such organizations more often than most of us would like. Large-scale, complex organizations typically provide us with the basic necessities of life: food, shelter, clothing, protection from "enemies," knowledge, relaxation, etc. Most of us spend our working lives in organizations, in return for a potpourri of physical and social rewards. The ability to organize—to routinely engage in interlocked behaviors that allow us to transcend our individual limitations—is one of humanity's most highly developed talents.

Academicians have, by and large, parceled out segments of these organizing processes for careful scrutiny. Some of this effort is spent "to learn how things work"; other effort, often in concert with the first, is spent on applications of this knowledge to important, immediate organizational problems. For example, there is much work going on in such areas as employee satisfaction and morale, motivation, enrichment or simplification of organizational tasks, finance and accounting, improved management skills, organizational development and change, and bargaining and negotiation.

Our particular interests concern the *communication processes in organizations*. By this we basically refer to the processes for gathering, processing, storing, and disseminating the communication that enables organizations to function. Organizations need to collect messages to help their members decide what to do and how to do it. Once gathered, these messages must be processed—selected or rejected, according to the procedures in effect at the time. Some messages are retained, i.e., stored for future use, while others are distributed to members of the organization or to the environment outside the organization.

The authors have conducted research in a wide variety of settings, under the auspices of academia and as direct consultants to organizations. We will report some of the results of our research in this book in order to illustrate selected points. Our *primary* emphasis, however, is on presenting a synthesis of our views on how to conceptualize key communication processes in organizations. Success at this level is a necessary prerequisite for productive research and effective organizational communication problem solving.

There are four major reasons why we have prepared this book. First, the operation of organizations at the societal level is, in our opinion, a critical factor in determining the long-term ability of humanity to survive. To the extent that we can make a contribution to the improvement of organizational functioning—or assist others in doing so—we will feel rewarded.

Second, when we turn to the question of the emergence of robust communication theory, we consider organizations to reflect some distinctive features that should help us broaden our knowledge about communication in general. For example, person-to-person *communication networks* are critical to the functioning of organizations, but they are more accessible for study and theory-building in organizations than in society as a whole.

Third, communication in organizations is appearing as a distinctive area of scholarly interest. Increasing numbers of people from various academic disciplines have begun working in this area and a "snowball" effect seems to be taking place. As the area has become more clearly recognized as societally important so the need to develop communication theory becomes more urgent.

Fourth, the fruits of work in organizational communication offer a number of practical, pragmatic implications for the current operation of organizations. Some direct benefits that the work in this area offers include improving the quality of life of organizational members and improving the production/profit aspect of certain organizations.

A more cautious interpretation of these comments is also in order. We do not pretend to offer a systematic theoretic conceptualization of communication processes in organizations. Nor do we feel that the problem-definition and problem-resolution approaches we have used readily answer all of the communication-related difficulties that organizations now face. It would be inaccurate as well as pretentious to indicate success on either front. Our hope is to convey what we have learned and to inspire others to take our initial efforts and significantly improve them. Given this caveat, we will return to a more optimistic portrayal of the role and importance of communication in organizations.

Today, it is no longer surprising to learn that "communication processes (and problems) occupy an increasingly large part of the activities engaged in by members of an organization." The trend is clear, and unlikely to reverse: more and more of the resources and energies of an organization are being devoted to communication activities such as seeking information, reading, writing, listening to talks, maintaining personal contacts inside and outside the organization, attending committee meetings, and "pushing papers." As this trend continues, a larger proportion of employee evaluation will depend on their efficiency as "communication managers" in different organizational settings. Since a larger proportion of organizational resources is devoted to communication activities, these activities necessarily become one of the larger segments of the organization's overall budget. Currently, the organization often attempts to control these expenditures by issuing such low-level orders as "don't use the photocopy machines too much." Organizational members are increasingly expected to show the specific *performance* achieved by their communication activities: they are expected to show the linkage between their use of communication resources and the work they complete.

What are other trends that will alter the nature and importance of communication-management skills in organizations? One trend involves the management of "communication networks"—the movement of messages throughout the organization. "Network management," as one part of "communication management," confronts the organizational member with increasing impact and urgency. It seems clear that as organizations grow in size, complexity, and sophistication, there are increasing levels of specialization among their members. These factors make the role of coordinator (or liaison) an increasingly important one if the various organizational "parts" are to mesh coherently. In turn, the role of communication becomes more critical. The tolerable errors of today will become unacceptable in the future.

One kind of "unacceptable error" may occur if the organization's communication networks and the policies governing the movement of messages through these networks lag significantly behind the internal changes in the organization and/or the changes in the external environment. Examples of this are seen today where organizations grow very rapidly, yet attempt to use networks and procedures that were adequate only for small-scale operation.

Another example of the network problem area is found in organizations where "adhocracy" (to borrow Toffler's term from *Future Shock*, 1970) has arrived. By adhocracy is meant the conscious recognition and use of communication networks in a highly flexible and goal-oriented manner. Rather than treating organizational working arrangements as fixed and immutable, short-lived "mini-organizations" within the parent organization emerge to meet particular goals. They strive to meet these goals, and then their membership is redispersed to meet other organizational goals. The person in charge of creating, directing, and dissolving these networks must have a clear and rational knowledge of the type of network that is required, the points of interface between the mini-organization and the larger parent organization, and the types of arrangements that are best suited to get certain goals accomplished.

Another important trend in communication that has considerable impact on organizational members involves changes in the *types* of messages that move through the organization, and in the *values* associated with different types of messages. These changes can be seen clearly if one traces the particular emphases given to the role of communication in major organizational theories. In the early classical "machine theory" writings, the emphasis is solely on *task-related* communication. As one moves from the classical theories to more contemporary writings, there is a fairly steady broadening of message-content emphasis to include new types of communication. There is much greater concern for messages about *innovation* matters (new ideas and practices), and there is also a much greater emphasis on messages that help maintain or improve *social skills* and *self-concepts* among organizational members. The organizational members of today—especially the managers—have complex demands placed on them for competence in communicating in a wide variety of situations.

A major *value* change now underway is in the relative importance attached to "memory" skills (the long-term storage of knowledge) versus "communication-processing" skills. Communication, as a commodity, appears to have a shorter and shorter life span. It becomes obsolete very quickly; the "facts" of today are outmoded and of little import tomorrow—*some* of them are outmoded, at any rate, and it becomes critical to have a good rule to determine which messages to store and which to discard. The sheer quantity of available messages is beyond the capacity of most individuals to store and retrieve, and so success will fall more to the persons who can organize, file, retrieve, collate, and synthesize communication, rather than merely store vast amounts in their heads.

The skills involved in communication processing, then, are those that involve learning how to choose which items to retain and which to discard, how to store material in such a way that it is readily retrievable, and how to instruct others where to find the proper items.

These brief comments illustrate the type of issues which will be discussed in later chapters. Throughout, our aim will be to provide a context for analyzing communication behavior. The communication system of an organization is an increasingly powerful determinant of the organization's overall effectiveness, and it may have a limiting effect on the ability of the organization to grow, to perform efficiently, or to survive.

APPROACH OF THE BOOK

Shortly, we will describe how a communication analyst might approach each of three typical communication "problems." But first we want to stress that the approach taken in this book is designed to eliminate some of the "mystique" that currently accompanies the use of the "communication-problems" label. Much of this mystique arises because many undesirable aspects of organizational activities are categorized as communication problems, when actually they have little or nothing to do with communication (in the terms in which we define it).

A particularly glaring example of an inappropriate use of communication is the assertion that "everything is communication," and that all organizational problems are therefore communication problems. Taking such a position is nonsensical; to equate all organizational activity with communication renders one of the terms unnecessary. In particular, this view eliminates the concept of communication from further use as an explanatory or analytic device. For communication to be a useful diagnostic and evaluative concept in organizational settings, we must be able to differentiate between problems that are primarily communication related and those that are not. We have already noted our focus on message gathering, processing, storing, and distributing as major referents for communication.

Our approach to communication is one that treats it as neither the *sole* overriding malady of contemporary organizations, nor as an insignificant and trivial adjunct to "more fundamental" organizational processes. We will concentrate on some of the major, serious communication problems that can occur in organizational settings, and we will describe the concepts which help to diagnose these problems. We will also indicate some of the methods that can be used to estimate their degree of importance in specific settings. We will then suggest some of the tactics and strategies that can be followed to avoid these problems or to reduce their severity when they do occur. Finally, we will argue for the importance of regularly monitoring the communication activities in an organization so that diagnosis and "treatment" are a routine part of management.

Our approach to communication is a *behavioral* one—behavioral in the sense that we focus on the specific message-handling activities of organizational members. We will discuss communication problem areas in terms of the concrete, referential aspects of message exchange, message movement, interaction, and other parts of the overall communication process. We will, in effect, strive to reduce many of the abstract aspects of communication to discrete elements which can be assessed and potentially altered to improve the total communication system.

There are four important features about this book that should be kept in mind as it is read:

1. The basic concepts included in the terms "communication" and "information" are derived from a powerful conceptual framework, a form of systems theory with a lengthy history, *structural-functionalism*. Organizations are viewed as processors (via input-throughput-output mechanisms) of energy, materials, and information. Structural-functionalism provides an appropriate framework for discussing the relationship between information and communication. It also provides the guiding logic for dealing with organizational communication structure, communication function, and the operation of communication structure and function at differing system levels. Relevant principles and hypotheses are available in the systems literature, and some are presented in the book.

2. The managerial dyad, linking hierarchical levels in an organization, has long been recognized as the basic "unit" of instruction, report, and performance appraisal. Our distinctive focus here is on the communication relationship in this dyad—on the rules and procedures that govern and constrain the communication between manager and managed. The book provides an extensive discussion of both the theoretical background of this topic area and the research results from it that are useful to managers.

3. One of the more innovative areas of research in which the authors have collaborated concerns the description and analysis of human communication *networks* in large-scale organizations. As noted above, it is through these networks, often based on face-to-face interaction, that messages move throughout the organization. The networks vary according to the type of message content they transmit (e.g., task versus personal or social topics), and in their extensiveness, capacity, redundancy, etc.

Organizations sometimes have specific policies concerning the persons who are to function in a liaison role (i.e., act as coordinators of communication between units). Also, there may be organizationally defined communication requirements for various jobs, and we will discuss how one conceptualizes such networks. We draw our conclusions from a number of network studies in actual organizations and the uses made by managers of the results of these analyses. This part of the book is based not only on the existing "network" research literature, but also on our research and consulting experiences, journal articles, reports, and papers presented at professional meetings.

4. The fourth distinctive feature of the book is its emphasis on some of the <u>practical applications</u> of the concepts and methods we use for analyzing communication in organizations. All too often, "practical" suggestions appear in the form of "how to do it" statements—whether to use an intercom or not, which photocopy machines are least expensive, and the like. While this type of information is definitely useful, our "practical" suggestions refer to the <u>application of communication concepts and principles to actual situations faced by managers.</u> For example, once the basic concept of communication networks is presented in Chapter 8, and the important network attributes are described, the discussion will turn in Chapter 10 to the issue of the practical uses to which network analysis can be put.

ANALYZING "COMMUNICATION": SPECIFIC EXAMPLES

The term "communication" is often used as a modifier in a phrase that describes one of the most widespread and pernicious "maladies" of contemporary organizations, the <u>communication problem.</u> This term often surfaces in discussions of any of a wide variety of undesirable incidents, unfortunate events, or troublesome mishaps in an organization. People in organizations lament that "bad communication" plagues them frequently. They discuss, in rather unpleasant terms, how "communication breakdowns" hamper their effectiveness. All too often, the need for "better communication" is seen as a cure for every organizational ailment. Here are three examples of what are often "communication problems": First...

> *Manager:*
> Okay, George, let's hear your problem ('phone rings, boss picks it up, promises to deliver a report, "just as soon as I can get it done"). Uh, now, where were we—oh, you're having a problem with your secretary. She's (...secretary—the manager's—brings in some papers that need immediate signature, so he scribbles his name where she indicates; secretary leaves)...you say she's depressed a lot lately, wants to leave...is she pregnant, maybe (laughter)? I tell you what, George, why don't you ('phone rings again, lunch partner drops by)...uh, take a stab at handling it yourself...I've got to go now.

Let's discuss some ways we might go about *analyzing* this situation to allow us to develop strategies to reduce the likelihood of its future occurrence. Perhaps the manager just doesn't care about George and, if he cared more, he wouldn't treat him so abruptly. Perhaps George's manager can be encouraged and/or trained to care more about his subordinates. Or, the blame might be placed on George—perhaps he should handle these issues on his own.

In this situation, the manager is clearly *overloaded* with messages and with the demands made on him from a variety of directions. Poor George receives rather short shrift. The problem with the secretary is not resolved, and the conversation does little to strengthen the work relationship between George and his manager. George's morale may suffer if he begins to worry about whether he should have been in his supervisor's office, asking the questions in the first place. The manager probably went off to feed an ulcer. The whole conversation was a rather dismal affair.

In evaluating this, the communication analyst would focus on the concept of *overload*. He or she would first recognize that the <u>level and intensity of communication flows and demands into (and out of) the manager's office were seriously in excess of his capacity to handle them.</u> Then the analyst would make a detailed scrutiny of the types of communication demands coming into the office, the time-to-completion expectations put on them, the quality and consistency of communication processing that was expected, and other aspects of the flow. Next the analyst would study the manager's own strategies for coping with communication flow—where was he efficient, where was he "sloppy," what did he do when the load became excessive, and what were the consequences for him (and for the organization) of his handling of the communication-load problem? Such an analysis not only provides a better understanding of the situation in which the manager operates, but also provides a rational approach to handling the communication-processing demands placed on him. Second...

Manager:
Well, Gerry, I'm glad to have you on board here. It's going to take you a while to learn the ropes, but there's one thing I want to make clear—my door is always open to you if you've got a problem with your work, or even something else, for that matter. Feel free to stop in and see me. Marge here will take you around the rest of the place. (Marge and Gerry go off.)

Gerry:
Is he serious about that...is he really that open and available, usually?"

Marge:
Well, I might as well tell you now, before you find out the hard way. He thinks he's open, and he tells everybody that, but nine times out of ten if you take him up on it you'll find he gets impatient and cuts you off. Most of us don't think he's accessible at all. We don't even *want* him to be...otherwise he'd be nosing into our work and personal life too much.

In this case, the manager might feel that his subordinates just don't *understand* him properly, and that if they took his statements at "face value," then the whole operation would run more smoothly. So he might take Marge and some of the others out for a drink, have them to his home, mingle with them more at work, and so on.

This example illustrates another topic in communication that is a frequent source of problems and difficulties. The manager, Marge, and the new employee (Gerry) had different expectations about availability or "openness."

The relevant conceptual area for this topic is that of *communication rules.* These rules (or, in many instances, "norms" that have not been formally codified into rules, but are powerful nonetheless) guide and limit the communication relationship between a manager and his subordinates. Communication rules deal with such matters as the conditions under which it is appropriate to initiate contact with the manager, the acceptable topics of discussion, the "leadership" or control of the conversation, the length of the conversation, and the setting in which it takes place. A major part of the socialization of a new member of an organization, regardless of entry level into the hierarchy, is the acquisition and use of the rules for "appropriate" interaction.

Knowledge of the communication rules in the organization is not, however, in itself, a sufficient base from which to analyze the situation. We must also consider: first, whether there exists *agreement* among the members of the organization with respect to what these rules actually are; and, second, whether the members of the organization are *accurate* in their perceptions of how the rules are viewed by the others. In the example, the factor of agreement is missing: the manager and Marge do not agree that an "open-door" policy exists. Furthermore, the manager is inaccurate in his perception of how Marge views the rules: he wrongly thinks that Marge accepts his "open-door" policy. This is clearly a situation where misunderstandings and "communication breakdowns" are likely to occur.

The analyst would approach this situation by determining the rules that are in effect in the organization (or some component area within it), the extent to which these rules are known by other members, and the levels of agreement and accuracy about these rules among organizational members. From this information, the communication analyst could generate strategies (such as one-on-one briefings, or training sessions with larger groups) that could do a great deal to alleviate this type of problem. Third...

Manager:
Now, team, let's get down to work. The purpose of this meeting is to decide how to handle that new account. You all got that report I sent around, I presume, so let's start off with your reactions. Remember, in it I asked you to coordinate with those three branches to help us put

together a pool of information. We need a good solution on how to handle the new account. (Silence, some uneasy movements.) You did get the report didn't you...and you did get together the material we're going to need to meet that deadline, yes? (More shifting in seats, looking from one to the other.)

In the third example, the manager might decide that her people should *listen* and *pay attention* more, so that these unfortunate incidents wouldn't recur. The manager might be tempted to remedy the situation by giving motivational speeches about the importance of *good listening* and *constant attentiveness*.

The third communication problem illustrated above presents a much different and, in many ways, more complex issue. In the example, the message-distribution network apparently failed to get the crucial report to the right individuals at the right time. In addition, the committee members were expected to fulfill a particular role in the communication network, that of *liaison* or coordinator among several groups. Within these groups, knowledge relevant to the committee's problem—how to handle the new account—was to be collected. The initial timing failure in the distribution of the report apparently led to the coordination failure by the committee members.

In this type of problem, the communication analyst would focus on the concept of *communication networks*—the networks for transmitting various types of messages throughout the organization. The analyst would obtain reports to use as the basis for the preparation of a "map" of the networks to determine where various groups were connected in the networks, how rapidly messages moved, what persons were included in (or excluded from) various networks, how extensive was the distortion or "noise" in the network, whether there was adequate redundancy at certain points, etc.

The analyst would understand how to create networks to meet specific needs or goals of the organization, and how to "manage" the flow of messages through them. This knowledge would be accumulated by regularly monitoring the existing networks in the organization, their performance, and their problem areas. Routine assessment could be made of whether the appropriate individuals were included in various networks, and whether effective liaison or coordination was taking place. Several training options, personnel reassignments, or other strategies could be invoked to deal with the network problems.

These three examples were presented to illustrate some of the types of communication problems that frequently occur in organizations. A parallel illustration is also given to show how a communication analyst would go about tackling each problem. With these examples in mind, the next section describes how the remainder of this book is organized to provide a more detailed exploration of communication in organizations.

PLAN OF THE BOOK

There are three parts to the book. Part I, which includes the present chapter, contains the conceptual framework. In Chapter 2, the basic conceptualization of organization, information, and communication is presented. Arguments for the use of structural-functionalism as an overall strategy for analyzing organizational communication are given in Chapter 3. Chapter 4 draws on a series of major organizational theories, and explicates the communication model that is implicitly or explicitly included in each theory.

In Part II (Chapters 5 through 8), four major organizational communication topics are discussed, using the approach of Chapter 3 as a framework for presenting the comments. The four topics are: the effects of "load" on individuals or larger aggregates of persons, communication "rules" in the managerial hierarchy, communication processes in groups, and "networks" of communication in organizations.

Then, in Part III, the discussion turns to ways to diagnose communication problems (Chapter 9), practical applications of network analysis (Chapter 10), and the role of communication "manager" in organizations (Chapter 11).

Organization, Information, and Communication

2

At the broadest level, the three key concepts in this book are *organization, information,* and *communication.* For this book to be useful to the reader, we must carefully present the key features of each concept. The linkages between the three concepts must be clearly identified. You, the reader, must come to share essentially the same meaning for these concepts that we as authors do. You may want to disagree with our views, you may want to alter them, or you may want to endorse them. In any circumstance, the important point is to acquire a thorough understanding of the three concepts and to carry this knowledge through the remainder of the book.

ORGANIZATION

Important Elements in the Concept of Organization

It is commonly known, but not trivial to consider, that most of our lives are spent in association with organizations. Whether we are born at home or in a medical setting, other people acting interdependently facilitate the process of birth. Our rearing takes place amidst a maze of organizations: some that educate us; others that provide food, clothing, and shelter; others that give us emotional or spiritual support; still others that provide us with fun things to do... the list seems endless. In today's world, one must work very hard to sustain a life-style that does not require involvement with some organization or another.

What do we mean by the concept of "organization" or, more specifically, "human organizations"? There are many well-known definitions, but they will not be recited here. Instead, we have abstracted five key elements in the concept, and by discussing these elements we hope to bring the concept of organization into clearer focus. The elements are:

- two or more individuals;
- who recognize that some of their goals can be more readily achieved through interdependent (cooperative) actions, even though disagreement (conflict) may be present;
- who take in materials, energy, and information from the environment in which they exist;
- who develop coordinative and control relationships to capitalize on their interdependence while operating on these inputs;
- and who return the modified inputs to the environment, in an attempt to accomplish the goals that interdependence was meant to make possible.

For shorthand labels, these five elements in "organization" will be termed *size, interdependence, input, throughput,* and *output*.

For an organization to exist, there must be some minimum number of persons who also demonstrate by their actions that they meet the remaining four conditions noted above. The minimum size is two persons—the dyad—since the condition of interdependence obviously cannot be met by an isolated individual. From this minimal two-person organization, we can extend the notion of size to much larger settings. Some organizations have hundreds or thousands of members. Religious and military organizations may have membership levels that are in the millions.

But the importance of size as a key aspect of organizations extends beyond the fact that some are larger than others and that some are very large indeed. Many of the other aspects of organizational functioning emerge as important, serious, significant, and even limiting factors as size increases.

For example, consider two central aspects of organizational behavior—coordination and control among members. As size increases, dealing with both of these factors becomes much more complicated. If messages must pass through the hands of many persons for a critical act of coordination, they may become distorted and the coordination effort may fail. If control messages must be broadcast to many individuals in a short time period, no existing communication mechanism may exist which can do the job.

As size increases, longer time periods are required for messages or materials to move within the organization. Growth in organizational membership poses a multitude of problems, not the least of which is the need to integrate new individuals into the present organization. It is for many reasons, then, that size is a key aspect of organizations: it is an important element in itself, and it may provide a bridge to other organizational processes that are closely related to size.

The second important aspect of organization is interdependence, i.e., the interlocked, reciprocal, mutually influential relationships among the organization's members. Why is interdependence so important? Precisely because it reflects that set of behaviors that distinguishes a collection of isolated individuals from an organized set of individuals. A collectivity, an aggregate, a mass of individuals—by definition—lacks interdependence: the behavior of one member is not influenced or constrained by that of someone else in order to achieve some common goal. In the strictest sense, members of a collectivity use only their individual abilities, and link with no one else to accomplish a goal. However, to the extent that interdependencies do arise, then (minimal) organizing is present. Without interdependence, organization (and hence larger goal achievement) is impossible. But if isolated individuals begin to act cooperatively, to join in a common cause, they make the transition to an organization.

There can be several bases for interdependence in an organization. One is authority—the bond between manager and subordinate—where one person seeks to control the behavior of the other while the other person accepts the control. Task relations form another common basis for interdependence; individuals whose work coincides, or meshes together, form bonds which express their interdependence. Interdependence based on mutually supportive attempts to bolster self-concept or self-esteem is yet another example.

The answer to the question of why interdependence arises in the first place is a complicated one, with a long history of answers. Perhaps the main point to be emphasized is that interdependence occurs when individuals realize that at least some of their goals can be better achieved through interlocked activities, rather than solely through independent efforts. By accepting control in an authority relationship one may be admitting that, through guidance and direction, one's goals will be better achieved than if no control is accepted; conversely, from the manager's point of view, by offering guidance, it is recognized that goals beyond the capacity of the individual will be achieved. By working together it may be possible to achieve output greater than the sum of the independent efforts of two or more individuals; similarly, by providing one another psychological support, the self-concept of each person may be more positive than the individual can achieve entirely alone.

Thus far we have described two aspects of organization—size and interdependence. Now we must consider the inputs received by the organization from the environment in which it exists. Any organization has a boundary which differentiates it from its larger environment. The boundary is usually specified in terms of who is a member of the organization, or who belongs to it at a certain place and time. Inputs, then, originate in the environment outside the organization, and enter the organization through openings in the boundary.

For example, a manufacturing firm may be defined in terms of its members at a specific time period working in specific plant locations. Inputs may consist of raw materials arriving at unloading facilities by truck, rail, waterways, or other means. Other inputs may be energy, supplied by power utilities. Still other inputs may be in the form of revenue, as indicated by the collection of sales receipts. Information is another important input to the organization, as we shall describe more fully later in this chapter.

Given inputs, the next important aspect of an organization is what its members do with the inputs—what *throughput* activities they perform. The term throughput refers to the passage of materials, energy, and information from point to point within the organization, up to the exit. As this movement takes place, the control and coordination procedures used by the members come into play; they touch, manipulate, ponder, modify, process, alter, and perform actions that are ultimately expected to provide the organization's members (at all hierarchical levels) with the often diverse goals they seek to accomplish. It is the throughput activities, under the control and coordination procedures that are in effect, that are intended to enable the eventual "payoff" to organizational members. The "payoff" (salaries, satisfaction, etc.) is what makes their interdependent activities worth the time and energy they personally devote to them.

Control processes are established to govern and regulate the ways in which the throughput activities take place. These processes include assigning work, implementing quality standards, detecting and correcting errors, and all the other activities required to see that the tasks of the organization are followed through to completion.

Coordination refers to the strategy that seeks to make each member of the organization, each component part of it, work in harmony with the others. Tasks must be done in the proper sequence, critical items must arrive where needed at just the right time, and new members of the organization must step in and smoothly take over the tasks being performed by former members.

The final aspect of organization that is of interest here is its output activities: the return to the environment of the materials, energy, and information that have been processed by the various members of the organization. This is the point in the organizational "cycle" where the members expect to reap many of the rewards or goals they sought during their participation in the organizational process.

How are we to judge "how well" the organization has conducted its activities? In organizations that operate to make a profit, the concept of "efficiency" is often used; roughly, the greater the output per unit of input, the greater the efficiency, and hence the more possible it is to achieve goal satisfaction.

If the organization is one that is devoted, for example, to recreational activities, to voluntary social work, or to supplying a "good" education to students, then definitions of efficiency and the precise relationships between participation in the organization and the "rewards" gained from it are much more complex. Nevertheless, we can still express these rewards in a somewhat rough fashion. For example, the members of an organization devoted to raising funds for underprivileged children may have a certain "inner self-satisfaction" goal, and to the extent the members raise funds, this goal becomes satisfied.

We should also recognize that certain goals of individuals or of organizational units may be achieved internally, without a necessarily direct linkage to the results of the output processes. Power in decision making, or personal satisfaction in meeting one's own standards of "doing a good job" are examples of these latter processes.

The Distinction Between "Organization" and "Organizing"

In the preceding discussion, we argued that "organization" implies issues of size, interdependence, and input-throughput-output of materials. We also noted that control and coordination are vital aspects of the ways the organization approaches the activities in which it engages.

It is important to make a distinction between "organization" and "organizing" (Weick, 1969). The term "organization" is typically used in a static, fixed sense; it does not take *time* into account. The term organization is used as a nominal label for a static description: General Motors is an organization; the Fraternal Order of Red Men is an organization; Michigan State University is an organization.

While this is a useful descriptive term, it is far more important, for both theoretic and practical considerations, to use the term "organizing." This shift represents much more than a semantic quibble over labels. *"Organizing" is used to denote the processual, sequential, time-varying nature of the behaviors of members in an organization*, while "organization" is a static term that usually denotes a particular system at a given point in time. "Organizing" draws particular attention to the processes of function and structure in an organization, to the uncertainties that accompany the day-to-day life in an organization, and to the fundamental point that organizations are not fixed, unchanging entities.

An organization, then, should be viewed as the *result* of the processes of organizing. At a given point in time, the configuration of behaviors and relationships in an organization reflects the action of many organizational processes, including communication. Some of these processes may be relatively stable over time, and would show a "static" organization. Other processes, more time-variant, will lead to changes in organizational configurations over time.

Perhaps an example will help clarify this distinction. A given office building is inhabited most weekdays by a set of individuals who form what we term the organization. It could be a city mayor's office, a manufacturing firm, a church mission in a ghetto area, a department store, a "Listening Ear" crisis center, or any other organization. "Organizing" refers to the sequence of activities that takes place in the course of each day's operation of that organization. It encompasses the work the members do, the meetings they attend, the conversations they have, the thinking they do, the reading and writing they perform, and the time spent operating machinery. All of these ongoing activities are among the referents of the term "organizing," as distinct from "organization."

Given that we view organizations to be often in a state of change or flux, the concept of organizing enables us to deal directly with the question of how much *structure* (predictable activity) is found in an organization. At one extreme, where structure is minimal, specific events or patterns are not predictable. Some might call this maximal freedom, others anarchy or chaos. In more current terms, we find the situation where everyone in the organization "does his or her own thing." This represents minimal structure, or, conversely, maximal uncertainty or unpredictability as to what activities will take place in the organization at any given point in time.

At the other extreme, maximal structure, each member's activities are clearly spelled out and are to be followed precisely. Military organizations often seek to have a high degree of structure in order to prepare themselves for future battles; creative and innovative "brain-storming" groups in advertisement firms often have minimal structure, so that each member has a full opportunity to speak out, regardless of status differences, job security, or any other factors that typically influence the level of structure in an organization. Different situations, therefore, may warrant greater or lesser degrees of structure to be most efficient in goal achievement.

What we ask, then, is that when you examine an organization you view it as a dynamic entity, changing its input-throughput-output activities over time. As each day begins, or as each new work shift arrives, people engage anew in a series of interlocked behaviors which, while largely constant, are also subject to change and alteration. At each work cycle new control and coordination decisions must be implemented, and these too will vary across time. Organizing goes with "time-varying," while organization is a label for organizing that has been momentarily frozen in time.

INFORMATION: A BASIC DISCUSSION

Thus far, we have given little attention to either of the concepts of information or communication. Instead, we have attempted to present a view of organizations which will be compatible with our conceptualization of information and communication. We want to draw close parallels between information, communication, and the broader set of activities mentioned under the discussion of organization and organizing.

Information, like oxygen, is something most of us would quickly testify we cannot do without. We sometimes have too much information, and become "overloaded." Sometimes we suffer from "underload." Often, we don't get the information that we need to do our work at the right time, or in the right form. We are routinely warned about the "information explosion," and we learn about "information-retrieval systems" to help us keep track of all that information.

But if we are to deal effectively with the concept of information in the organizational setting, we must begin with a clear understanding of how information evolves in the first place. In other words, we need to move very carefully from our previous discussion of "organizing" to "information," and finally to "communication." Our goal in the remainder of this chapter, then, is to present the major elements in the concept of information, to begin our discussion of communication, and to link both of these discussions to our prior commentary on organizations and organizing.

How Information Arises

Let's first return to the notion of organizations as the recipients of materials and energy. Better yet, since Albert Einstein's work over a half-century ago showed that the two are interchangeable, we will bypass, at the conceptual level, the distinction between matter and energy, even though it is obvious that different organizations input, throughput, and output matter and/or energy of very specific types.

Now, imagine that you are seated at your desk in a new office, provided for you by the firm you have recently joined. There is an intercom on your desk, with lines connecting you to five other offices. There are several lights on the intercom, one of which glows whenever someone tries to contact you. At first, when a light glows and you press the button that enables you to hear the person contacting you, it is completely unknown who will be at the other end of the line. After several days and quite a few calls, however, you learn to anticipate who the caller will be.

Although this is admittedly a rather simple example, it does illustrate the fundamental difference between basic matter/energy flows and the simplest conception of information. Energy was required to make the light glow whenever someone called, but initially those lights meant very little to you—you didn't know who the caller would be. Only after repeated exposure to the calls did *patterns* in the energy flows begin to become established in your mind. If the first light glowed, it was probably Anne calling; if the second, Gerry; the third, George; and the fourth...someone else. However, sometimes Anne did not use the first line (when she called you from a different office), so you can never be completely sure exactly who the caller is. The term "pattern" is particularly important here, because *one of the primary ingredients in the concept of information is the discernment of pattern in the matter/energy flows that reach an individual.*

Let's pursue some of the implications of this point. We are arguing that the first and highly critical distinction between any matter/energy flow and information is that information evolves *only* when at least one member of an organization perceives a particular pattern in the flows of matter/energy into, through, or out of the organization. In basic information-theory terms, the perceptual link you make between the intercom lights and the persons using each line represents the total set of *alternative patterns*.

Furthermore, you can easily determine the *relative* frequency of each alternative by summing the total calls received and then dividing the number of times a particular caller uses each line by the total of all calls.

Let's review what you have accomplished. You have identified one particular source of matter/energy input to you—the electricity flow along the intercom lines to your desk. Superimposed on that matter/energy flow are a series of "patterns," which in this case are the lights associated with the names of the persons who contact you. The total number of names gives you the number of alternatives in this situation, and the relative frequency of appearance of each light tells you about the probability of who is calling.

Now put this example into a broader perspective. There are many other matter/energy flows in the organization. Some of them are very rapid (like electricity), while others may be extremely slow (such as the decay of the office furniture on which you sit). But in all of these instances, whether they be the sound waves along which oral speech travels, printed memoranda, video tapes or cassettes, or growth, change, and decay processes, *these matter/energy flows have the capability of carrying patterned signals.* But while they may be carrying patterned signals, only when you (or someone else) recognize them can you begin to talk about information.

Some patterns are more widely known than others. Sunrise and sunset are nearly universally known. The three-phase traffic light (red=stop, yellow=caution, green=go) is a common pattern for most drivers and pedestrians. Air travellers can usually distinguish among the dozen or so jet aircraft now in service. Classical music fans can often discern the musical period, composer, and specific composition from a brief exposure to the music.

Why put so much emphasis on discerning patterns? We do this to highlight the fact that only those patterns which are known to individuals, which they acquire during their life, can be recognized by them in any of the matter/energy flows in which they exist. The recognition of patterns is a basic fact of our growth and maturation as individuals. As infants we learn aural patterns that are the components of spoken language. In early years of schooling we learn visual patterns that enable us to read and write. We learn to detect subtle patterns that tell us of the joys and sorrows of others, of their hopes and aspirations, of their intents and desires. We perceive patterns through our senses, singly or in complex interactions. During our lifetime we acquire the ability to perceive thousands of patterns—perhaps tens or hundreds of thousands.

The precise number of patterns is not as important as the recognition that these patterns reach us via the movement of matter/energy flows. The flows act as "carriers" of patterns, and it is our task to perceive them where they occur. The same electrical energy that drives a power saw can also be used to convey the complex patterns that appear as sounds and images on a closed-circuit television screen. In the first example we perceive no pattern, so no information is possible; in the TV example, most of us would detect patterns, and thus the potential for information is present.

Furthermore—and this is also a critical point—the patterns which one individual recognizes will *differ* from those that another might recognize. Each person, with a different background and set of experiences, will perceive patterns somewhat differently. Thus we are saying that information, which at this initial level of discussion requires only the discernment of pattern in the matter/energy flows reaching an individual, may well change across time and space for a given individual, and will probably differ from individual to individual.

Finally, note that there are no "objective" patterns that exist apart from the ability of at least one individual to recognize them. The pattern that signifies a "danger signal," if not perceived by anyone in the organization, can have disastrous consequences. The significance of this point will be underscored when we later discuss the concept of an "information space" for the individual, and for an organization as a whole.

But patterning and information are not synonymous. Another element must be introduced to provide the union between the recognition of patterns on the one hand and information on the other. This is the concept of *uncertainty*. Uncertainty is the term used to express how confident or sure you are about something. Uncertainty refers to the predictability or structure of some set of events, such as the presence of one or more patterns: the less predictable, the less structured, the more uncertainty is present. Randomness is another way of expressing uncertainty: if the presence of patterns is random, if there is little that is definite about what patterns there are, then we have uncertainty. In summary, the more uncertainty in a situation, the less knowledge we have about it; the less we can say about it, "for sure."

In the strict statistical sense of information theory (Shannon and Weaver, 1949), there is a direct relationship between uncertainty and information. Information theory gives a measure of the uncertainty in any situation on the basis of two factors: (1) the number of alternative patterns identified in the situation, and (2) the probabilities of occurrence of each alternative. The greater the number of alternative patterns, the greater the uncertainty, since it is harder to predict exactly which pattern will appear in any given instance. The more the patterns are equally likely to occur, the greater the uncertainty; uncertainty is greater when there is an equal chance of patterns appearing than when one pattern is more likely than others to appear.

Then how do information and uncertainty relate? The more uncertainty present in a given situation, then the more "information value" a pattern has when it appears. Given all the possible outcomes in a particular situation, when you learn which specific pattern occurs, your uncertainty is reduced; you have gained information. Thus, the more predictable a situation, the more information we have about it—and thus the lower its uncertainty. Conversely, the less structured a situation, the higher its uncertainty—so when a particular pattern does appear, uncertainty decreases and hence more information is obtained. Information can be viewed, then, as the use of pattern to reduce uncertainty.

One systems theorist (Buckley, 1967) relates information to the movement of patterned matter/energy by emphasizing the distinction between matter/energy as a "carrier" and the patterns which the carrier is capable of transmitting:

> ...though "information" is dependent on some physical base or energy flow, the energy component is entirely subordinate to the particular form or structure of variations that the physical base or flow may manifest. In the process of transmitting information, the base or carrier may change in many ways—as in the production or reproduction of sound via phonograph records—but the structure of variations in the various media remains invariant over the carrier transformations.*

From Information to Communication...

There are a number of important points yet to be made about the concept of information, but this discussion can be presented more clearly if we first de-

---

*William Buckley, *Sociology and Modern Systems Theory*, © 1967, p. 47, Prentice-Hall, Inc., Englewood Cliffs, New Jersey. Reprinted by permission.

scribe important distinctions between information and communication. In short, what are the ways in which information and communication differ?

Some of the basic ingredients in communication have already been indicated, since communication involves *all* the elements of information—matter/energy flows, patterns, varying probabilities, uncertainty, and uncertainty reduction. However, the concept of communication has some additional unique requirements of its own.

The first additional requirement is that the patterns—the set of alternatives—be expressed in a *symbolic* form that is widely known and understood by potential communicators. A language requires a symbolic system (along with other necessary components, such as a grammar); within languages, English uses a particular collection of symbols. Morse code used in telegraphy is another symbolic system; and the manipulation of semaphore flags by personnel on military vessels to communicate with other vessels is yet another example. For communication to be possible, then, the first additional requirement over and above that of information is the presence of a symbolic system that is shared by potential communicators.

In addition to sharing the same symbolic system, another highly important condition must be present. This is the associations that are established between the symbols and their "real-world" referents. To the extent that persons use the same symbols to refer to the same phenomena, effective communication is more likely. Conversely, to the extent that different individuals (who may use the same symbolic system) differ markedly in the "real-world" associations they give to various symbols, communication is impeded if not made impossible. To summarize, a symbol represents something else, while a referent is that which a symbol represents, and a shared symbol-referent system is a necessary step toward achieving effective communication.

Let's review some examples of these two additional requirements: first, we argued that shared symbolic systems are vital. An English-speaking individual confronted by a Russian-speaking individual cannot communicate because of the barrier set up by the lack of shared symbolic systems. They may, however, be able to achieve rudimentary communication by signs, gestures, and other nonverbal means, but that is a precarious basis at best for communication involving more complex ideas, goals, and needs.

But suppose that both speakers are similarly versed in the same symbol system—a lower-class white laborer speaking with a middle-class black professional. Here, in addition to any differences in symbol systems that occur between the two, there will probably be quite distinctively different symbol-referent relationships. Terms like "dignity," "love," "rights," "manhood" and many others may be mapped onto their "real-world" referents quite differently, and thus may impede communication between the two individuals. For other terms, such as "wife," "money," "apples," etc., their relative mappings may be much more in common.

In sum, then, *communication refers to the exchange of symbols that are commonly shared by the individuals involved, and which evoke quite similar symbol-referent relationships in each individual.* Communication processes therefore become a subset of information processes because of these two extra limiting conditions imposed on the movement of information. Yet communication can still be related back to our initial comments on the flows of matter and energy into, through, and out of organizations.

It should be noted that most writers who use the term information are, in our terms, referring to communication. Shared symbol systems and the presence of similar symbol-referent relationships are typically implied in their use of "information." It is primarily in such topic areas as coding theory for information channels (i.e., the transmission of "bits" of information per unit time) that the concept of information is used in its original, statistical sense. We feel, however, that the distinctions between information and communication are of such fundamental importance that we will use communication (in the sense we have described it) throughout the book. However, where other authors use "information" where we would use communication, we will point out that fact.

And Back to Information: Absolute versus Distributed

One of the most important distinctions in types of communication was pointed out by the physicist Leon Brillouin over ten years ago (Brillouin, 1962). His conception of "information" appears quite similar to our use of "communication." He differentiated between *absolute* and *distributed* "information." Absolute "information" exists as soon as one individual has perceived a new, unique pattern in the phenomena of life. We will call these "pieces of knowledge," recognizing that to the degree they are expressed symbolically (and with known referents), they are capable of use in communication. The polio vaccine was once a new, unique "piece of knowledge," the rotary combustion engine was once a new, unique piece of knowledge, as were many thousands or millions of other patterns in our history. Typically, these "pieces of knowledge" are expressed symbolically, with specific referents associated with them.

Distributed information, on the other hand, refers to the relative dispersal through a system of a particular piece of knowledge. In Brillouin's terms, distributed knowledge is determined by locating the number of persons who possess a particular piece of knowledge (absolute information) out of a potential population which might possess it.

These two types of information can be easily applied in an organizational setting. If we survey the number of different pieces of knowledge that are present among the organization's members and contained in documents and other forms of storage, then we would know how much absolute information the organization possessed. Assuming a perfect job on our part, we could enumerate all pieces of knowledge. If, after our survey of levels of absolute knowledge, we then determined how widely known each piece of knowledge was, we would be able to determine the amount of distributed information in the organization. We might find that some of the pieces are known to one or a few persons, while others are known to nearly all. (It is quite possible that in our initial composition of the list of items of knowledge we found some that were known only to us as outsiders.)

This is much more than an academic exercise. *What* is known in an organization, and *who* knows it, are obviously very important in determining the overall functioning of the organization. We have encountered the following situation many times while conducting research in an organization: we ask subordinates whether their managers usually give them the information needed to do a good job. All too often, the reply is, "No, they have the information I need, but they just don't give it to me."

But when we query the managers on this point, a quite different story emerges. Often, the managers will say, "It's not a matter of me not giving them the right information...I just don't have it to give. Nobody else around here does either." In these instances, then, the subordinates define the problem as one of inadequate distribution of information, while the managers define it as inadequate absolute information.

The absolute-distributed distinction also illustrates another point about the concept of communication. Earlier in this chapter we noted that the various parts of an organization are linked together through control and coordination mechanisms. Further, the communication processes provide the vehicle or means through which control and coordination are made possible. Now, given the absolute versus distributed distinction, we can examine the organization from several perspectives.

First, we can ask whether anyone in the organization (including persons knowledgeable about storage) has a particular piece of knowledge that is required to meet objective A or to complete task X. If the answer is negative, then for that organization, an "absolute" problem exists. The organization's members must look *outside* the organization for this information. They may find it in other organizations, in specific information repositories such as libraries, or elsewhere. The role of "consultant" is created in part to increase the absolute-information level of many organizations.

The same question of absolute-information needs can also be asked at the level of each part of the organization, or of the units within the larger components. Is the information that a unit needs to perform its work adequately actually present within it, or can it be found at a higher level? Thus it should be clear that the distinction between absolute and distributed information depends on whether you scrutinize the whole organization or just parts within it. What may be an absolute-information problem at a lower level in an organization may simply be a distributed-information problem if one moves to a larger, more encompassing level of the system.

This point can be carried outside the organization as well. Suppose that you are dealing with one firm within an industry, and that a specific absolute-information lack exists for that firm. At the higher "whole-industry" level the information may exist, and thus in principle could be distributed to the particular organization in need.

It is also possible, however, that the needed information simply does not exist at any system level. Out of such definitions of information needs arise the large research and development programs funded by many organizations.

But next let's assume that there is no problem of information, in the absolute sense. What appears to be the important problem is one of information *distribution*. We can, as we pointed out above, compute the amount of distributed information by multiplying the number of distinct "pieces of knowledge" by the number of persons who possess them. From an organizational manager's point of view, however, that result indicates only the very "tip" of the larger issue of how to distribute information adequately throughout the organization.

One alternative that a manager might consider is that everyone within the organization should be knowledgeable about all major phases of the organization's activities. This kind of approach appears in various forms, some of which are in the literal floods of memos, talks, meetings, "house organs," etc., to keep everyone "fully informed" about what's going on in the organization. Often this approach is developed as a response to member complaints about "never knowing what's going on." Dissatisfaction is to be overcome by opening the communication floodgates.

An opposite strategy is to be highly restrictive in the distribution process. Hoarding may be practiced by members at various levels in the organization, or rigid procedures may be established to restrict communication from passing from unit to unit. These conditions are common in military or intelligence operations, or when organizations are in the process of developing new products that they want to keep secret from competitors. Sometimes hoarding takes place because organizational members want the pleasure (or power, protection, or advantage) to be gained from knowing things that their subordinates—or superiors—don't know.

Most commonly, however, failures in distribution policies are due to failures by managers to identify which groups of personnel need to know certain things, or to establish where these groups are supposed to be able to obtain the information they need. Initially, the burden of this problem may be placed entirely on the shoulders of management. This need not always be the

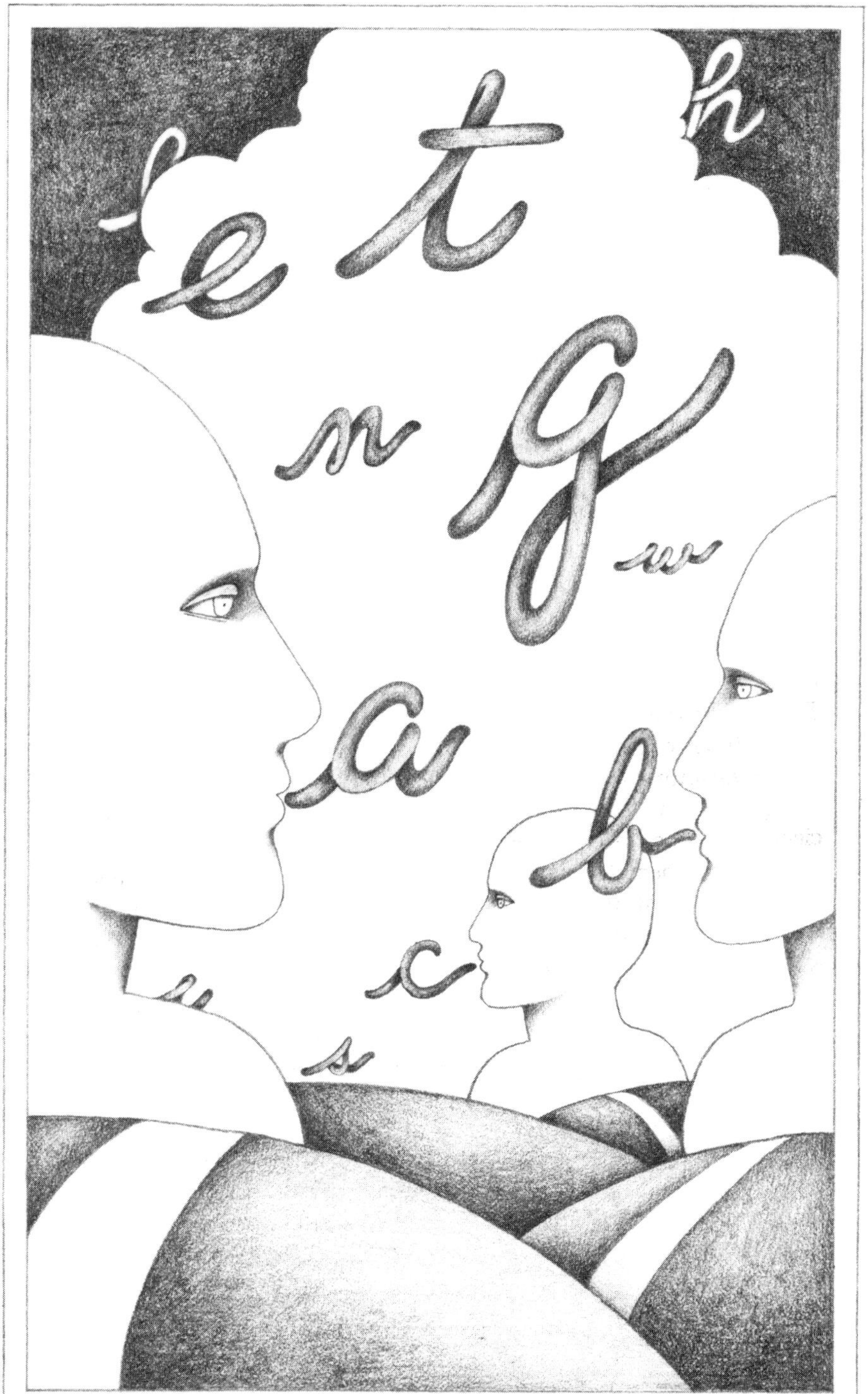

case—one of the goals of much of the so-called "participatory management" approaches is to get personnel to define their own communication needs and to learn where to seek the desired items, rather than merely waiting passively for the communication to be fed to them.

Many managers we have encountered firmly believe that the problem of how to distribute communication adequately in the organization is one that will largely "take care of itself." We are tempted to call this the "woodwork" theory of distribution—that what is needed by organizational members to function adequately resides in the walls, machines, and atmosphere surrounding them; and that by some natural (although mysterious) process, it will be made known to the relevant employees at the relevant times.

Another common failure of managers is to equate what *they* themselves know with what others in the organization know. Managers may automatically assume that their subordinates can "read their minds" and know precisely what is needed to get on with their work. These views find genuine support much less frequently than some managers think.

Environmental, Motivational, and Instructional Communication
There is yet another entirely different set of important perspectives about the concept of communication which is relevant here. This is found in the work of Ackoff (1957), and in Ackoff and Emery (1972), who are concerned with three types of communication—environmental, motivational, and instructional. The basic distinctions are found in Ackoff; we have reordered the quote to fit our preference for the sequence in which to discuss them: "We shall say that a communication which changes the probabilities of choice, *informs*; one that changes the value of the outcomes, *motivates*; and one that changes the efficiencies of the courses of action, *instructs*."

Environmental communication provides descriptions of actions, events, or processes that observers detect in the world in which they live. This might be in their own work groups, in their movement through the remainder of the organization, or in some event in the world outside the organization. Examples of environmental communication are: "The stock market rose 20 points yesterday," or "Our enrollment figures in undergraduate courses are down 10 percent this term," or "There's a rumor out that our competitor is going to bring out a new product that will compete directly with our current main profit-maker," or "I see a growing sense of despair and boredom among the workers on the line." The unifying thread that runs through these four statements is that each gives a descriptive report of some aspect of the phenomena that an individual observes; each *informs* us about the world in which we live.

Motivational communication is quite different from the environmental-descriptive category. Motivational communication refers to statements that assert specific *goals* or *values*. We can use the four descriptive assertions above and construct four parallel motivational assertions: "Making a profit on the stock market is critical to maintaining my desired life-style," or "To operate the kind of department we believe in, we need an increase, not a decrease, in student enrollments," or "Our survival as an organization may be seriously jeopardized if the competition's product cuts heavily into our market share," or "The achievement of personal growth and development of our employees, and the rise in their feelings of self-worth, is a major goal of this organization."

Again, each of these assertions has presented a particular value or goal, and, furthermore, we have linked the environmental-descriptive statements to the goal-expressive statements. By doing this we have completed an example of two of the three types of communication.

The third type, instructional, is in some senses the most important of the three. Instructional communication consists of assertions that provide *courses of action* which link the motivational and environmental statements together. Instructional statements indicate particular approaches that can potentially achieve the goal, given the environmental description as the starting point.

Here are four more statements, instructional in nature, which provide the linkage between the preceding pairs of statements. First, given the rise in the stock market, and the desire for profit, the instructional statement might be, "Sell your shares in Company A and use some of the profit to pay for that new car you want. Use the remainder of the money to buy shares in Company B." In the second case, given the decline in student enrollments and the need to raise them to continue operating as an academic unit, the instructional message might be, "Let's lower the minimum grade point required for enrollment into the program, and thus attract more students."

The third case involves the new competitive product that may potentially cut into the firm's sales and reduce its profitability to bankruptcy levels. Here the instructional message might be, "Let's put our market researchers to finding some comparative advantage that our product has over the other one, and then step up our advertisement campaign using those results as soon as the other product appears." The final instance involves the perceived frustration and boredom of line employees vis à vis the goal of increasing their feelings of self-worth and dignity. Here, the instructional message might be, "Let's genuinely commit ourselves to some large-scale changes in their work life, and devote enough money to a program to get done what's needed, even if we have to bring in outside help."

In each of these four examples we have provided environmental, motivational, and instructional statements, and attempted to link them together in a logical sequence. Of course, each of the four cases has been greatly simplified, and the instructional messages we have proposed may not be the most appropriate ones for linking the expressed goals with the initial environmental description. Nevertheless, these sequences are meant to illustrate the main differences in the three types that are proposed by Ackoff and others.

Examples of messages that confuse or abuse these three categories are all too prevalent in organizational settings, as many individuals we have described these concepts to have testified. Perhaps the most common abuse is in the motivational message which has no accompanying environmental or instructional components in it. The organization's members may be exhorted to "boost the firm at every opportunity," or to remember that "profit is our primary motive," or "let's beat our competitors every chance we get."

While motivational messages are often important, and may have commendable values underlying them, it should be clear that they can be quite ineffectual if the recipients (a) do not know the environmental conditions upon which the motivational message is based, and/or (b) have not received the instructional guides to tell them how they might actually achieve the goals in the motivational message. Many organizational members (including the present authors) have experienced that pit-of-the-stomach feeling when someone in the hierarchy announces that we are to be subject to what we know will be...yet another...motivational speech.

Links Among these Distinctions in Communication
In the preceding pages we discussed the basic concept of information and then distinguished it from communication. Then we divided communication two more ways—absolute versus distributed, and environmental, motivational, and instructional. We can increase the usefulness of these distinctions by evaluating communication on both dimensions at the same time; i.e., by examining instructional attempts in terms of their distribution, or by determining the total (absolute) amount of motivational communication present at a point in time. We will now combine the preceding discussions into an example that illustrates some of the practical uses to which this conceptualization can be put.

Let's suppose you are told by your boss that "there's a growing concern among our management that the firm should consider purchasing some new computing equipment for the salespeople to use, both in their field work and in their offices." You are assigned the task of investigating this possibility, and are to turn in a report in time for the next managers' meeting, some ten days away. The obvious implication in this assignment is that if you do a good job, your prospects in the organization will brighten considerably, while if you do poorly...a number of the higher-level managers will see the evidence before them as they peruse your report.

Let's begin with the three columns in Fig. 2-1, and ask the following question: "Is your purpose in the report simply to present descriptive information about the kinds of computing equipment currently available on the

	Environmental communication	Motivational communication	Instructional communication
Absolute communication			
Distributed communication			

Fig. 2-1. Simultaneous comparison of two types of communication.

market?" If so, you clearly need a great deal of environmental description. You need to know what kinds of equipment are available, their costs, their capacities, the service facilities available if breakdowns occur, and a variety of other details about the equipment.

As you begin to make this list of environmental needs, it is likely that some motivational or goal-related questions will arise. One quite probable one is a rather normal desire to "do well" on your part, i.e., to be praised for the quality of your work and perhaps to receive other forms of organizational rewards.

But the more immediate goal-related issue deals with how you are to *judge* the information you will soon be gathering to answer the first set of questions you've enumerated. What *are* the goals or values underlying the environmental items you are about to search out? Do you want to minimize the immediate purchase cost...or the long-run costs including maintenance and operating costs? How important is portability in the equipment; does it matter if the equipment is a bit heavy to carry around? How easy should it be to learn to operate the equipment? Is it important that you have a clear understanding of what the desires of the sales people are in this situation, or doesn't that matter? These questions are examples of goal-related or motivational issues that could arise in this assignment.

At this point in your formulation of the assignment, you could very well decide to ignore these goal-related issues entirely, and simply stick to the environmental-descriptive questions that were initially suggested. You could provide the managers with the descriptive results of your search for computing equipment, and let them decide what values to express and how to go about selecting the final choice. But when you turn to your manager with this possibility in mind, you soon learn that you are not to be let off so easily—you are to carry on and make a *complete* report. It should present descriptive details about the computing equipment, make clear what goals you consider important in the choice, and present a specific recommendation, i.e., an instructional message about what course of action to take. You should learn how to go about obtaining the equipment which, given your selected and expressed goals and the relevant descriptive material, is the "best choice."

The task has certainly become much more formidable. It would certainly be easier to stick to the descriptive level and let the managers do what they will with the basic report you provide. But that option is no longer available to you.

Your next step is to return to the list of questions you had been formulating concerning the descriptive aspects of the equipment. You also begin to list the criteria (motivational guidelines) against which you will ultimately have to evaluate the descriptive results. At the same time, given the broad nature of the assignment, it is also pertinent to consider the descriptive topics that should be covered. The managers expect your report not only to describe the available equipment, but to evaluate it as well. Furthermore—and this is where the instructional comments become important—you are expected to indicate how the organization might best go about obtaining the new equipment and getting it utilized by the sales staff.

By now your list of information needs is rather lengthy, and is also quite diverse. At this point, if not sooner, you should begin to pay some attention to *locating* this information. Here the distinction between absolute and distributed communication becomes important. You will need to evaluate the environmental, motivational, and instructional needs in terms of whether you have absolute- or distributed-communication problems.

A simple initial assumption is that the information is already within the organization, but is not readily available (i.e., not distributed) to you. So you begin to search among your coworkers, your manager, the sales personnel, and other areas of the organization (perhaps files on this type of information are available somewhere). You begin to compile some answers to your questions, and you get a clearer understanding of the questions for which there are apparently no useful answers within the organization—clearly a problem of absolute needs, in these instances.

By this time you have a set of alternatives (the different kinds of computing equipment elicited by your search within the organization, plus additional material on the cost, performance, and other features of the equipment). You also have some statements about the relative importance of cost in purchasing the equipment, the preferences for ease of use and performance capability from the sales personnel, and some leads to persons outside the organization who can provide additional help.

Going outside the organization seems definitely feasible at this point. You might contact sales representatives of firms that produce such equipment, and get reports from them. You may have friends in other organizations that have had experience with this type of problem. Rather quickly, you begin to assemble a rather sizable "mosaic" of the pieces that should fit into a final report.

It's time at this point to review once again the set of questions you established for the descriptive, goal-related, and instructional aspects of the task, and the knowledge about these questions you collected from first searching within the organization and then looking outside it. As you review the situation you should readily be able to spot areas where your uncertainty is still quite high. For example, you may not be very sure about the reliability of some of the equipment, even though it offers other advantages in cost or performance. This "uncertainty analysis" pinpoints your greatest areas of need, and thus guides your final search.

In all likelihood, you will not fully satisfy all the requirements that were established in the initial set of questions, given the time constraints under which you have been operating. Most of the time in the "real world" we are in the position of performing less adequately than we would like, of "satisfying" rather than "maximizing." But the procedure that you have just gone through has a number of built-in safeguards, since it forces you to examine, from two quite different perspectives, the kinds of communication that are needed to complete the task that was first outlined. In addition, this general strategy provides a framework for the actual preparation of the report, since it provides logical connections between the descriptive statements you make about the computing equipment, the goals or values you argue are most important in choosing among the alternatives, and the mechanisms or actions by which the equipment can be obtained once the final decision has been made. It is now time for you to complete your task by writing the report, turning it in to your supervisor, and awaiting the outcome of the managers' meeting.

The "Information Space" Outside the Organization
Our discussion to this point has been restricted primarily to the concepts of information and communication within the context of the organization. These concepts need to be broadened, however, since it is not only their operation *within* an organization that exerts influence on organizational activities, but (perhaps even more importantly) their operation *outside* the organization that exerts a highly important degree of influence.

What is meant by "space"? This point may be clarified if we return to the initial view of how information is first "recognized" by an individual within the organization. We asserted that information is basically dependent on the recognition of distinctive, repetitive patterns that occur in the flow of matter/energy into and through the organization. Only when such patterns are recognized by at least one individual in the organization can information be said to exist. When some of those patterns are expressed in symbolic form and regularly associated with specific referents, communication becomes possible.

This same view can now be extended to the environment in which the organization exists. Each member has a set of information and communication perceptions that are finite in number and which represent a particular view of the surrounding environment. The accumulated perceptions of all organizational members represent a bounded "space," or limits to the conception an organization has of its environment.

This concept puts an active perspective on the role played by the organization's members in arriving at a definition of what constitutes the limits of what is perceived and what is communicated about outside the organization's boundaries. Weick (1969), for example, calls this the "enacted environment." He also emphasizes that this is a composite enactment, based on the various viewpoints of the organization's members, and cannot be considered to be an "objective" phenomenon that exists independently of the organization. Thus while "outsiders" may define the environment differently, it is the views of members that influence internal operations. The term "enactment" puts a definite emphasis on the fact that an "information space" is something that is literally *constructed* by the members of the organization, and hence is subject to change from time to time, and liable to differ from member to member.

One of the most elegant descriptions of the enacted environment, although he does not use the term, is given by De Chardin (1961). He uses instead the term "noosphere" to describe the layer of information that surrounds us all, whether in an organizational setting or not. This layer is as pervasive as the air we breathe—so pervasive, in fact, that most of us remain generally unaware of it and recognize only portions of it at best. We take the "noosphere" for granted; we do not consciously recognize that we "enact" the information space in which our organizations exist.

Types of "Information Environments"
Emery and Trist (1965) have given careful consideration to the environments in which organizations function, and developed four main types of environments. Each of these environments is based on a significantly different conception of the information and communication aspects of the environment in which the organization operates.

In the simplest type of environment, both the goals toward which the organization strives, and the dangers it seeks to avoid, are considered to be relatively constant and distributed randomly throughout the environment. This first type is called the *placid-randomized* environment, and the best that an organization operating under this assumption can do is to cope with events as it encounters them, one after the other. Trial and error provide the main source of "learning" on the part of the organization's members; i.e., sensitizing the members to those environmental factors that they need to consider important as they enact their environment.

When environmental goals and dangers are not viewed as randomly distributed, but instead are clustered together, Emery and Trist call this second situation the *placid-clustered* environment. Here the environment takes on new properties, because it becomes vitally important to the organization's survival to learn how to detect quickly the cues that indicate potentially rewarding (or potentially damaging) conditions. Hence a longer time-horizon is needed on the part of the organization's members, because it is recognized that pursuing only short-run positive goals may in fact lead the organization into a much larger region of clustered noxious factors, a situation which can be enormously damaging to the organization.

At the point when there are a number of other similar organizations in the same general environment (and even this fact must be consciously recognized by the organization), then the third type, a *disturbed-reactive* environment, is present. Additional information must be obtained because now the organization must deal with "competitors." It becomes particularly important to learn "what the other guys are doing." The organization must alter its activities in such a way as to minimize the impact of its competitors, while at the same time continuing to operate its basic input-throughput-output activities. Important aspects of the environment for these firms are the patterns or "cues" that denote any encroachment by the competitor organizations, as well as anything that will help the organization develop strategies to thwart possible inroads by its competitors.

The fourth and final type of information space—where organizations see themselves as operating in a *turbulent* field—represents the most difficult and complex of the four environments. These organizations must learn ways to recognize and avoid unpleasant conditions, to maximize their goals, and to cope successfully with their competitors; their space also provides the patterns or cues that show how the very *nature* of their organizational activities must change. In the three prior examples, the information space dictated no basic change in the fundamental purpose of the organization. In a turbulent environment, the very reason for existence becomes an important component determining the appropriate space—a space that will facilitate survival if not growth.

We have personally observed a fairly large manufacturing firm going through a painful redefinition of its relevant information space. In this case, its upper-level managers shifted from a disturbed-reactive space to a definition of a turbulent space. The manufacturer, well known for the quality of its products, began to feel increasingly pressured by other, larger competitors. Attempts to maintain an adequate organizational level of performance by meeting the competitors on common grounds were less and less successful. At that point, the question that began to percolate through the organization was, "What are we really in business to do?" Numerous alternatives were discussed in terms of their desirable and undesirable consequences, and new alternatives were provided by going to outsiders who understood the business they had been conducting and who also had a wider view of the industry of which they were a part.

The result of this process was a fairly radical redefinition of the major activities—of the "primary mission"—of the organization. No longer were they to be mere purveyors of products. Instead, they began to redirect their operations so that they could provide clients with a much wider range of services. Their clients had previously been involved in building new facilities and/or redesigning existing ones, but now, instead of providing only certain equipment, the firm provided additional services: space planning, acoustics, a wider variety of equipment, flexibly arranged facilities, etc.

In terms of their "enactment" of the environment in which they had been operating, then, this firm moved from a definition in which they were in a disturbed-reactive situation, to a turbulent one. They no longer sought to compete directly with their former opponents; instead, they redefined the nature of the services they would offer and thus deliberately moved to a considerably different type of operation. Their communication needs had altered, their communication-seeking strategies changed, and their provisions for distributing communication within the organization changed as well.

There are some important points to highlight in this discussion of the information and communication spaces in which organizations operate. The first one, which appears to be obvious but which is almost always overlooked by an organization's members, is that what they *collectively* discern as "information" in the environment outside the firm directs and determines their behavior. Information arises during the interaction between the individual and his or her perception of patterns and uncertainties in the environment. The patterns of interaction by the members of the organization, the distribution of power among members, their acceptance of change, plus other factors taken together determine how they will view their environment. Control and coordination processes within determine their responsiveness to the environmental definition and changes in the definition.

This is not to say that all of the individual information spaces generated by members of the organization will equally influence the behaviors that are performed. Some organizational members' view of the information space is more influential than others'. But at basic levels it still remains as a fundamental point that organizations do not exist in any "objective" information space, but rather in a "subjective" one that grows out of their evaluation of the environment.

It is quite possible, for example, for the members of an organization to define their environment as a placid-clustered one, even though an outside observer might argue otherwise. The observer might feel quite confident that the organization operates in a turbulent environment, but be unsuccessful in convincing the main decision makers in the organization that this view is the more appropriate one. Without resolving the question of which one is the "correct" view, it is nevertheless clear that many organizations have clung persistently to a particular definition of their environment, when in fact it was quite different in the eyes of many observers. Many of those organizations have also ceased to exist.

A Strategy for Processing Information from the Environment

Given that an organization has a particular definition of the environment in which it exists, we can then turn to the question of the strategies that are useful in systematically scanning the environment, processing information into the organization, and using some in communication. Reindl (1970) provides an excellent conceptual "flow chart" by which an organization can review its information-processing activities. This sequence is shown in Fig. 2-2.

He begins by reminding us that there is far more "patterned matter/energy"—information—in the environment than any organization can ever hope to input. In the figure, this is represented by the area lying outside of the diagram. But it is highly unlikely that any such attempt would even be made since, as we have indicated, only a portion of that environment falls within the information space of a particular organization. The arbitrary shape noted as (1) represents a hypothetical space. Reindl then presents a series of interlinked decision points by which we can follow the strategy an organization uses to actually incorporate a subset of the information available to it.

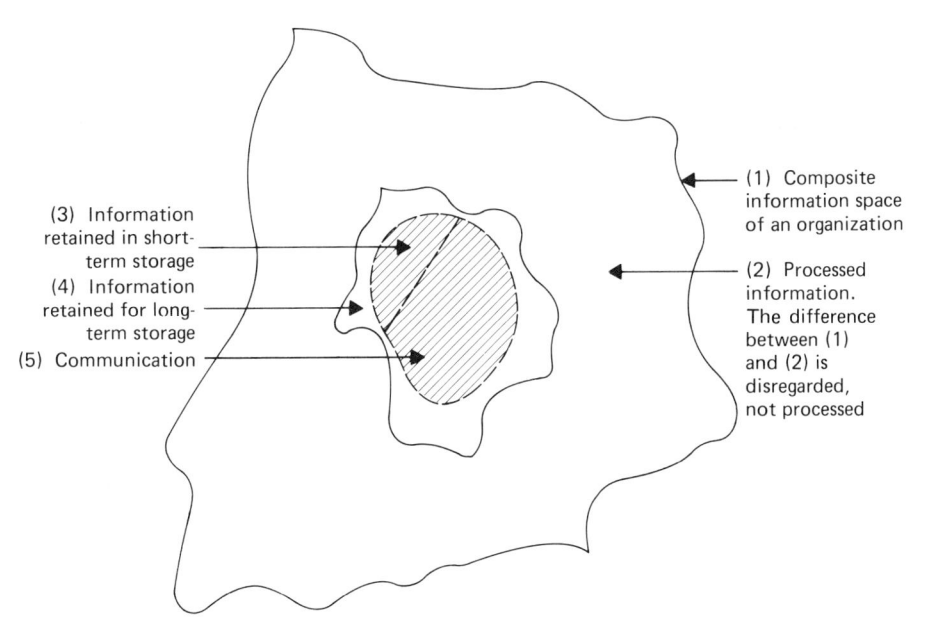

Fig. 2-2. Processing environmental information and communication-processing rules.

The total information available to an organization first goes through a processing step as it reaches the organization's members by any of several different channels. These channels include reading, listening to others, observing activities outside the organization, attending to the mass media (newspapers, radio, television), and conversations with friends, colleagues, and other individuals. A certain amount of information is encountered purely on a chance or random basis.

These input channels may be quite systematically designed and utilized by the organization. Various journals and periodicals may be subscribed to on a regular basis; there may be a research and development component in the organization; public relations activities may include a systematic scanning for relevant information from many sources; the organization may subscribe to a newspaper-clipping service that will send it materials relevant to predefined topics, etc. The shape marked (2) represents the information actually processed into the organization. We would expect that most of this information would be communication, in our sense of the term (note the broken lines surrounding the cross-hatched area).

A critical decision point in the organization's information-input strategy is "What do we keep...and what do we discard?" One easy answer, and a frequently proposed one, is "Let's keep it all!" But that is a nonsensical approach, for several reasons. Any organization that attempts to retain all the information input to it soon finds it physically impossible to store it all. Use of document-reduction devices, (e.g., microfilm, microfiche) is one way to increase storage capacity, but that still may only temporarily delay the time at which it is no longer possible to store additional materials.

But even if it were physically possible to store all information, it is clearly unwise from an economic standpoint. It requires scarce resources to store and then to retrieve it later. These resources are being drained off from other areas where they might be put to more productive use. *So a critical point in any assessment of an organization's processing strategy is the type of rules it follows in deciding what to keep and what to discard immediately.*

Unfortunately, there is no easy answer to this question, no "magic formula" to apply to the situation. Perhaps the best approach is to have individuals with detailed knowledge about various aspects of the organization meet regularly and review what information is being input, and what is not, and to establish guidelines and procedures that, at least in the short run, appear to be most appropriate. The key to the effectiveness of this approach lies not only in the individuals who perform this task, but in the fact that it is done *periodically*. This makes possible changes in the processing strategies that are aligned with any changes in the organization's definition of the environment in which it operates.

At this point the initial *available* information has been reduced by processing it in terms of specific filtering rules. The next important decisional area centers on the immediacy of the information. Should it be put into short-range storage (step 3 on Fig. 2-2), where it is readily accessible, or can it be put into longer-range storage, where it is available when needed, although extra effort is required to retrieve it (step 4)?

Some information, by its very nature, must go into short-range storage. It may be highly "perishable," i.e., it may lose its value very quickly. Current weather reports, the latest stock-market quotations, and present sales levels are often put into short-range storage. Other items readily suited to short-range storage are those which are needed immediately to help resolve issues in ongoing activities, e.g., the newest method for estimating man-months of work required to complete a project; the organization may be in the process of preparing a number of project bidding proposals, and need that method to complete their proposal.

Again, it is easy to conclude that *all* items that survive the initial processing should be put into short-range storage. That would make them always readily accessible. But cost factors involved in storage may make it far more economical to differentiate between quick accessibility and long-run retention. One good decision process for deciding when to use long-run storage is based on the costs involved in retrieving information from the environment once again. It may be far more costly to retrieve the information (i.e., to spend time in a search through a library file for a relevant document) than to photocopy it and keep it on hand. Sometimes external rules and regulations (e.g., federal income tax laws) dictate how long information must be stored.

The final decision area in this sequence (step 5) is that of information *dissemination* within the organization, and at this point our discussion has now returned to the conclusion of our earlier discussion of absolute and distributed information. The dissemination issue, then, refers to the rules and procedures that are followed to determine who gets what information, in what form, and with what priority.

THE CONCEPT OF COMMUNICATION: SOME FURTHER DISTINCTIONS

What are some important ingredients in our view of communication that need further highlighting? First, when Person A seeks to communicate with B, A must produce some set of symbols that represent what A intends to convey to B. These symbols (in the form of oral speech, a letter, or any other form) are received by B and interpreted or "decoded." To the extent that B shares the same symbol system with A (i.e., speaks the same language), then successful communication is possible. But perhaps even more importantly, to the extent that B's symbol-referent linkages are similar to A's, then communication will have been achieved with greater success than if these linkages are highly dissimilar.

Some Impediments to Communication Success

It should be clear from this view of communication that it is a process replete with potential impediments—with "communication problems" or "breakdowns in communication." This comes about largely from the fact that the symbols produced by A have no inherent linkages with "real-world" phenomena until a decoding process is undertaken by B.

What are some other impediments that may be introduced into the communication exchange between A and B that may serve to further increase the difficulty of their communicating with one another? One of these is *noise*, which is technically defined as the introduction of random alterations in the symbols (the "message") as it moves to B. In a telephone conversation, for example, noise may be introduced by background factors—the humming, buzzing, garbling factors that can reduce two persons to frustration and rage as they attempt to converse over the telephone.

A second major impediment to the effective movement of a message is *distortion*—the addition, deletion, or altering of parts of the message. This is typically a problem when messages are relayed through several individuals. Even when they have the best of intentions regarding accurate relay of messages, distortion factors often creep in. There are numerous studies of message distortion that show how remarkable these changes can be. A favorite party game is to construct a message, and have it relayed in turn to each guest, who then writes down his or her version. Under most circumstances, it is quite likely that after several relays the message will have become drastically altered. In organizational settings this process is more than an amusing exercise, however. It can be a vital and distinct source of many significant problems, particularly in communication that cuts across status levels in the organization.

There is at least one important concept that serves to minimize the negative effects of noise and distortion—*redundancy*. There are two main types of redundancy: one is to repeat, within the message, the main points that are meant to arrive unchanged at the message's destination; the other approach is to send the same message along alternative paths and then have them compared upon arrival. If they differ substantially, the recipient can query the original source about the discrepancies. Or, if this is not possible, the message can be sent along three separate channels and the recipient can look for agreement among the messages on the main points—and assume that if the same point is made at least twice, it is the point that is meant to be conveyed.

Summary Views on Communication

The issues noted above are a sample of the kinds of specific aspects of communication upon which this book is based. There are other important aspects of communication to consider, and they will be introduced at later points. But to conclude this chapter we would like to indicate some of the general views one should hold regarding communication in organizations.

First, the chances of achieving exact communication are close to zero, if not completely impossible. We define exact here to mean that A has transmitted a message to B which has elicited in B an exact reproduction of A's original intention. There are at least two reactions you might have to the assertion that the likelihood of exact communication is zero. The first is, "Well, if what you say is so, then how come so many things involving communication still seem to work out rather well, as I intended them to?"

Our response to that is first to offer our congratulations, but second to warn that many potential impediments to effective communication remain *constantly* present, and can at any time create error and havoc in your communication relations with others. In effect, then, we are arguing that by improving your knowledge of the communication process you can increase the level of success you have in your interaction with others. An increased knowledge of potential communication problems, and an increased sensitivity to the ever-present possibility of their occurrence, will help you and those with whom you communicate to operate at a much lower level of communication difficulty.

A second view you might adopt from the concept of communication we have presented may be that, "Well, isn't *everything* communication, because can't these 'patterns' you speak of appear in many other guises—like nonverbal ones, for instance?" Our reply to this question is somewhat more equivocal than to the one above. It has been clearly established through a considerable amount of research in the nonverbal area (which involves such aspects as body movements, time, dress, gestures, etc.) that these dimensions do play an important role in the communication process. Nevertheless, our main focus is on that aspect of communication for which well-established symbolic systems are already well known. Much of the work in the nonverbal area is still involved in the primary investigative problems in "breaking the code" for such areas as gestures, postural movements, etc. Hence much of this work is still at the presymbolic level, and we have chosen to concentrate on those aspects of communication where this is not the main problem.

A third point to be drawn from our view of communication is that its focus is primarily on the *message-exchange* process that occurs between two or more individuals. The primary focus of communication inquiry is on the "linking system" between individuals, and not their internal states—such as attitudes, beliefs, knowledge levels, motivation, and personality dimensions. Clearly these latter areas are highly important for a complete understanding of organizational behavior as a whole, and it is also clear that there are many important associations between communication processes and these other organizational elements. But these other areas have received a great deal of attention by social scientists and organizational practitioners over the years, while communication processes have, all too often, been relegated to a minor role on the assumption that individuals will somehow "naturally" evolve appropriate communication patterns and practices.

But the weight of evidence against giving communication a minor role in organizational settings is growing rapidly. As organizations become more complex, as the problems and costs of communication management become more important in determining organizational success (if not survival), then an understanding of communication becomes a vital part of any overall assessment in an organization.

The final point we would like to emphasize is an *economic* one. By referring to our conception of organizations as processors of materials and energy and to the evolution of the concepts of information and communication, it should be quite evident that communication always entails *costs* in an organization. This fact is often overlooked, yet communication activities may account for two-thirds or more of the total time spent by members of an organization.

Seldom is attention given to treating communication as a resource-consuming aspect of organizational behavior which must be assessed against the value to be received from such expenditures. The most common approach we have encountered to this is reminders (in multiple copies) from management that communication costs are to be reduced by restricting access to stationery supplies. Quite often, firms involved in the selling of communication devices assume that the more of them you have, and the more elaborate they are, the "better" your communication will be. Try asking for a competent benefit/cost analysis of that assertion from the next salesperson you deal with; unless clear indications can be provided that effective communication improvements can be achieved through additional hardware, then we suggest that perhaps a second look at the sales proposal might be in order.

We can look elsewhere in the organization for other areas where communication exchange is seldom treated in terms of achievements versus costs incurred. Meetings, for example, are seldom assessed in terms of any accomplishments that come out of them versus the dollar expenditures in man-hours of time consumed (let alone in terms of alternative ways in which those members might have been spending their time more profitably). The value of individual preplanning before meetings is often overlooked. Even the basic concept of an "agenda" is often ignored. There is a natural tendency to meet on a regular basis, rather than on an "as needed" basis. When meetings occur, they often follow Parkinson's law and continue until the predesignated ending time, no matter what trivia occupies the meeting.

We are definitely not arguing here for an end to meetings, nor advocating a "magic formula" for optimizing communication-resource allocation in an organization. We are arguing at a much more basic level—we want organizations to begin to recognize the importance of considering communication as a cost-related aspect of overall organizational behavior. We want organizations to rationalize and investigate the nature of the communication activities in the organization. We advocate the concept of an "information manager" or a "communication manager" as a central part of organizational activity, whether this is an individual, a group, or a responsibility that is allocated among several members. Our intention is that, as the reader proceeds through this book, it will become increasingly clear what this task involves, what some of its major dimensions are, and what its potential benefits to the organization can be.

SUMMARY

Organizing is the label for the processes by which individuals come together to accomplish goals that are beyond their reach as independent entities. Organizing involves the input, throughput, and output of materials and energy. Superimposed on this matter/energy flow are patterns, perceived by members of the organization, occurring at various levels of probability. The concept of uncertainty refers to the unpredictability of outcomes; information is a measure of uncertainty reduction depending on how predictable an outcome is. When common symbolic systems and shared referents between the patterns and "real-world" referents are present, we have established some basic prerequisites for communication.

Internal to the organization, communication provides the mechanism for the control and coordination processes by which the members transform the inputs into useful, effective outputs. Part of control and coordination requires understanding information or communication as an absolute versus distributed entity, or as environmental, motivational, or instructional in application.

External to the organization, we define the information "space" in which it exists as the composite, aggregated space of the individual members. Furthermore, we indicate four types of general environments into which the information space can be classified: placid-randomized, placid-clustered, disturbed-reactive, and turbulent. The behavior of organizational members is described in markedly different terms depending on which environment they consider themselves to occupy.

Finally, we review some of the impediments to successful, effective communication—noise and message distortion—and one useful counterbalance to the problems they can create—redundancy. The chapter concludes with some comments about the cost implications of communication, and offers some perspectives from which to consider the question of costs.

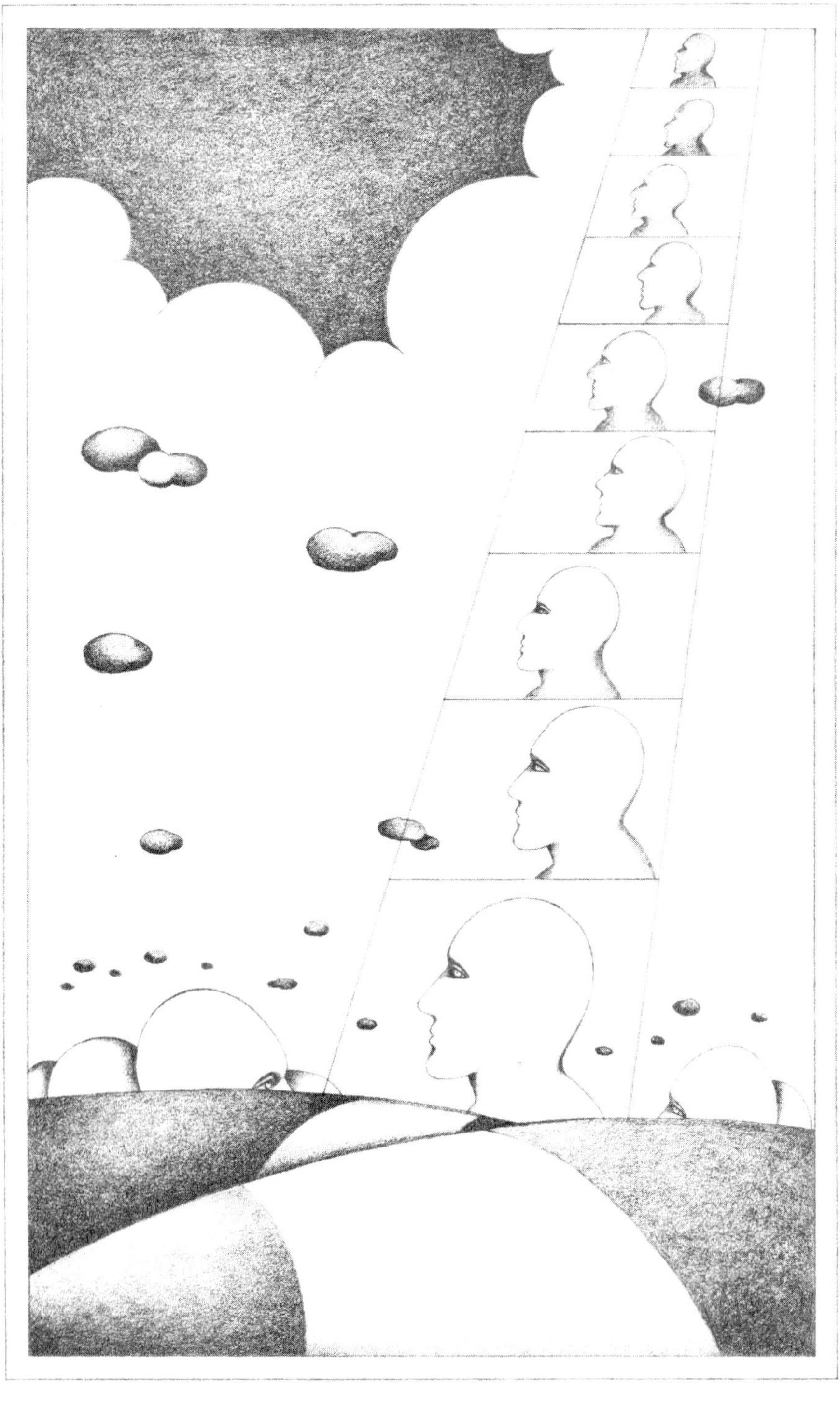

A Structural-Functional Framework for Organizational Communication 3

In the previous chapter we discussed three concepts that are fundamentally important to understanding the objectives of this book—the concepts of organization, information, and communication. Some of the immediate ways in which these concepts could be used in an organizational setting were illustrated; for instance, we gave an example using the distinction between "absolute" and "distributed" communication.

Once these central concepts have been presented, however, a different kind of need becomes important to the reader. It is one thing to discuss these concepts in isolation from one another, or from other organizing processes; it is an entirely different matter to deal with them in the framework of a logically consistent perspective that helps reveal *how* they operate and *why* they operate, not just *what* they do. There is a need for a coherent framework that relates the concepts of information and communication to the larger set of activities involved in the processes of organizing.

Thus we want to provide the reader with some broader perspectives that will help integrate the concepts of information and communication into the context of organizing. By doing this, the reader should be better able to understand the substantive material in Chapters 5 through 8. But, in addition, the reader should also acquire a way of viewing communication that will carry through the concluding chapters and apply to communication topics and problems that are not specifically dealt with here.

We will present a conceptual framework in three parts. First we will briefly discuss some of the terms and concepts that are commonly used in a "systems" approach to communication analysis. Then we will describe a three-way taxonomy whose main purpose is to provide a means for integrating existing knowledge about organizational communication. And, finally, we will review one systems analytic perspective, *structural-functionalism,* as a useful starting point for dealing with the questions of *how* and *why* communication operates in organizations.

SYSTEMS TERMINOLOGY

In Chapter 2 five crucial elements of organization were specified: size, interdependence, input, throughput, and output. The basic concepts of information and communication evolved directly from this view of organizations. It was stressed that communication played a critical role in the control of the flowthrough processes of the organization and in the coordination of the various parts of the organization.

Contained within this discussion are the main features of most definitions of systems: *systems* are composed of interdependent parts (components) that are separated by a boundary from their surrounding environment. The notion of interdependency has already been discussed. "Parts," or components, are the units within the system, such as individuals, work groups, or larger subdivisions of the organization. As noted earlier, "boundary" refers to the "perimeter" or outer limits of the organization; boundaries may be defined in terms of membership, or the physical, spatial, and temporal aspects of the organization.

One key feature of boundaries is their degree of permeability—how easily they allow materials, energy, or information to enter or leave the "system," i.e., the organization. To the extent that a boundary has very few "openings" to the environment, it is said to be relatively closed. Only a limited amount of matter, energy, or information can enter or leave. If there are no openings whatsoever, the system is (by definition) completely closed, completely self-contained. Most human social organizations, however, are relatively open systems. Even cloistered, contemplative religious orders, or isolated tribes in the most remote areas of the world, are minimally open to the outside world.

The greater the openness or permeability of a system's boundaries, we have said, the more readily materials, energy, and information can enter and leave. It is important to recognize that increases in openness may have consequences on the system itself that go beyond a mere increase in throughput. As systems change in their level of openness, important changes in the internal characteristics of the system are typically found. For example, increases in the openness of a system may lead to internal changes in the degree of complexity of the system (Danowski, 1974). Internal rearrangements of the system under the impact of increased openness can increase its capacity to handle more inputs and more types of inputs.

One issue which is often raised about the concept of "boundary" is "How do we know exactly where the boundary around the system is?" The answer to this is straightforward, although the implications are not: boundaries are *arbitrarily* defined by the person conducting an analysis, whether this be an academic researcher or a manager bent on solving a particular problem. Initially, there is no right or wrong way to define a boundary around a system; the analyst must develop his or her own precise definition. Only as the purpose of an analysis is made clear can a boundary definition be drawn and then evaluated.

Suppose a manager wants to learn how many messages about work topics are passing between two parts of the organization, Division A and Division B. It will be necessary to develop some clear rules that define whether a given organizational member is in either division or in some other part of the organization. Only when this step is accomplished can the manager proceed to identify messages: where they originate, the paths along which they flow, their points of destination, etc. If the system of rules mixes the membership together, however, the manager will not be able to answer the initial question about flow between the two divisions.

The *size* of a system is also determined by the investigator, depending on the problem under study and the way the boundary is drawn. For example, interaction patterns in one manager-subordinate dyad might be the "system" one chooses to study, so that the work group becomes the immediate environment, the division further removed in the environment, and the organization removed further yet. Or the organization itself might become the system that is to be studied, with the other organizations it interacts with serving as the immediate environment, and the larger economy the environment further removed.

In the second example, where the organization itself is under scrutiny, we want to introduce another important pair of systems terms, *subsystems* and *suprasystems*. Subsystems are parts of larger systems which themselves show interdependence and boundaries, i.e., the properties of systems. The suprasystem is a larger system that incorporates the system under scrutiny. In an organization, divisions might be subsystems, and work groups in a division, subsystems of the division. The organization might belong to a suprasystem composed of the other organizations in the same industry. The point of both these terms is to show that it might be possible to decompose any system into subsystems (whose behavior may significantly impact on the system), and that the same system may exist in a suprasystem (whose behavior may also significantly impact on the system). Consequently, a thorough systems analyst looks both to higher levels (suprasystems) and lower levels (subsystems) to see if their behavior is an important influence on the system being studied.

COMMUNICATION: BY LEVEL, FUNCTION, AND STRUCTURE

Let's return to our main topic—communication. There are a large number of specific variables within this basic concept, and in order to provide the reader with a framework for organizing and categorizing these variables, we will use a three-way classification scheme. We will discuss organizational communication as distinguished by the *system level* of analysis, by the *function* that communication performs in the organization, and by the *structure*, or patterning of communication among system members.

System Level

A comprehensive review of the research and writing about organizational communication indicates that there are four major system levels that are most commonly used (see Guetzkow, 1965; Downs, 1964; Katz and Kahn, 1966; Porter and Roberts, 1972; and Redding, 1972). First there is the individual, communicating to and receiving communication from the larger environment in the organization. Then there are the two-person units, the dyads, such as manager-subordinate, friend-friend, and two coworkers. The third important system level is the group, a set of individuals bound by common work relations, friendship relations, or other reasons for aggregating together. Finally, there is the organization as a whole, where its collective behavior is of interest.

What do we find when we examine the organizational communication literature concerned with each of these system levels? In terms of sheer amount of effort expended, the bulk of the work has been done on individuals, treating them as isolated entities in the larger organizational setting. Literature concerning group communication is next most prevalent, with discussions of dyadic and whole-organizational levels of communication least common. As a rough estimate of distribution of effort, about 60 percent of the literature deals with individuals, 25 percent with groups, and the remaining 15 percent with the dyadic and organizational levels. We will next point out the distinguishing features of the variables studied at each of these levels, describe some of these variables, and raise some comments and criticisms about where future research efforts ought to be expended.

At the individual level, where the greatest amount of work has been done, there are typically two types of research approaches that are used. In the first, different types of messages, or different combinations of channels and messages, are directed at the individual organizational member and an assessment is made of the effects this has on the individual's opinions, knowledge, or behaviors. For example, does exposure to the company newspaper raise the level of knowledge members have about the top officials of the organization? Or is the morale of workers boosted by exposure to a series of video-cassette tapes whose contents explain the purposes and goals of the organization, and which exhort members to work harder so that company (and individual) goals can be met?

The second approach involves the assessment of individuals on a selected series of characteristics to see if their subsequent communication behaviors can be predicted. Does a test of information-processing skills indicate which individuals will perform adequately in tasks that demand high levels of processing? Do certain personality tests predict which individuals will make effective group leaders, or effective managers?

Some of the specific communication variables that have been assessed at the individual level include *amount of communication*, as measured by frequency and/or duration of interpersonal contact and exposure to organizational printed materials; use of various *communication channels* (e.g., interpersonal, print, and mediated); *levels of knowledge*; and *communication skills* (e.g., interpersonal, writing, and listening).

The key theme that runs through such studies is the stress on *individual* differences, rather than on any concern for the individual as an *interdependent* part of a system. These studies focus on changes in the individual, or on changes that the individual may create, but are conducted in such a way that the fact that they are organizational members is almost irrelevant. Given our basic position that organizational behavior requires control, coordination, and interdependence, studies that ignore these phenomena may make greater contributions to general communication theory than to theory in the organizational setting. This is not to deny the value of studying individual communication behavior in an organization, but simply to stress that a significant amount of theoretic and pragmatic value remains untapped in research at the other system levels. We hope to explain this criticism shortly.

A second major criticism about this research, often called "individual-difference" research, is that it is largely atheoretical; i.e., it is often not derived from any particular theoretical proposition or a larger theoretic formulation. Hence results from such efforts generate unintegrated (and perhaps unintegratable) findings that may have little value to either the researcher or the manager. Perhaps the major exception to this criticism comes in the research based on the psychological "balance" theories, although most of that research does not deal directly with communication in the sense of message reception, production, and exchange, as we have described it. In Chapter 5 we deal with one individual-difference phenomenon, communication *load*.

Table 3-1. Weick's hierarchy of organizational sizes, with explanatory comments on the unique aspects of larger organizations.

Number of persons	Distinctive features of each organizational size
1 to 2	The basic unit of social interaction is formed, and departure of one member destroys the system.
2 to 3	Coalitions are now possible, with the obvious implication for control processes.
3 to 4	While a dyad cannot necessarily rule, stalemates can occur.
4 to 7	Although two dyads can coalesce for control, a triad can achieve its will if the dyads do not unite; minority rule is possible.
7 to 9	Perfect symmetry in terms of the above; with three triads there can be coalitions at two levels.

The argument that it is important to study communication processes at levels other than that of single individuals is not a new one, however. Some 18 years ago, Coleman (1958) used the arguments we have been citing in an indictment of the use of individual differences and aggregative statistical analyses in the study of social processes, such as communication. The core of this criticism is that it is not appropriate to theorize about processes while using research procedures that do not reflect the time-varying nature of these processes. More recently, other authors (Krippendorf, 1970) have reopened this issue and urged that research of much more significant theoretic and practical utility is available to those who wish to investigate processes, including information or communication, at higher system levels than is typically the case.

If the argument is accepted in principle, then the question becomes one of implementation. What *are* the most fruitful system levels for the study of communication? Weick (1969) contends that the crucial transition points in organizational size occur in the five instances shown in Table 3-1.

These distinctions are quite intriguing, not the least for their ability to capture basic organizational processes. Unfortunately, the available literature does not break easily into precisely those categories, so we have elected to use a simpler system, with the loss of precision that entails. Beyond the individual, the level we will first evaluate is the *dyad*, since it is the fundamental social unit in an organization. Furthermore, the dyad is an essential "building block" in the composition of groups and larger networks in organizations.

What variables distinguish a dyad from two isolated individuals? For the purpose of analyzing organizational communication, there is at least one major type of communication that emerges in a dyadic setting, and which is not present among isolated individuals. This phenomenon is known as *relational control* through communication; it refers to the use of communication to signal the degree of influence or direction one person has over another. The important point to note is that control requires two persons, one who attempts it and the other who accepts.

When two individuals exchange messages, there are two separable aspects of this exchange. The first is well known; it is the referential or "content" aspect of the message. It refers to the "real-world" referent of the message. In the earlier discussion of the relative merits of office computing equipment, it is the objects themselves that are referenced by the "content" aspects of the interaction.

A second and equally important part of the interaction (particularly in the organizational setting) is the relational-control aspect of the exchange; i.e., those elements in the exchange in which the two persons define and carry out the relationship that will exist between them. A simple example of the control dimension is shown in the following exchange:

Manager:
By the way, what's the status of that memo you're writing for me? Is it ready to go out?

Subordinate:
Yes, it's done and ready for your review.

This type of exchange is called a *complementary* one (Watzlawick, et al., 1967), and shows that the first speaker had control of the interaction, at least at that moment in time. The first speaker asked a question (made a statement that offered a control definition of the relationship) that the subordinate responded to in a manner that indicated that control was being accepted (the question was answered in the affirmative). The exchange might have gone otherwise however:

Subordinate:
Are you actually ready to read the memo? I need to know before I can answer you.

This type of interaction is called *symmetrical*, because the control definition offered by the manager was not accepted by the subordinate. By responding to a question with a question, the manager's control maneuver was countered by a similar attempt on the part of the subordinate.

Whether relational control in a dyad remains constant or shifts over time depends on a number of factors (see Chapter 6). The important point to note here is that a new communcation phenomenon has emerged in the interaction of these two individuals—and this phenomenon is not available for analysis at an individual level. Problems of relational control are at the heart of many of the communication difficulties that are encountered in life, particularly in the organizational setting. Often it appears that two individuals are arguing at the content level when in fact they are engaged in an intense dispute over who will *control* the interaction.

Another concept which emerges at the dyadic level of analysis is the set of communication *rules* that guide and shape the interaction between two persons. The concept of rules applies to all dyads, although the nature of the rules and their relative importance changes for different types of dyads. Examples of rules are those that deal with when, where, and how often to interact, who makes these decisions, what topics are appropriate under various circumstances, etc.

Finally, two other dyadic concepts are worthy of mention, both of which developed from the well-known "coorientation" model of Newcomb and others. The first concept is *accuracy*, a measure of how precisely one person in the dyad knows how the other views a particular aspect of their interaction. The second concept is *agreement*, which indicates the extent to which members of a dyad hold the same view about what the appropriate rules are, their importance, etc.

We do not want to present a "shopping list" of variables at this point. Instead, we simply want to illustrate the fact that organizational communication analysis has many areas which are underdeveloped, but which, if developed, will provide exciting new contributions to both the theoretic and the applied aspects of communication. Chapter 6 is devoted to a fuller explanation of communication at the dyadic level.

The next-higher system level of interest is the *group*. Groups are important in organizations under several types of definitions; i.e., work, friendship, kinship, or "tribal groups" (see Jay, 1971). Group processes have attracted the attention of many individuals. For organizational communication purposes, groups offer the opportunity to study additional communication phenomena.

One important phenomenon is communication *structure*, a term which refers to the patterns of repetitive interactions that occur among members of a group. When structure is minimal, every member feels free to talk with everyone else, making it impossible to predict who will be communicating at any given moment. Conversely, when structure is maximal, interaction is constantly directed to just one individual. The degree of communication structure in a group is one important property in determining its ability to process incoming messages, conduct its own internal operations, sustain its morale, or continue its output. Structure is treated more fully later in the present chapter, and Chapter 7 is devoted to group-communication processes.

In the preceding pages the focus has shifted from the individual to the dyad, and from the dyad to the group. At the final level, that of the whole organization, our interest is primarily in the networks of interaction that exist among the members—networks that enable work-related communication to occur, that enable social communication, gossip, rumors, and other types of messages to flow. It is important to learn not only the networks themselves, but their relationships with other aspects of the organization's activities. Hence Chapter 8 deals exclusively with the topic of networks.

There are two concluding points to be drawn from our discussion of system levels. The first point is that individual-difference research has accounted for much of what has been done under the heading of organizational-communication research. We have tried to indicate, as our second main point, that a considerable body of useful information about organizational-communication processes lies before us when we examine dyadic behavior, group behavior, and network behavior. Chapters 5 through 8 deal with these four topics, in turn.

The Function of Communication

While system level provides one dimension of our attempt to deal with the study of organizational communication, function and structure provide the main substance of our interest at each level. Here we turn to function.

Goals and objectives can differ widely at the individual, dyad, group, or organizational level. Communication provides a means by which at least some of these goals can be reached. We use the term *function* to refer to the use of communication in different settings to achieve various goals and objectives. Function refers to the effects or consequences of communication in the organization. More simply, the term function is used to help answer the question, "What is communication supposed to *do* in the organization?"

One important factor in considering the function of communication is the viewpoint or perspective from which the functions are established. Katz and Kahn (1966) provide one of the classic illustrations of this point in their discussion of two separate functional typologies. The first posits a series of organizational subsystems into which functions can be classified: production, maintenance, adaptation, and management. This scheme takes the perspective of the entire organization; it is useful for managers trying to operate and integrate all four functions, or for an analyst studying the whole organization.

But Katz and Kahn also provide a separate set of functions that are intended at the dyadic level—between manager and subordinate. In this setting the functions of communication concentrate on job instructions, job rationale, organizational procedures, and the indoctrination of employees into organizational goals. Notice that the two sets of functions are not at all incompatible; the second is a translation of the first into the specific one-on-one setting at the dyadic level. This illustrates the important point that communication functions can vary by system level, and that it is also possible to "translate" them from level to level so that they comprise a coherent and integrated whole.

Numerous authors have written about organizational functions, and have developed their own variations of functional categories. The diversity of their efforts illustrates that there is no functional category system which is necessarily "best" for a given organization; what is appropriate in one setting may

Table 3-2. Functional categories given by twelve authors, arranged into five groups (From Martha A. Jacob, "The Structure and Functions of Internal Communication in Three Religious Communities," unpublished doctoral dissertation, Department of Communication, Michigan State University, 1972. Reprinted by permission.)

	Communication functions	
Authors	*Work*	*Maintenance*
Katz and Kahn	job instructions	organizational proceedings and practices job rationale organizational goal
Redding	task	maintenance
Haberstroh	control (prevent dysfunction)	
Berlo	production	maintenance
Thayer	instruct	inform
Barnard	effectiveness	efficiency
Wickesberg	problem-solving instructions	information transmission
Ackoff	inform	instruct
Parsons	production	maintenance
Johnson(H)	goal attainment	pattern maintenance and tension management
Etzioni	instrumental information cognitive orientation	instrumental information cognitive orientation
Maslow Argyris		

not be appropriate in another. Jacob (1972) reviewed twelve category systems and was able to group them into five different headings (see Table 3-2).

Inspection of the first column shows categories that deal primarily with task relations, with getting work completed. The second heading deals with the support or maintenance activities needed to bolster production efforts. Next is a small number of functions with a motivational quality to them, followed by a column that reflects the integration of the individual into the larger organization. The final heading clearly refers to the innovation, change, or adaptation function.

Communication functions

Motivation	Integration	Innovation
	indoctrination of employees: social-emotional	
	human	
		innovation
influence	integrate	
approval	scuttlebutt	
motivate		
	management support	adaptation
	integration	adaptation
	expressive values, norms	
	self-actualization	

To clarify the concept of function, we will concentrate on three commonly used functions: production, innovation, and maintenance.

What is meant by "communication that achieves production"? The term refers to that subset of the total message flow in the organization that is directed toward the achievement of the organization's output or production goals. Production messages are those that direct, coordinate, and regulate the activities of the organization's members in such a way as to bring about the desired end results. This includes messages that specify the type and amount of output for units or individuals in the organization, as well as its overall goals. This also includes messages that deal with any problems in the work flow, any errors or error trends, or any of many other possible impediments to organizational success. The flow of production messages is typically along the lines of formal authority, as depicted in the "organization chart."

In contrast to messages that govern or affect ongoing work activities, messages that deal with innovation or with maintenance are usually much less common yet much more complex when they do occur. "Innovation"—the generation of new ideas and behaviors for improving the organization—is seldom treated as a central part of the communication system of an organization. In other words, higher management rarely makes an explicit attempt to obtain and evaluate new ideas and practices from their subordinates; there may be no formal mechanism (especially if the so-called "suggestion system" is not considered) for allowing a flow of such messages to move throughout the organization. It would be inaccurate to accuse all organizations of this deficiency, but it does appear to be widespread in a very high proportion of organizations.

In large part, the importance of communication intended to bring about innovation is based on the degree to which the organization's managers believe that their environment is a rapidly changing and/or unstable one. To the extent that the environment is seen as either disturbed-reactive or turbulent (using the Emery and Trist typology described in Chapter 2), innovation will be treated as one of the important functions of communication.

There are two clearly separable aspects of the innovation function. The first deals with eliciting or generating proposals, suggestions, and/or new ideas for changing organizational practices in such a way as to increase efficiency, morale, or other important goals of the organization. It is this type of message that "suggestion systems," or "task forces," or "research and development" units may provide. But often the main body of organizational members are considered a source of new ideas and practices which, if managers were more aware, could be drawn on to improve the organization.

The second aspect of the innovation function is often included with the first, although it actually deals with a considerably different type of problem. Here we refer to messages which deal with the issue of *implementation* of new ideas and practices. Thus while the first type of innovation message (which might also be labeled "creativity" message) centers on the problem of finding new things to do, this second type treats the problem of getting organizational members to *adopt* and carry out new ideas. In essence, the second type of innovation message can be more easily treated as a subheading of the basic production-related or persuasive aspect of communication, and there is an extensive body of literature on the diffusion of innovations through social systems (Rogers and Shoemaker, 1972).

Maintenance communication, on the other hand, serves a purpose which is quite distinct from either production or innovation communication. Berlo (1969) discusses the maintenance function in terms of three subcategories: (1) the maintenance of the individual's self-concept, (2) the maintenance of interpersonal relationships with others in the organization, and (3) the maintenance of the production and innovation functions themselves. Another way of stating these three categories is this: maintenance communication is that which (a) affects the member's feelings of personal worth and significance, (b) changes the "value" placed on interaction with coworkers, supervisors, and subordinates, and (c) alters the perceived importance of continuing to meet the organization's production and innovation needs.

Thus we are arguing that production, innovation, and maintenance are three of the functions which communication is meant to perform in an organization. Furthermore, the responsibility for the development and continued operation of communication practices that influence these functions is primarily that of the organization's leadership—management and/or union. This is not meant, however, to reduce the importance of nonsupervisory personnel in formulating and implementing effective communication practices. Finally, we should note that over the past 50 years organizational theory has tended to encompass more and more of the innovation and maintenance functions. We discuss this in more detail in Chapter 4.

The Structure of Communication
Let's shift the discussion from the concept of the function of communication to that of the structure of communication. In discussing communication functions, we are dealing with the substance or content of messages as they move through the organization. When we discuss communication *structure*, however, our concern is with the patterns or regularities observed when these messages move, rather than with the content of the messages themselves. Both function and structure are intimately linked together, and major breakdowns in either can render the communication system of an organization inoperative.

What do we mean by communication structure? Assume that you are able to observe the behavior of an organization's members over time, as they go about their work activities. The overall work flow includes frequent acts of interdependence among the organization's members. As part of the ongoing work flow, the exchange of messages also takes place. It is these repetitive, recurring patterns of message exchange that comprise the basic *structure* of communication among the members of an organization.

Communication structure can be readily seen if we examine the telephone network within an organization. Once we learn who calls whom, and which telephone lines are easiest to use to reach a certain individual, some basic characteristics of the network have been determined. We can derive many measures of the message "traffic" along these lines.

But communication structure in organizations has a much broader application than simply those networks established by formal communications hardware. In addition to the hardware networks are the networks based solely on face-to-face interaction, such as discussions among coworkers, reports and orders given in a manager-subordinate exchange, and regular meetings of certain groups. It is these "people" networks that are at least equally as important as the organizational networks based on communications devices.

How can we describe, in general terms, the nature of the communication networks in an organization? First, we should recognize that the networks can be based on any of several types of channels besides telephone or intercom; memo distribution systems, group meetings, face-to-face encounters, and other types of channels are possible. Second, the type of information moving along these networks can also vary, as can the speed, accuracy, freedom from distortion, and other aspects of the message flow.

The basic concepts and properties of organizational networks are described more rigorously in Chapter 8. For the moment, however, it is important simply to recognize that such networks are a vital part of organizational functioning, and that they may be examined and appraised even when person-to-person networks are involved, rather than hardware networks alone.

The concept of structure is closely related to the level of predictability or patterning of the communication exchanges among the organization's members. In a situation where everyone talks to virtually everyone else, there is a minimum of structure; there is virtually no *restraint* on the communication patterns and very little in the way of a network emerges. Conversely, where communication is more restrained, where predictability of interaction patterns increases, then communication structure increases as well. At this level, the important questions include, "How much structure best organizes our overall efforts?" and, "What types of structure are best suited for achieving various goals?"

STRUCTURAL-FUNCTIONAL ANALYSIS

Structural-functional analysis, with its roots in biology, is one of the major systems approaches that have been adapted to the social sciences. One of the distinctive virtues of structural-functional analysis (or "functionalism," for short) is that it contains an explicit, step-by-step set of procedures to be followed in conducting such an analysis. The essential steps in this process are given by Monge (1972), as synthesized from a number of authors; the steps appear in paraphrased form below:

1. The system under study, as well as the component parts and their interrelations, must be specified. Not *all* the parts of the system require identification, just those included in further analysis.

2. The system's environment must be specified; in particular, those aspects of the environment which affect the system's behavior must be clearly noted.

3. The attributes or traits of the system which are considered essential for its continued existence must be determined.

4. The different amounts or values which each trait may assume, and in particular, the range of values within which the trait must stay for the system's continuation, must be indicated.

5. The mechanisms by which the system's components collectively keep the trait within the limits required for the system's existence must be discovered. The mechanisms must also be understood in terms of the potential impact of internal system changes or of changes in the environment.

Before we discuss these points in greater detail, there are three distinct needs that they highlight. First, it is clear that we must be able to tell what key traits keep the system operating at any given point in time, and we must know what the "critical" levels of the key traits are, i.e., when the system is in danger of collapsing or being destroyed. Second, we need to know rather precisely about the bonds between the system's component parts and the key traits, since it is these bonds that act to keep the traits within the desired limits. And, finally, the important environmental factors must be identified and their impact on the system must be monitored.

Earlier in this chapter we discussed three functions that communication commonly performs in an organization—production, innovation, and maintenance. Let's take a hypothetical *manufacturing organization* as a system and use it to illustrate a functional analysis of communication, beginning with production or task communication.

The first step—specification of the system—has already been completed. Next we want to identify the component parts. We might do this by noting the existing divisions, such as sales, marketing, finance, production, and research. Or, alternatively, we might conduct an analysis of the task or production *net-*

work through which all work-related messages move. This network indicates what types of messages move, to which people, at which times, through which channels, and at what costs. By identifying groups of people communicating about work, and the people who link the groups together, we can produce a "map" of the movement of production messages in the organization. These groups can be treated as the "components" of the system.

Our next step is to identify the environment in which the organization operates. We can do this from the vantage point of the members of the organization, using their composite "enacted environment," as defined in Chapter 2. In addition, we may want to construct our own definition of the information space of the organization, compiled by examining competitors, future market conditions, uncertainties in supplies, and management styles and capabilities—in short, by building a counterpoint view to the information space used by the organization's members. The purpose of our efforts will be to identify key factors that might affect the production-communication function of the organization.

The next step—identification of the essential (existence-determining) traits of the system—is crucial. This effort can proceed at two distinct levels. We can identify such traits as total profit, return on investment, growth in value of assets, ability to attract capital, and efficiency, each of which economists or financial analysts might consider essential. But because analysis at this level is beyond the scope of this book, we must assume that these decisions have been made by the appropriate individuals (and that "good" production communication is necessary to accomplish them) and turn to the question of whether the production-communication system is properly operative. We consider the flow of production communication, therefore, essential to the survival of our hypothetical manufacturing organization.

For example, suppose this organization earns most of its income through the manufacture of products for sale in the mass consumer market. Each of its managers is enmeshed in a network of task-related communication. How rapidly are the products now being sold? What are the top manager's profit goals? What are the latest developments among competitors? What does the firm's economic-research unit have to say? What are the latest odd bits of rumors that affect an individual manager's job? How much communication does he or she have access to, and how much is useful? What channels provide what communication? What time lags are involved in the receipt or dissemination of communication?

While we may eventually reduce these questions to a simpler set, they comprise a partial list of the traits of the production-communication system from the perspective of this one individual. The performance of this system affects the performance (career) of the individual, and ultimately the organization (its viability).

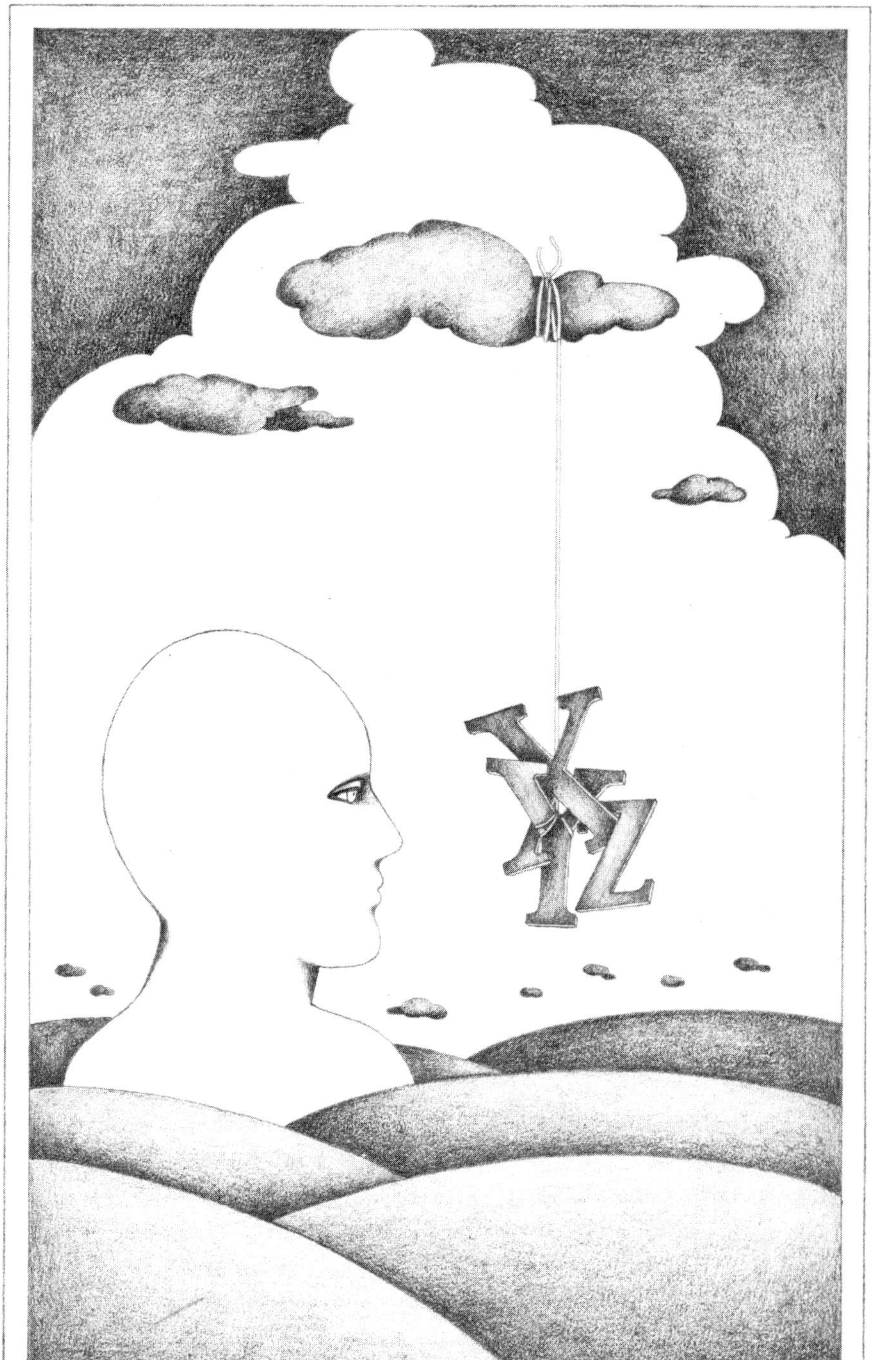
XYZ

The major traits would include type of communication quality, timeliness, and completeness. Are they all *essential*? Perhaps. Are they an *exhaustive* set? Probably not. But as we study the problem more thoroughly, we will obtain more complete answers to these questions. *The issue of essentiality requires that we learn whether in fact the absence (or excessive presence) of one of these traits can lead to a collapse in the person's performance or, ultimately, a collapse of the system itself.* If the answer is "yes," the trait is an essential one.

In certain instances, failures in production-communication systems have been given considerable blame for the failure of entire organizations. The collapse of many brokerage houses in the late sixties and early seventies has been attributed to their inability to process the enormous volume of stock and bond transactions the market was then experiencing.

A fear of the *possible* failure of communication processing in large-scale computerized health-care delivery systems has been responsible in part for the reluctance of the medical profession to adopt them for hospital use. While the existing "paper-and-pencil" record-keeping systems are known to possess their own distinct faults, the potential damage that could result if a computerized system "crashed" has led to minimal adoption of such systems.

In many instances it seems clear that some aspects of production-communication systems do not have the dramatic "life-or-death" quality demanded in the biologically derived functional-analysis guidelines. But it is equally important to note that there can be many instances where malfunctions in the production-communication system reduce output, cause costly mistakes, lower efficiency, and otherwise impair the organization's performance on its more basic traits. Each aspect of the production-communication system needs careful review to determine the degree of its potential impact on the organization.

Step four in functional analysis requires the determination of the range of values which the communication system's traits may take on, and, more importantly, the range required for the system's continuation.

Let's use a library as an example. Among their various duties, the staff receives a certain number of requests per hour for assistance, and returns a certain number of previously withdrawn items. In order to function in such a manner as to continue to receive income, both sets of demands must be met. A balance must be maintained.

If output exceeds returns too greatly, the library will soon have no further materials to provide. If all resources are spent handling returns, dissatisfaction with unfilled requests may create serious problems. Empirically, over time, the library management may find that when the imbalance reaches 20 percent, strong corrective measures are needed to restore the system to proper balance.

In this example, then, two points are illustrated: (1) knowing the range the trait *may* assume in the system, and (2) knowing the range it *must* assume in order to remain viable.

Step five is the essential aspect of the entire analysis process—establishing the *mechanisms* that operate to keep the trait within the desired range.

Suppose that "timeliness" of message receipt is one of the system's key traits. The range of times when a certain message reaches an individual should be determined, as well as when that message is needed. At some point, at least for selected messages, there may be critical deadlines which cannot be exceeded if the messages are to have any value at all. Items that reach the person after the deadline are considered to have no importance in reaching a particular decision—they are too late. Or, if the message arrives too early, it may be overlooked when decision-making time comes. Perhaps ideally the message should arrive three days before the decision.

The system can be inspected to determine the mechanisms or procedures for getting the messages to the individual. Perhaps they are phoned in (are the lines ever tied up for lengthy periods?), or mailed (how long does it take to reach the person; how often is it lost?), brought by messenger (how reliable is the service?), or even obtained by the individual (with what rate of success?). So we can identify the different ways that the critical message can arrive, and isolate some of the potential trouble areas in the delivery system. We can also find out how often a message actually reaches the person too early or too late to be of value, by each of the mechanisms actually used.

Normally, in such a system, if the "error" rate reaches levels that are considered excessively high, there are corrective actions that can be taken. Perhaps a note to the individual's manager will provide authorization to develop additional back-up systems that can be used whenever it seems that a failure may occur. Perhaps the manager will put some pressure on the subordinate to take the issue more seriously and engage in some immediate corrective action. The point here is that, once given the trait and some idea of the mechanism by which it functions, the final step in functional analysis is to learn as much as possible about the control processes that will keep the trait in the desired range of values—and ultimately, of course, be able to influence the trait whenever it seems to be deviating excessively from its desired range.

To summarize, then, functional analysis requires that we complete five tasks when we analyze communication in an organization: (1) identify the organization, its component parts and their relations, and, in particular, identify the communication system in the organization; (2) identify the important aspects of the environment which affect the performance of the organization; (3) determine the communication traits (among the possible set of traits) that are essential to the organization's survival; (4) find out the range of desired and acceptable values for these traits; and (5) learn about the mechanism which determines the values these traits take, its potential problems, and the means for correcting these problems.

The example we have just reviewed involved one trait—timeliness of information, which was considered essential since certain key decisions in the hypothetical organization required getting certain messages by a certain time. We determined how those messages reached the decision makers, and we identified the possible sources of delay or distortion that could prevent the messages from arriving when needed. We also mentioned corrective steps that could be initiated if the system is found to be defective. These specific steps, then, are an example of the application of functional analysis to the communication system of an organization.

Although we could go on to give other examples of traits in the flow of work-related communication that seem essential to the overall survival of the organization, we prefer to turn to the other functions of communication, and to present a brief discussion of each of them, using the same analysis scheme.

Earlier we defined innovation communication as that subset of overall communication that elicited new ideas and practices within the organization's overall framework. Some of these innovations might be related to the production process, others might be related to the innovation process itself, and still others might be related to maintenance communication. An important point to consider before any further functional analysis is attempted is whether innovation communication can be said to be vital or essential as a trait of the organization's communication system. To many managers it is clearly not important—they do little to encourage the generation of new ideas, and even less to reward those who provide them. Alternatively, however, there are many managerial systems which establish cash rewards for innovations, which give recognition to innovators in internal publications, and which include this aspect of performance in a person's review for raises and promotion. In a parallel fashion, we will show in Chapter 4 that some organizational theorists stress innovation, while others do not.

The key here seems to lie in the way managers (or organizational theorists) view their environment, their "information space." If environmental conditions are unstable and potentially threatening to the organization, and if the organization's members are perceived to have a reservoir of useful new ideas and practices, then innovation is an encouraged component of communication. It is treated as an essential trait. To the extent that this is not the case, the innovation function receives little or no attention.

Thus we begin our discussion of innovation communication with the forewarning that its status varies from organization to organization. But if we assert that it *is* to be a function of communication in a given situation, we can then proceed with a functional analysis. We will follow exactly the same steps as before, but we will probably find that their actual implementation is considerably more difficult.

For example, we must again define the key traits, this time for innovation communication. Will the traits be the number of innovations generated, the cost-savings value of each, the breadth of applicability of the innovations, the total number of persons involved, or what? When we dealt with production communication, we linked the traits directly back to the economic aspects of the firm. Here we can emphasize either the economic aspects, as before, or the "human factors" aspects, in which the important function of innovation communication is the creation of the feeling that organizational members are valued for their ideas, even though many of their ideas are undesirable or unworkable. We are not faced with a dichotomous choice—economic versus human concerns—because the two can be blended. What we are faced with is the need first to come to a clear decision about the purpose or purposes of innovation communication in the organization, and then to use that decision as an organizing principle around which we evaluate and/or build the innovation system.

What are some of the mechanisms that can be used to foster innovation in the organization? Perhaps the most effective is to make innovation communication a clear part of the job responsibility of each successive level of management. This means that managers at each level routinely gather new ideas, suggest them to others, discuss them with peers, subordinates, and supervisors, and are generally held accountable for the accomplishment of the task in the same way that they would be held accountable for the completion of a report or some other task-oriented project.

Beyond this, there are a wide variety of "add-on" systems that have been used, with varying degrees of success. One of these, for example, is an independent "suggestion system," in which members fill out forms describing their idea and eventually get some word back about the idea's acceptability, including the possibility of a cash award.

Communication intended to maintain the self-image or the attitudes of the individual toward work and the organization—the maintenance function—also is interpreted and applied in a wide range of ways by different managers and different organizational theorists. Its importance to the survival of the organization is the subject of a great deal of debate. Some consider only the monetary aspects of employment while others regard the job as a means of developing or actualizing the human potential within each organizational member. Needless to say, under the first view the maintenance system is virtually nonexistent, while under the latter much greater emphasis is given to developing a sense of participation and belonging among organizational members by such means as involving them in decisions and implementing nonmonetary ways of enhancing their self-concept, ego, and status.

If, however, maintenance-communication practices do exist in a given organization, our analysis of these practices would be parallel to our analysis for production (and perhaps innovation) communication. We would define the critical maintenance traits (e.g., the level of morale below which serious employee unrest would occur), determine the mechanisms which govern these traits (e.g., the amount of direct contact with one's immediate supervisor, and the positive reinforcement gained from that contact), and operate on these mechanisms to keep the trait within the desired levels.

SUMMARY

In this chapter we have presented an overall conceptual framework for the analysis of communication in organizations from three perspectives. First we reviewed and discussed some of the terminology that is basic to any discussion about organizations as systems and communication as part of a system.

Then we presented a simple, three-way taxonomy for arranging the existing knowledge about communication: we discussed different communication phenomena at the individual, dyad, group, and whole-organization levels. We noted the theoretic shortcomings and advantages present at each level. We then discussed the concept of communication function, where our interest is in the purpose or consequences for communication in the organization. A dozen functional typologies were presented. Next we reviewed the concept of communication structure, i.e., the repeated patterns of interaction that make up the relatively stable "networks" through which communication moves in the organization.

In the final section of the chapter we outlined the logic and procedures for conducting a structural-functional analysis of communication in an organization. We presented the main steps in the process, and then provided the example of a manufacturing organization whose production communication was vital to its performance. The application of this set of procedures was briefly extended to innovation and maintenance communication.

After completing Chapters 1 to 3, the reader should by now have developed a conceptualization of communication as the movement of patterned matter/energy with symbolic referents through an organization. Communication should be treated as the vehicle or mechanism by which processes of control and coordination are carried out while the organization's members go about their general organizing processes.

Communication itself should be seen in structural-functional terms, with the reader recognizing that this approach includes a framework for examination of key aspects of organizational processes. There are, however, alternative conceptualizations of the role of communication in organizational theories, and we turn to these more traditional approaches in the following chapter.*

---

*Those readers already acquainted with systems concepts and terminology may well question why the structural-functional perspective is used as an analytic framework, rather than cybernetics or general systems theory. At least as far as concepts are concerned, this chapter has, in fact, drawn upon all three paradigms. For example: trait, range, and mechanism are derived from structural-functionalism; the concepts of components, boundaries, and system levels are clearly adopted from general systems theory; and control and feedback are borrowed from cybernetics.

Furthermore, general systems theory presents a useful category scheme for labeling the parts of any complex phenomenon, structural-functionalism provides a reasonably sophisticated and sufficiently general theoretical mechanism for explaining how the phenomenon operates, and cybernetics offers a restricted but well-developed analytic framework for studying the special properties of coordination and control. Given the current, relatively low level of sophistication of research directed toward organizational communication and the complexity of the phenomena we intend to examine, structural-functionalism seems the most appropriate. Additionally, since the logic of structural-functionalism has not yet been clearly articulated and applied to dynamic problems, it seems to have particular merit as an important perspective to introduce into the communication discipline.

In a recent book, Hage (1975) argues that the focus of structural-functionalism has been on the identification of static structures rather than dynamic processes, and he urges that structural-functionalism be abandoned in favor of a cybernetic approach. While we will not debate his analysis of past research, we do take issue with his conclusion, for there is nothing inherent in the logic of structural-functionalism which requires a static approach. In many respects, the differences existing between cybernetics and structural-functionalism may well be differences of degree rather than of kind; i.e., a structural-functional and cybernetic analysis may well produce the same kinds of results, but the structural-functional analysis is appropriate when the analyst is limited in insight and information, while the cybernetic analysis requires highly accurate and precise knowledge about how a certain process operates. Whatever the final resolution of these differences in perspective, the critical distinctions should not be terminological; one should, rather, employ the analytic tool that is most appropriate for both the problem and the level of analysis required.

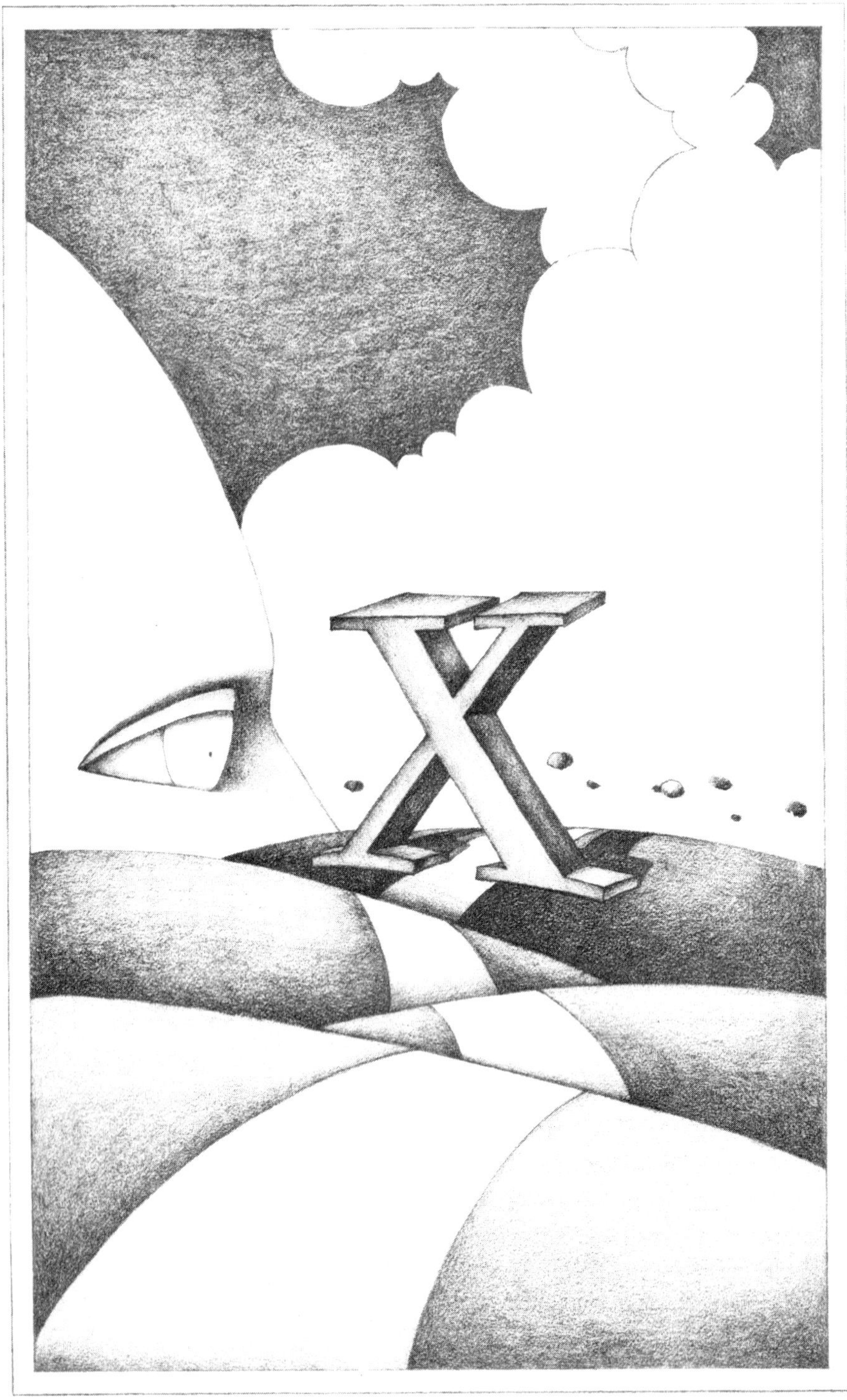
X

Some Communication Implications of Major Organizational Theories 4

> ...in an exhaustive theory of organization, communication would occupy a central place, because the structure, extensiveness, and scope of organization are almost entirely determined by communication techniques.
>
> (Barnard, 1938)

In reviewing the history of organizational theories and the attention given to communication by various theorists, we find Barnard (1938) is one of the first theorists to mention the importance of communication in the functioning of organizations. Writers then and, more often, now point out the ubiquitous nature of communication in organizations. Communication is said to be pervasive, ever-present, and closely linked to other functions of the organization.

Sometimes this broad-spectrum conceptualization leads a theorist to dismiss communication as a concept not worthy of further study. If *all* behavior is included under the heading of communication, no further analysis is possible, since we are dealing with a very general notion, one which does not readily lend itself to scientific study. But we have argued throughout this book that communication ought not—and need not—be treated in such global terms. In place of a global view, we have discussed a variety of communication concepts which focus on specific, discrete behaviors, such as information load, communication rules, group communication phenomena, communication networks (structure), and communication function. These concepts vary from situation to situation, and we are accumulating a growing body of evidence for their relationships to other organizational phenomena. By treating communication in such a way that specific phenomena can be identified, isolated, and studied, it will be possible to advance scientific knowledge about communication as well as to increase the practical utility of the knowledge. Without such efforts, however, communication will truly remain an ambiguous "background variable."

There is another serious problem that often occurs in the writing about communication processes in organizational functioning. Often, theorists will pay lip service to the importance of "good" communication, and then let the issue rest there. Good communication, apparently, is what one has when there are no "communication breakdowns," or when the major "pitfalls" to achieving good communication are avoided. Writers usually make fairly general comments and devote relatively little attention to a systematic elaboration of the communication concepts, principles, and practices—the particular "model" of communication—underlying a given organizational theory. So on the one hand there are writers who dismiss communication as unimportant, while on the other hand there are those who praise it yet still do not accord it the specific treatment needed. It is precisely this latter point—that communication can and should be treated as a distinctive and influential aspect of organizing—that is of main concern in this book.

The critical need for a detailed elaboration of the basic communication model underpinning any organizational theory seems obvious. Why? Because the communication behaviors of the organization's members must reflect the thrust of an organization's operating philosophy—its "theory"—in order for the philosophy to have impact. Suppose that the managers of an organization decide to adopt one of the human relations approaches—McGregor's "Theory Y," for example, with its emphasis on openness of human relationships. Operationally, openness typically means that face-to-face exchanges are characterized by greater self-disclosure of internal feelings, greater willingness to provide information rather than withhold it, and fuller and more frank discussions regardless of distinctions of power or of status between and among participants.

Consider a situation where, following a training program to enhance openness, organizational members find themselves subtly ridiculed for revealing their private feelings. The members find that information they share is used for the betterment of others, at their own expense. Their salary raises and promotions suffer from their frankness in conversations with managers. Here we have conflict: the "Theory Y" approach implies one set of communication behaviors, while the behavior of individuals in the organization represents a quite different model. Without a consistent application of an organizational theory to the appropriate communication behavior, the theory will have a distorted impact on the organization.

A second example should show how this same phenomenon can work in exactly the opposite fashion. Consider a military campaign, complete with battle plan, targets and objectives, supplies, manpower, a command structure: the full complement of items needed to wage war. A tightly knit plan of operation is drawn up and put into motion; coordination among units becomes essential.

One field captain, however, finds himself faced with field situations somewhat different than he had been led to expect. He decides to redirect his men toward a different target. He informs his supervisors, somewhat ambiguously, but they do not realize what he is doing. The captain feels convinced that his redirection will definitely help the overall effort. What he fails to realize is that by pulling out from his assigned position he leaves two other units with exposed flanks, and consequently they lose valuable men, supplies, and terrain that had been costly to acquire. Here again we have a conflict arising between the communication model implicit in the military organization (which presumes fast, accurate, and complete interaction with field units) and the actual communication behaviors expressed by one individual, with tragic and unfortunate consequences.

In military organizations, generally more than in many other types of organizations, communication procedures and policies are spelled out and penalties are imposed for not following them. This is more the exception than the rule for organizations in general, however. And for organizational *theories* (which we clearly realize are distinct from the operating philosophy ["theory"] of real-life organizations), the same discrepancy typically exists: the communication model implied by the theory is either sketchily described or given no attention at all.

One plausible explanation for this situation can be found by quickly reviewing the history of organizations since our early days. The first human organizations were small hunting and/or food-gathering societies that required relatively little interaction or coordination, if we use current and projected organizations as our point of comparison. The city-states, church organizations, and military operations that followed had increased needs for control and coordination—and hence for greater communication—but many of their activities were routinized, consistent, and predictable. Under conditions of certainty, the need for communication is restrained. The industrial revolution provided a transition to larger, more complicated organizations, but even here much of the early large-scale organizing (such as in the automobile industry) stressed mechanization and routinization of work, and

74   Implications of Major Organizational Theories

thus required only moderate increases in the nature and functioning of communication.

Increasingly in recent years—and clearly in most projections of the future—the complexity and nature of organizations are undergoing radical changes. Organizational environments are becoming more and more complex, creating greater uncertainty for any given organization and raising the need for appropriate communication mechanisms to process the messages that will reduce this uncertainty.

The trend to very large organizations (conglomerates and multinational corporations) points to greatly increased problems of control, coordination, and effective interdependence, and hence requires increased communication activities to accomplish these goals. Technology, mechanization, and computerization are themselves becoming more complex, so the interdependence among organizational members using these facilities must rise if effective coordinated action is to take place.

The sheer number of organizational members whose work is solely information processing ("paper pushing") rather than handling of

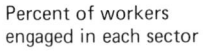

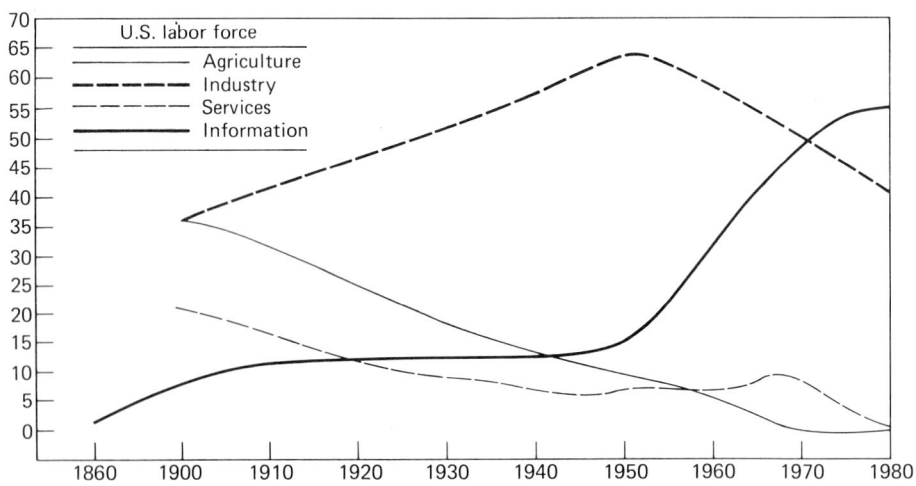

Fig. 4-1. U.S. labor force from 1860 to present: four-sector aggregation showing tremendous increase in percent of workers engaged in information production (adapted from Porat, 1975).

matter/energy is rising as middle management expands, as the insurance industry grows, as governmental bureaucracies grow, etc. Machlup (1962) estimated that approximately 29 percent of the U.S. economy in 1959 was devoted to the production, distribution, and reproduction of information. Recently, Porat (1975) undertook a reaggregation of the "information sector" (he includes all machines, workers, and services devoted to the production, reproduction, and distribution of information) and found that approximately 50 percent of the U.S. economy was then devoted to this information sector rather than to the production of material goods. Porat's sector breakdown of the U.S. economy is shown in Fig. 4-1. This trend underscores the increasing competence in communication, and it also suggests the increasingly important role to be played by communication in the overall organizational philosophy under which an organization functions.

The purpose of Chapter 4 is to help the reader to interpret existing organizational theories in terms of the communication "model" that is presumed by them. The chapter focuses on a set of structural and functional communication concepts that, in the authors' opinion, are of consistent importance across major organizational theories. Five selected organizational theories are compared on a set of communication concepts, and a sixth, systems-based theory ("contingency theory," which appears to offer an excellent capability for integrating communication with other aspects of organizational theorizing) is also discussed.

ORGANIZATIONAL COMMUNICATION: CONCEPTS

In Chapters 1 and 2 we ordered our approach to organizational communication along three dimensions: structure, function, and system level. We presented arguments for the use of structural-functionalism as a general theoretic perspective from which to approach the analysis of communication in organizations. A central aspect of this approach is the specification of key communication traits which are vital to the operation of the organization. In the present section we will use the same logic to discuss six organizational theories. What kind of communication structures or networks are implicit in the theory? How are the functions of communication treated? On what system level or levels does the theory focus?

For structure, four communication traits or concepts will be discussed; these are traits which tend to be systematically treated across theories, and which appear on their face to be important to organizational operation: (1) degree of network flexibility, (2) directionality of message flow, (3) initiation of messages, and (4) amount of communication processing.

1. *Degree of flexibility of communication structure or network.* Various theories treat in different ways the questions of who can communicate with whom, and what specific pathways messages are to take. In some instances, the theories contain rule systems which are highly codified and have little flexibility, while in other instances, communicators have a large measure of freedom or flexibility in their choice of communication partners or networks for sending messages. The degree of flexibility will be expressed along a continuum ranging from "minimal" to "high," and examples of these differences will be given.

2. *Directionality of message flow.* Here the pattern of message flow is related to the formal organizational structure. Messages directed from higher management echelons to lower ones in the formal hierarchy are described as vertical-downward messages. Those from lower echelons to higher ones are called vertical-upward messages. And those between components or echelons at the same hierarchical level are called horizontal or lateral messages. The theories will be described as either primarily vertically downward in emphasis, bi-directional vertically, horizontal primarily, or all-directional.

3. *Initiation or sequencing of messages.* This dimension distinguishes between messages that are more *imposed* (initiated from the top down, irrespective of the wants or desires of lower-level personnel) and those that are more *sought* (where individuals at all management levels foster and encourage upward communication by all organizational members).

4. *Amount or load of communication being processed.* We are interested here in the emphasis given to expending the organization's resources on communication processing compared with processing matter/energy. This can be shown by noting the proportion of resources specifically budgeted for communication activities, e.g., the volume of paperwork processed, numbers of meetings held, memos written, and frequency of contacts between supervisors and subordinates. In this discussion load will be characterized as ranging from minimal to high.

For communication function, we will continue to use the three major categories that were described earlier: (1) production, (2) innovation, and (3) maintenance.

1. *Production.* Communication involving the work being done, the work waiting to be done, problems in the work (such as errors), and problem detection and correction.

2. *Innovation.* Communication involving the elicitation of new ideas for doing work, new ways to do the work, new types of work that might be done, and new procedures and policies that would improve the operation of the organization or the overall environment.

3. *Maintenance.* Communication that improves or enhances the individual's concept of self, or the nature and quality of interpersonal relations, or the identification with and loyalty to the company; in addition, maintenance includes communication that supports the production and innovation functions as well (e.g., that it's good work to do, or that it's important to come up with new suggestions.)

And for system level, we will also use the same four levels we used before.

1. The *individual*, as an entity operating within the larger organization.

2. The *dyad*, in particular, the supervisor-subordinate dyad and the friend-friend dyad.

3. The *group*, whether work group or friendship group.

4. The *whole organization*, as a complete entity.

SELECTION OF ORGANIZATIONAL THEORIES

As Mouzelis (1967) notes, the literature on organization is both extensive and somewhat confused by a multiplicity of viewpoints. Each school tends to consider a slightly different system level and to focus on relatively unique aspects of the organizational structure or process. In particular, as Litterer (1969) emphasizes, there is considerable difference in terms of which system level receives most attention. Unfortunately, these levels differences are frequently overlooked in many of the arguments on the relative merits of different theories.

One classification scheme for organizational theories which makes distinctions that appear to have definite communication implications is proposed by Barrett (1970). Barrett distinguishes among three *goal-integration* models; each model focuses differently on the relationship between the goals held by the organization's members and the overall objectives of the organization.

1. *The exchange model.* Barrett proposes that, under this model, a fairly explicit bargaining relationship prevails between the individual and the organization. He notes that the model is more concerned with relating personal goals and organizational objectives than with ways of integrating them. There are several distinct subsets of theories within this grouping. In particular, the theories of Weber (1947) and F. W. Taylor (1947) represent economic exchange. Those of Simon (1957) and Barnard (1938) stress the notions of balancing inducements and contributions; and those of Mayo (1949) and Roethlisberger and Dickson (1946) of the Harvard school use an exchange "currency" that stresses social incentives.

2. *The socialization model.* Barrett describes this model as being basically a social-influence model, with goal integration being achieved through persuasion or influence processes. The individual member is encouraged to value activities that contribute to the achievement of the organizational objectives. Barrett suggests that much of the theory proposed by Likert (1967) and by Blake and Mouton (1964) fits within this model.

3. *The accommodation model.* In this model the stress is on the organization taking *individual* goals into account in developing procedures to attain the organizational objectives. Among the theorists advocating this approach to management are Herzberg (1966), Argyris (1964), and McGregor (1960, 1968). Also, as Barrett notes, Likert's theory incorporates some of the notions of accommodation. In the accommodation model, the organization does not try to "buy" the member, or "persuade" him or her (however subtly), but instead "comes to" the member and tries to make an arrangement that satisfies the individual *and* accomplishes the organization's goals at the same time.

The classification offered by Barrett offers a basis on which to select a limited set of theories for more detailed consideration: *Weber's* bureaucratic theory represents economic exchange, *H. A. Simon's* administrative-behavior theory represents the inducement/contribution theories, and the *Harvard "Human-Relations"* theory represents social exchange. Renis Likert's *"System IV"* represents the (idealized) socialization model, and Douglas McGregor's *"Theory Y"* represents the accommodation model. Finally *"Contingency Theory"* will be considered, which may offer an integrative conceptualization above these other theories.

ANALYSIS OF ORGANIZATIONAL THEORIES

Max Weber's Bureaucratic Model. Weber is generally recognized as having developed the single most powerful theory of organization, and his "ideal" type of bureaucracy has been the starting point for almost all considerations of organizational theory in the last 30 years. Weber recognized that his view of bureaucracy was of a "pure" type that would seldom be found in its entirety in concrete situations; nevertheless, it provides an extremely useful analytical tool.

Weber describes the core of the bureaucratic type of organization as being a system of control based on rational rules. These rules regulate the whole organizational structure and process on the basis of technical knowledge, with the goal of maximizing efficiency. These principles can be seen in the basic characteristics of the ideal type that Weber presents (1947):

1. Fixed and official jurisdictional areas as applied to regular activities, authority to give commands, and the continuing fulfillment of these duties.

2. A firmly ordered system of super- and subordination, with monocratic hierarchy.

3. Management based on written documents.

4. Thorough and expert training and consequent specialization.

5. Official activities demanding the full working capacities of the members.

6. Management follows rules which are more or less stable and exhaustive, and which can be learned.

Weber also stresses the impersonality of relationships and the clear differentiation between private and official lives of members of the organization.

These statements, and the exhaustive literature on the bureaucratic model, portray a communication model whose level of formalization is very high; i.e., flexibility over lines of communication is minimal. The directionality of message flow follows the classic "command-and-report" sequence, in which orders or commands emanate from the top of the management levels and reports of compliance with the orders return upward. Horizontal communication is nonexistent. Message initiation, correspondingly, is from the top downward. Given the emphasis on formal, known rules, rigid codification of communication procedures, and a stable work environment, the amount of communication is relatively low.

The function of communication in such a model is primarily if not exclusively directed toward production matters. Innovation is not seen as the concern of organizational members (except perhaps those at the very top), and given the strong emphasis on creating job positions whose incumbents are relatively easy to replace, maintenance communication is of scant importance.

The system level here is clearly focused on the individual, since all aspects of his or her job are treated in "machine" fashion, and hence, like parts of a machine, the person can be removed and replaced without disturbing the overall hierarchy more than momentarily.

We can thus summarize the communication implications as follows:

Weber's Bureaucratic Model

Structure

Flexibility:	Minimal
Direction:	Vertical down
Initiation:	Imposed by superiors
Amount:	Minimal

Function

Functions: Production

System level

Individual

Whole-organization authority network

The Harvard School Human-Relations Theory of Organization. While Weber's bureaucratic model is acknowledged as the originator of modern organizational theories, the results reported by Mayo and his colleagues (in the "Hawthorne studies") have been the main inspiration for the tremendous development of the field of human relations. It was these studies that, despite subsequent severe criticism of their findings, focused attention on system levels and organizational functions that were different from those customarily studied under the Weberian viewpoint.

Schein (1970) summarizes Mayo's assumptions as follows:

1. Man is basically motivated by social needs and obtains his basic sense of identity through relationships with others.

2. As a result of the industrial revolution and the rationalization of work, meaning has gone out of work itself and must therefore be sought in the social relationships on the job.

3. Man is more responsive to the social forces of the peer group than to the incentives and controls of management.

4. Man is responsive to management to the extent that a supervisor can meet a subordinate's social needs and needs for acceptance.*

Mayo (1949), and Roethlisberger and Dickson (1946) demonstrate the existence of informal groups within an organization, and further show that the norms of these informal groups could strongly affect production. They point out the importance of the manager-subordinate dyad, and the need to socialize new members of the organization. They argue that an organization should be regarded as a social system with two major functions: producing a product (formal achievement), and creating and distributing satisfactions among the individual members of the organization (maintenance, e.g., group-need satisfaction). They emphasize that many of the actual patterns of human interaction have no formal representation in the organizational chart.

Unlike the earlier models, the human-relations model focuses on informal group interaction and stresses oral communication; it also minimizes the importance of formal rules. Similarly, there is a direct focus on peer (or horizontal) communication, recognizing the important contribution of interaction between equivalent members.

---

*Edgar H. Schein, *Organizational Psychology*, 2nd ed., © 1970, p. 59, Prentice-Hall, Inc., Englewood Cliffs, New Jersey. Reprinted by permission.

Mayo, and Roethlisberger and Dickson restrict their considerations almost exclusively to basic work groups. The theory suggests little additional hierarchical communication, and therefore an intermediate volume of communication. The model clearly stresses maintenance messages while tending to play down somewhat the importance of production messages. Little consideration is given to innovative messages.

The model does not explicitly discuss the flexibility in activated communication linkages, but appears to acknowledge the need for some flexibility while primarily concentrating on the somewhat stable relationships of individuals to their informal groups.

The emphases taken in this model place it in the intermediate categories on most dimensions. The overall communication volume in the organization is greater than in the Weberian model, with much greater stress on maintenance messages and peer communication. Similarly, more involvement is likely in the initiation of communication at all levels in the organization.

We can thus summarize the communication implications as follows:

Harvard Human-Relations Model

Structure

Flexibility:	Some
Direction:	Horizontal stressed
Initiation:	More sought than imposed
Amount:	Intermediate

Function

Functions: Production
Maintenance

System level

Individual (to gain self-identity)

Dyad (supervisor-subordinate)

Group (informal group acknowledged)

Simon's Administrative-Behavior Theory. A descriptive model of organizational behavior, Simon's theory differs somewhat from the others, which tend to be prescriptive. Simon's central theme is that organizational behavior is a complex network of decision processes that all have an effect on the behaviors of the ultimate operatives or employees. He argues that the essence of the organization is to be found in the distribution and allocation of decision making. He presents the following factors as mechanisms of organizational influence:

1. Division of work among members.

2. The establishment of standard practices (rules).

3. The establishment of systems of authority and influence to transmit decisions down through the organizational ranks.

4. The provision of communication channels running throughout the organization, through which communication for decision making flows.

5. The training and indoctrination (socialization) of members.*

Simon attempts to integrate the various aspects of organizational behavior that were treated in a one-sided way by the Weberian and human-relations schools. His theory is intended to reconcile the rational and nonrational aspects of organizational behavior.

Simon tends to focus his attention on the individual. Like the Weberian model, he stresses a rigid hierarchical system of coordination and authority and the provision of clearly designated communication channels through which messages can be disseminated.

The model stresses the detailing of formal rules and practices and the socialization of members. While acknowledging the existence of informal groups, Simon does not stress peer communication; therefore, the model primarily restricts communication to vertical hierarchical channels. Through clear, formalized rules, the total volume of communication is restricted.

Simon also stresses production messages and minimizes maintenance ones. He does not consider innovation messages other than to acknowledge the input of middle and lower management to organizational decision making. The model implies some initiation of messages by those lower in the hierarchy, but with the primary emphasis clearly towards upward communication in

---

*H. Simon, *Administrative Behavior*, 2nd ed., 1957, p. 27, Macmillan, New York, 1957. Reprinted by permission.

response to requests by top management for communication. The whole model emphasizes formal established communication channels; therefore, it tends to enforce a minimum of flexibility in communication contacts.

The administrative-behavior model can be viewed as *intermediate* between the Weberian and the human-relations models, on almost all dimensions. We can summarize the communication implications as follows:

Simon's Administrative-Behavior Model	
Structure	
Flexibility:	Some
Direction:	Vertical both ways
Initiation:	More imposed than sought
Amount:	Restricted
Function	
Functions:	Production
System level	
Individual	
Whole-organization network	

Douglas McGregor's Theory Y. McGregor epitomizes a series of theoretical writings which focus on the individual and on needs that are *not* met by the monetary-reward system or through group membership. Other theorists who have stressed this viewpoint are Argyris (1957) and Herzberg (1966). McGregor (1960) summarizes the basis for his theory in a series of assumptions about human nature:

1. The expenditure of physical and mental effort in work is as natural as play or rest.

2. External control and threat of punishment are not the only means of bringing about effort toward organizational objectives. People will exercise self-direction and self-control in the service of objectives to which they are committed.

3. The capacity to exercise a relatively high degree of imagination, ingenuity, and creativity in the solution of organizational problems is widely distributed in the population.

4. Under conditions of modern industrial life, the intellectual potentialities of the average human being are only partially utilized.

Theory Y clearly focuses on the individual and self-actualization. Since McGregor emphasizes individual self-direction, formal established rules are minimal; therefore, the model contains an emphasis on oral communication with a minimum of written messages. It does not stress peer or hierarchical communication, but rather independent effort; and therefore implies a relatively intermediate volume of communication.

There is an implicit suggestion that most communication will be initiated by subordinates rather than imposed by higher management. Message content is not restricted by the model, and innovative messages in particular are clearly advocated and encouraged. Therefore, a roughly equal proportion of production, maintenance, and innovative messages is expected. The model implies an equivalent stress on messages from members throughout the hierarchy, and thus there should be a relatively equal proportion of messages traveling in each possible direction, with a high degree of flexibility in interaction patterns.

The model focuses primarily on the individual and encourages a maximum of delegation to line workers, thus involving the total organizational membership. There is also a clear indication of minimum barriers to communication as reflected by high flexibility, high peer communication and a tendency for messages to be sought rather than imposed.

The communication implications can be summarized as follows:

McGregor's Theory Y Model

Structure

Flexibility:	High
Direction:	All
Initiation:	More sought than imposed
Amount:	Intermediate

Function

Functions: Production
             Maintenance
             Innovation

System level

Individual self-actualization

Rensis Likert's System IV. Rensis Likert is identified as a leader in the human-relations school of organizational theorists. He has been responsible for a large-scale research and consulting program directed towards management and leadership styles in industry. Of all the theorists considered in this chapter, Likert provides the program that is most solidly based in empirical research. He also deals most explicitly with the communication aspects of organization, although advocating, primarily in his "ideal" System IV, a type of organization that is seldom encountered in today's world.

His "ideal" theoretical position (1961 and 1967) is summarized in his participative or System IV system of organization, which includes these main points:

1. Superiors have complete confidence and trust in their subordinates.

2. Subordinates feel completely free to discuss things about the job with their superiors.

3. Superiors always seek ideas from subordinates and try to make constructive use of them.

4. Much communication both with groups and individuals.

5. Communication down, up, and with peers.

6. Downward communications generally accepted, but if not, are openly and candidly questioned.

7. Upward communication accurate.

8. Superiors know and understand subordinates' problems.

9. Interaction extensive and friendly.

10. Substantial cooperation throughout the organization.

The primary focus of Likert's System IV is on the group; however, the stress on involvement of individuals at all levels affords the opportunity for self-actualization.

Likert stresses group decision making and an absence of formal rules; therefore, the model implies a bias towards oral communication. Likert clearly advocates a high level of communication, both up and down and with peers.

The model calls for managers to solicit information from subordinates and for a minimum of barriers to the initiation of communication. The model

88 Implications of Major Organizational Theories

tends to stress production messages, but at the same time group situations are encouraged and superiors are required to be involved with their subordinates' problems. Therefore maintenance messages are accommodated in the model.

On the same basis, the involvement of all personnel in decisions that affect them encourages innovative messages, so even though production messages might dominate, there is also a high level of maintenance and innovative messages. The model indicates the establishment of a hierarchy of *interlocking* groups; "linking pins" (persons who are members of two or more groups) provide the mechanism for the interlocking effect. However, it accommodates a considerable amount of flexibility in communication patterns as a consequence of a general freedom and an overall delegation of decision making, and involvement of all relevant members in activities that impinge on their organizational lives.

We can thus summarize the model as follows:

Likert's System IV Model	
Structure	
Flexibility:	High
Initiation:	More sought than imposed
Direction:	All
Amount:	High
Function	
Functions:	Production Maintenance Innovation
System level	
All, especially organizational networks	

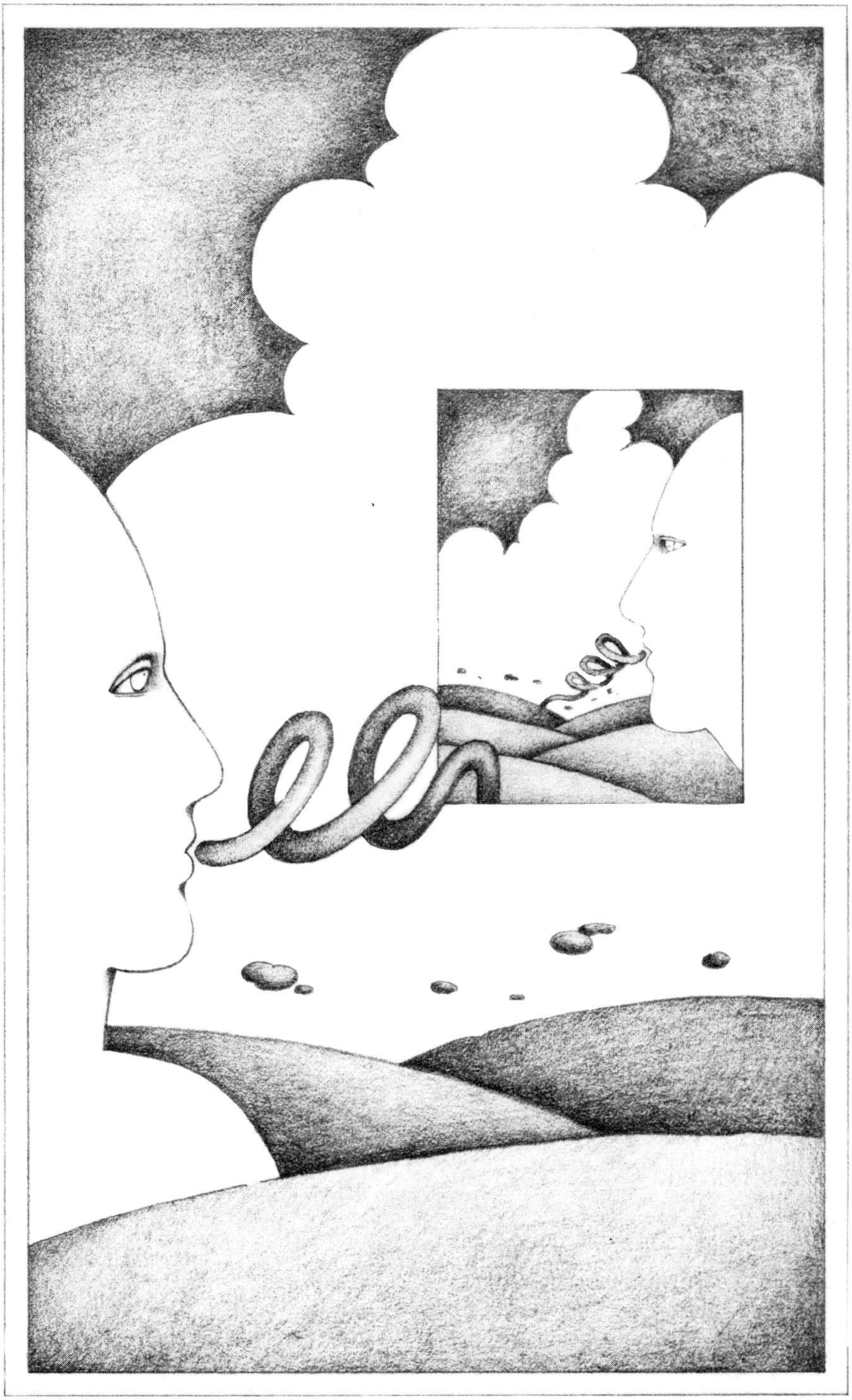

SYSTEMS THEORY—CONTINGENCY THEORY

We have reviewed five major organizational theories by comparing their main communication structure, function, and system-level characteristics. There are clear differences in each of these communication dimensions across the major theories. Perhaps the two most extreme are the Weberian bureaucratic model on the one hand and Likert's System IV on the other. The Weberian model builds in many restraints to communication—the permissible structures are highly limited, the content narrowly conceived, and the analytic focus is on the individual as a replaceable component of the larger organization.

The System IV model, in contrast, is the most open, unconstrained, and permissive of the group. Messages can travel along many different pathways; content is consciously meant to vary along many dimensions; and a wide range of the component parts of the organization are specifically treated,

Table 4-1. Summary of communication implications of six organizational theories.

	Exchange models		
Communication dimension	WEBER'S BUREAUCRATIC MODEL	SIMON'S ADMINISTRATIVE BEHAVIOR MODEL	HARVARD HUMAN RELATIONS MODEL
Structure FLEXIBILITY DIRECTION INITIATION AMOUNT	minimal vertical down imposed minimal	some vertical both more imposed restricted	some horizontal more sought intermediate
Function FUNCTIONS	production	production	production maintenance
System level	individual whole-organization network	individual whole-organization network	individual (to gain self-identity) dyad (supervisory) group (informal group acknowledged)

beginning with the individual and extending through the managerial chain to interlocking functional groups and finally to the overall organization. The Weberian model seems well suited to predictable environments and is easy on the organizational resource budget; the System IV model seems more designed for turbulent, uncertain environments and is definitely a high-cost communication system. These models are compared in Table 4-1.

There is one major organizational theoretic viewpoint which we have not yet specifically discussed, because by its very nature it does not readily lend itself to such comparisons. More specifically, the appropriate entries under the three headings that have been used (structure, function, and system-level) are all "variable," e.g., while all options are potentially useful, the specific result depends on the characteristics of each situation. There is no uniform, primary emphasis. This theoretical view is based on general systems theory (Buckley, 1967; Berrien, 1968), or, as it is usually called in the organizational literature,

Accommodation	Socialization	Contingency
McGREGOR'S THEORY Y MODEL	LIKERT'S SYSTEM IV MODEL	SYSTEMS MODEL
high all more sought intermediate	high more sought all high	variable variable variable variable
production maintenance innovation	production maintenance innovation	variable
individual (self-actualization)	all levels	variable

contingency theory. The rationale for contingency theory is presented succinctly by Tosi and Hamner (1974):

> To understand behavior in an organization, administrators should have a systematic set of concepts. The contingency approach to organizational behavior assumes that an organization is a system, or unit, of behaviors composed of subsystems or subunits that have identifiable boundaries within the system. Each subsystem can be analyzed as a unit of behavior in its own right, or as a subunit of behavior interacting with other subunits.
>
> ...a "contingency" approach is an approach where the behavior of one subunit is dependent on its environmental relationship to other units or subunits that have some control over the consequences (e.g., profit for the organization or recognition and praise for the individual) desired by that subunit.*

The contingency theory is similar to Simon's administrative-behavior model in that it does not carry with it a particular prescriptive view of how an organization "ought to be." It does not dictate "the" way an organization should be structured or administered. In effect, it asserts that there is no such thing as the "one best way," because what's best for an organization, or a subunit in it, is a highly complex function of many variables, many perspectives, and many intricate relationships. Only when the theorist knows important factors in the environment for any unit, as well as the internal operations of the unit, will it be possible to tell what's "best" in a given situation. Hence the label "contingency" theory for this particular school of organizational thought.

One point that the contingency model underscores is the need for tailoring the communication aspects of organization to the particular people, tasks, goals, environment, and uncertainty at hand. The Weberian bureaucratic model is just as likely a candidate for adoption as is the Likert System IV model when a new organizational situation arises. Under these circumstances, it is important that organizational researchers and/or administrators have a broad understanding of the flexibility in communication models that are available to them. The selection of appropriate models is even more complex when it is realized that the subunits within an organization as well as the entire organization must also be considered; furthermore, as time and personnel change, the communication-model requirements may change as well. The whole concept of a "fixed" solution to selection of communication models is fully discarded in the contingency-theory approach to organizational understanding.

---

*From Henry L. Tosi and W. Clay Hamner, *Organizational Behavior and Management: A Contingency Approach*, © 1974, p. 1, by St. Clair Press. Used by permission.

Contingency theory makes it possible to deal more comfortably with what is a recognized fact in most large organizations: that different parts may operate best under different philosophies. Contingency theory stresses the need to take the existing philosophy as a "given" and to seek ways to improve the situation, rather than attempt to apply a cure-all to the entire organization. Contingency theory encourages the study of problems such as the following: suppose you are dealing with a social-service agency, organized along functional lines. A crisis arises—perhaps a rapid change in federally-mandated service delivery. Given a crisis situation, new communication relationships may be needed. These may cut across the former boundaries and require a radically different set of communication and other operating rules. What should they be? Contingency theory encourages the research that will show the best configuration of communication practices and procedures in a given situation.

The transition from contingency theory to structural-functionalism is a relatively easy one, with an important exception. Contingency theory is largely nondirective (which can be an advantage) in that it does not point to specific aspects of organizational functioning in an analysis. As it appears to be currently used, however, contingency theory researchers do not follow the major requirements of general systems theory, nor of structural-functionalism or cybernetics (Monge, 1972).

In Chapter 3, the arguments for using structural-functionalism were presented, particularly the sequence of steps to be followed in conducting such analysis. Structural-functionalism requires that traits or concepts that are vital to the continuance and performance of the organization be specifically identified. Furthermore, the investigator is charged with the task of specifying the mechanisms within the organization that bring about the desired levels of those traits. Consequently, if degree of flexibility, directionality of message flow, message initiation, communication load, or the flow of production/innovation/maintenance messages are the traits under scrutiny, structural-functionalism requires one to search for those key factors that lead to different levels of each trait. As more is learned about the factors, it becomes more feasible to bring the traits under control and so effectively "manage" communication in the organization.

CONCLUSION

If we accept the predictions of Toffler (1970)—that organizations and their components will, to an ever-increasing extent, become shorter-lived, with a changing structure built on highly transitory human relationships—then the question of how to establish the most appropriate and efficient communication relations becomes crucial. As relationships change, difference rather than similarity becomes the rule, and more people may be hurt through misunderstanding the communication rules or through being tied to an inappropriate communication structure.

Our hope is that the reader, by review of the earlier chapters—especially Chapters 2 and 3—will become much sensitized to the communication options open in any organizational setting. Then, by selecting traits that are critical to the organization's performance, and exploring the mechanisms or means by which they may be brought under control, effective "communication management" will be possible.

Applications of the Conceptual Framework

II

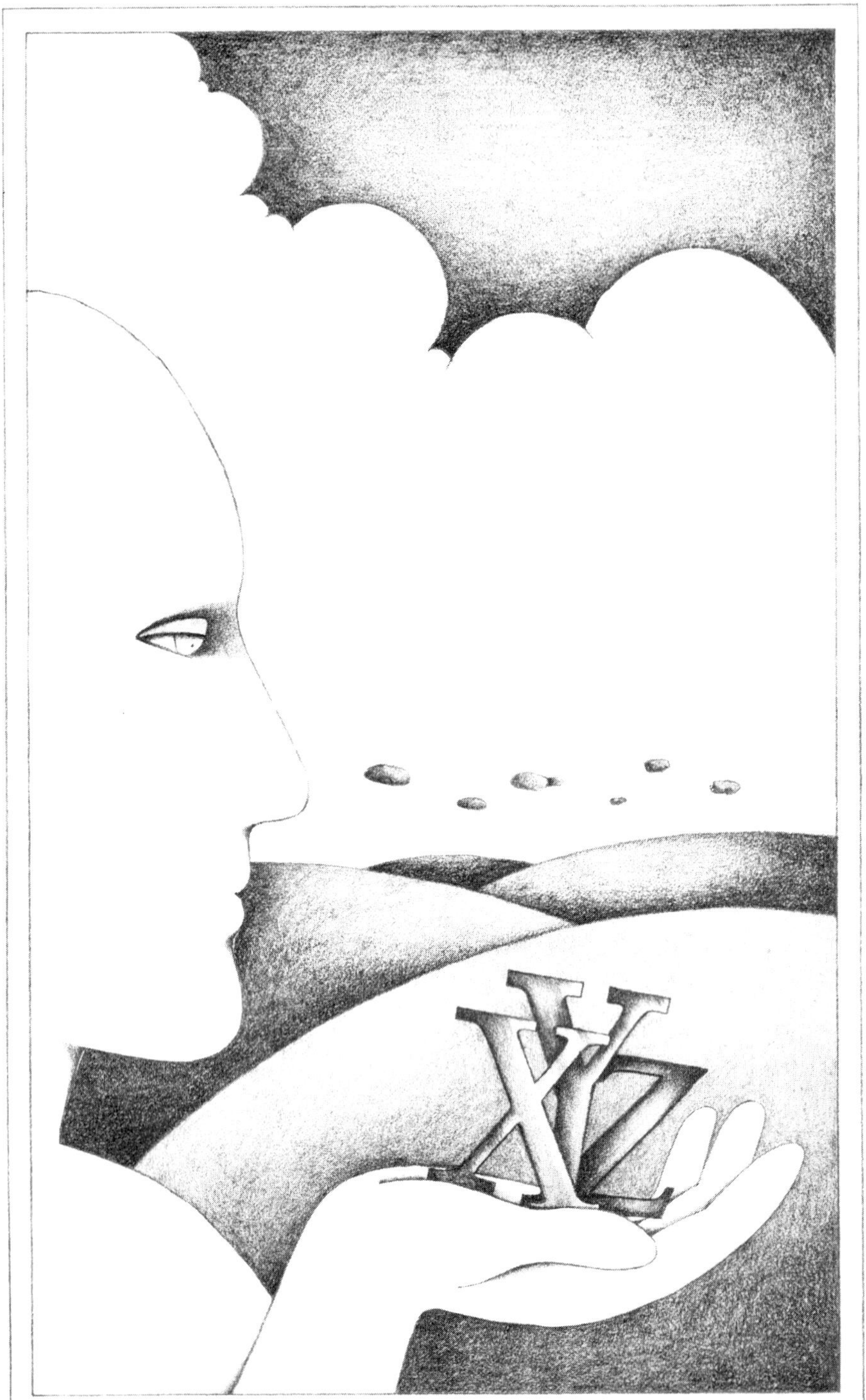

5
Communication "Load"

We can now begin to blend our conceptual view of communication (from Chapter 2) with the theoretic base of structural-functionalism (see Chapter 3). Organizations have already been defined as processors of communication (and other things). Processing occurs through the organization's networks, and is related to the achievement of organizational functions (goals, objectives, outcomes). Or, to make the point another way, *networks provide the mechanism by which communication flows, and functional considerations reflect the effects of that flow.*

In the present chapter, we will examine one key trait of the flow of organizational communication: load. As the chapter develops, the reader should obtain a clearer understanding of the importance of load in enabling an organization to carry out the functions its members desire to achieve. And it should become apparent that load can vary from a helpful, facilitative level to a costly, burdensome, even destructive condition that can seriously damage an organization's ability to perform and survive.

Here are some examples of different types of load situations that are common in organizations:

Manager:
Okay, George, let's hear your problem ('phone rings, boss picks it up, promises to deliver a report, "just as soon as I can get some other

things off my desk."). Uh, now, where were we, George—oh, you're having a problem with your secretary. She's (...secretary—the boss's—brings in some papers that need immediate signature, so he scribbles his name where she indicates; secretary leaves)...you say she's depressed a lot lately, wants to leave...is she pregnant maybe? (laughter) I tell you what, George, I'd like to help you, so why don't we (phone rings again, lunch partner drops by, indicates it's late)...have you take a stab at handling it yourself...I've got to go now.

What are some load characteristics of this situation? First, it's clear that the manager is receiving information inputs from multiple sources. The inputs seem to be arriving constantly. He gets a couple of telephone messages, his secretary brings in papers that require his immediate attention, and George stays with him in pursuit of advice on how to handle the secretarial problem. The manager seems to be reacting to the information inputs rather than actively dealing with them. Little information about George's specific problem is elicited, nor is any appreciable attempt made to do so. The situation is resolved by (a) flight, to a luncheon engagement, and (b) passing the problem back to the subordinate who came seeking help initially.

Let's review another situation, one involving a middle-level manager in the financial department of an organization. Here's how the manager is described by her peers and supervisor:

Janis arrives at her office each morning to find a stack of work left from the night shift. The size of the work to be done varies with the volume from the previous night and the diligence the night people mustered in tackling the job. It is expected that Janis will complete the work in front of her, with the assistance of two subordinates, by the end of the day. In addition, she will spend about two hours in meetings, and is expected to complete her work soon on the yearly charity-fund drive. Janis goes through the pile of work to be done, delegates portions to her subordinates, keeps the more difficult tasks for herself, and declines three phone calls while the work is being completed.

When the work is assigned, she returns the phone calls, skims through an assortment of memos, and retains some for closer reading. Then she begins work on her tasks, leaving orders that only a very select few people are to be allowed to interrupt her. By the time her daily meeting is completed she has also finished most of her work. The remainder gets first priority, and then she turns to other phone messages, memos, and minor tasks that are still to be completed. Some of the people who attempted to reach her are upset, but she chooses to ignore this. She spends some time socializing with her subordinates, reviews their work, and wraps up the day.

This sequence may sound a little idyllic, but it is not uncommon in many organizations. It is a processing style found in many public and private organizations where a member can be counted on to do an important task while warding off many potential interruptions. Janis has learned to deny the behavioral compliance implicit in telephone calls, memos, and passers-by. There is always a chance that this system will backfire if the "wrong people" are turned away, but Janis has implemented some elementary rules (an "always open to" list) that should protect her to a large extent. And it remains to be seen if Janis's behavior is more or less effective than George's, from either her own personal viewpoint or that of the organization's higher-level managers.

A third scenario is needed to illustrate still another major information-handling situation in an organization:

> Ken is a relatively new member of the organization, and he definitely intends to "get ahead." To rise in the organization, he must prove himself, and the way that is done is to work at lower-level jobs until his supervisors can trust him to do them without error. So Ken's current work consists mainly of checking the transfer of names from former common stock owners to the new owners. Basically, he considers it a trivial job, even though it's clear that both the former owner and the new owner (especially the latter) don't consider the transaction a trivial one at all. But after doing a few hundred of these, or perhaps a few thousand, Ken finds himself bored, sleepy, frustrated, and inattentive. He daydreams about his date that night. He contemplates a way to bring a good paperback into the work area without getting caught. He looks for idle conversation. He develops feelings of hostility toward his manager for criticizing him when these moments of absentmindedness are caught. He is not very happy.

Ken's situation is entirely different than either of the two prior examples. He is not swamped with inputs, as George is, nor has he come to terms with his communication environment, as Janis apparently has. Ken finds himself receiving far fewer inputs than he would like to have. He seems to be in a state of underload. While he knows the kinds of behaviors he must exhibit to move ahead in the organization, he finds it very difficult to keep his unwavering attention on the task itself. Ken actually *creates* inputs for himself by daydreaming, surreptitious reading, and extended socializing. It is likely that Ken's behavior is dysfunctional for the organization and, most likely, for himself as well, if he ever intends to advance in the corporation.

In this chapter, then, we will review a series of issues that are central to the topic of communication load in organizations. We selected load as a trait to discuss because, from a structural-functional perspective, it represents an essential aspect of communication which must be managed closely if the organization is to perform efficiently. Although precise quantitative measures are not yet available, the weight of research and relevant theory indicates that when load falls too low, the "organization" may cease to exist; when load is excessively high, stress, errors, discomfort, and other unpleasant consequences may render the organization ineffectual and perhaps also lead to its demise. Our procedure will be to define load in the section below, and then relate it to the three situations just presented. Then we will describe the measurement of load and discuss the consequences of different levels of load on individuals, groups, and organizations. Finally, we will present some of the options—and their implications—open for use under different types of load situations.

WHAT IS LOAD?

Anyone who has ever participated in an organization should have an intuitive feel for the concept of load. Put most simply, *load is based on the rate and complexity of communication inputs to an individual.* Rate is usually expressed as the number of communication demands (e.g., bits of information, or requests, messages, etc.) that are received, operated on, and resolved (i.e., "processed") in a given period of time. Complexity refers to the number of judgments or factors that must be taken into account while dealing with (processing) communication. If the level of input increases or decreases, and/or complexity alters, then load changes.

It should also be pointed out that the term "individual" here can easily be replaced with any of the higher system levels: dyads, groups, organization subunits, or organizations. The concept of load is applicable at all of these levels, and some of the most provocative research on load and its processing has come from studies that compare these processes at different system levels. Some of their conclusions, to be presented later, are rather sobering commentaries on the potential processing efficiency of modern, large organizations.

We have expressed the concept of load in terms of a rate of flow, and of a level of complexity of flow. As noted, flow can refer to "bits," requests, queries, commands, orders—any facet of interaction that demands the attention, resources, and processing capabilities of the receiving unit, whether individual or higher-level system. Presumably, the baseline or reference point is zero—the point where, for example, all message movement ceases and there are no further alternatives (and hence no complexity) in the system. At this point, interdependence, and hence organizing, would be impossible. The most common use of the term "load," however, couples load with an evaluative term—"overload" or "underload." "Over" or "under" is an evaluation of the load in a given situation vis à vis some desired level, or perhaps the maximum *capacity*, of the system to process communication. The term *overload* is used to indicate situations where the flow of messages exceeds the system's processing capacity. In today's highly complex and information-rich environment, overload has reached epidemic proportions and has consequently become the most frequently discussed and studied aspect of load.

Underload is just as much a part of today's organizational world as overload is, however. Underload is defined in terms of message flows which fall below the system's ability to process. Underload is said to be a factor in much of the dissension and strife among blue-collar workers who feel chained to the repetitive and simplistic tasks of the assembly line. Underload is a genuine white-collar problem as well, since many of the jobs that are considered white-collar have the same potentially boring, underloading aspects as some of the more traditionally designated blue-collar jobs do (Gooding, 1972).

Earlier in this chapter it was noted that the distinction between "load," and "underload" or "overload," is an evaluative one; i.e., in each case where a judgment of "underload" or "overload" is made, the decision must be based on an assessment of the processing capability of the individual (or a higher system level), in contrast to the load being placed on the individual. Where the load is higher than the individual can handle, then "overload" is present. Where it is lower, then "underload" is found. This may seem an obvious point, but it is a critical one, because an assessment of overload or underload cannot be made until both the communication load itself *and* the relationship between the load and the system's processing ability are known. One person's overload may well be another's underload, if only level of processing is known.

A return to the three examples given at the beginning of the chapter should be helpful. The first situation, concerning George, would appear to be a case of communication overload on the part of his boss. Telephones were ringing, papers were flying by, and conversations were superficial. Was this an example of overload? With the information presented in the example, it is not apparent whether the manager considered himself to be overloaded. He may have been operating at normal capacity; and even if he were above or below capacity, he may well have defined George's request for assistance as unwarranted and unworthy of his time and attention. Even if he had had nothing to do, he may have felt the problem was George's to handle and may have been attempting to ease George out of his office. So, from the manager's point of view, more details need to be gathered about his processing capacity before we can determine whether his treatment of George was a reflexive attempt to avoid processing one more request or a conscious desire not to engage in such a discussion.

George would probably want to define the situation as one where his manager was overloaded ("If he'd just had his work arranged better, he could have helped me"). From the organization's point of view, the situation is more complex. Higher-level managers may well feel it is management's responsibility to deal fully and carefully with such problems, particularly given the possibilities of sexist discrimination expressed in the situation. Higher-level management may have taken the position that this was inappropriate behavior on the part of George's manager and that, regardless of the press of other duties, the matter should have been handled fully. Whether this could be done by reordering the processing priorities of the boss, or increasing his processing capabilities, is an issue that requires further investigation.

In the second situation, Janis does not appear to be overloaded and in fact is able to accomplish important work. She does not appear to be stressed, nor does her work flow indicate sluggardliness. It is possible that she could drive herself to higher output levels, at least on a short-term basis. So, from Janis's viewpoint, her processing and load could well be in balance, an assessment which might be agreed upon at higher management levels. On the other hand, her subordinates might argue that she accomplishes this feat only by overloading them (a dysfunctional move from their perspective). Her immediate supervisor might consider her underloaded, a staff member with "talent going to waste." These comments again suggest that the question of overload or underload, as judged by the individual (or by members of the system being evaluated) may not be in accord with those at other levels of the overall system.

Ken's plight in the third instance looks like a classic example of communication underload. He shows many of the typical symptoms, including boredom. But notice his self-initiated attempt to redefine his communication environment by increasing his input rate through his own actions. His self-perception is that he is capable of doing much more processing, and he chafes at having to "learn the ropes" at what he considers tasks of minimal value. One way humans modify underload experiences is to engage in activities that will bring their processing levels up to more desirable conditions.

Measurement of Ken's processing capability may show that he is in fact underloaded; on the other hand, the possibility exists that his problem is not underload but an attention span so short that he cannot give his work the concentration it requires. Perhaps his attention span is what concerns his managers most, for it may be the basis on which they will make their decision regarding promotion. So Ken's case can also be viewed from at least two perspectives, one based on his appraisal of the situation and the other based on the appraisal of outsiders acting as judges of the situation.

HOW CAN LOAD BE MEASURED?

To discuss the measurement of load, the term will have to be presented in a fashion that lends itself to accepted procedures for measurement. To say that load is (in part) a function of the rate of communication movement to and from parts of an organizational network requires that load must be expressed as a "rate" in a precise way. One useful approach is to use the message as the basic unit of load, so that rate becomes the number of messages reaching an individual in some unit of time. An alternative is to use the utterance in spoken communication; a sentence or paragraph could serve as an analogue to an utterance. Demands or requests require processing and can also provide an index of load.

The basic units of information theory (as discussed in Chapter 2) are alternatives (different outcomes) and their probabilities. These same units can also be applied when we deal with communication, i.e. with messages based on a common language and shared symbol-referent relationships. Messages that are decoded into alternatives and probabilities reach individuals and interact with the uncertainty that already exists within the receiver. Sometimes the messages are translated into new definitions of a situation, with expanded or contracted alternatives or altered probabilities. Messages may reach the receiver via several channels: face-to-face, in meetings, by telephone, intercom or picture-phone, via personal notes or memos, etc. So there are many, many opportunities for uncertainty to increase as well as to decrease in the relationship between an individual and the larger organizational system. Content alternatives, probabilities of outcomes, conflicting messages, and variably activated channels all combine to enable highly complex message inputs to reach a given individual. Couple this complexity with the fact that the *rate* of input may increase or decrease, and the intricate possibilities of information-load conditions become more apparent. This complexity is even more apparent when each item of input or output may require different amounts of time and/or effort to process; i.e., when all inputs or outputs do not consume the same resources to deal with them.

The research on measurement of load is far more primitive than the actual "real-life" complexity of the situation demands. Most of the research has been done in the traditional information-theory paradigm, using the number of alternatives in a situation and their probabilities to calculate the "bits per second" in a given transmission. While this is vital for designing the technological hardware required to transmit patterned matter-energy, it does not bear fully on communication, when the concept includes common language and usage. Nevertheless, some of the research that has been done sheds important light on the main problem of measuring communication processing.

Most of this research has dealt with the judgment by individuals of uni-dimensional attributes, using experimental situations in which sound levels only are varied, or colors only, or size only, etc. Relatively few studies have simultaneously varied multi-dimensional attributes, i.e., colors and sizes and densities. For example, if individuals are asked to judge among four attributes, each of which has three levels, then the number of possible combinations to judge among is (3 x 3 x 3 x 3 = 81). It is easy to see that approximating the judgmental processes in real-life situations may require careful control of up to several thousand discriminations at once. This is a nearly impossible task, even in a controlled scientific setting.

The concept of *channel capacity* is invoked in research on human information processing in the same sense that it is used in research on communication-hardware devices; it represents the upper limits of the rate of processing that the individual can generally achieve while making few if any errors. The main finding to emerge from this research is that when individuals judge uni-dimensional attributes, their processing capacity is about three bits, or seven discriminations in all (Miller, 1956). To allow for differences in individual capabilities, as well as for problems in accurate measurement, this is usually expressed as "seven alternatives, plus or minus two."

Note that this conclusion is based on judgments along a uni-dimensional attribute. What about more complex judgments, involving multi-dimensional comparisons at the same time? Here there is but a limited amount of research, but its general thrust is that individuals can process more information in multi-dimensional situations than in uni-dimensional ones. Bear in mind this critical point, however; an individual's ability to process multi-dimensional attributes does *not* increase as the additive sum of his or her ability to process these same dimensions, taken one at a time (Miller, 1964). Instead, the rate of processing increases at *less* than the cumulative sum of the individual's ability to process uni-dimensional attributes. This limitation becomes important later in this chapter when the processing capabilities of higher-level systems are examined.

In a more practical mode, when the actual behavior of organizational members is considered, it is clear that they often process much more communication than these studies would seem to imply. How can we assess the load for a given individual, with at least sufficient precision to make use of this assessment in deciding whether optimal or nonoptimal load is present?

The single most important point to keep in mind in evaluating load is the number of decisions or judgments that the individual has to make. The more decisions, the higher the load (assuming that each decision takes equal effort). How do we tell how many decisions are to be made? One way to do this is to observe all incoming messages, noting which ones are acted on immediately, which ones are stored for later attention, which ones are integrated with other messages, which ones are discarded, and which ones are simply not attended to at all.

It may be possible to estimate the amount of time and effort that goes into handling each input. If additional information is available elsewhere in the system, it may be possible to make some rough, subjective judgments on the quality of the information processing taking place. The channels along which messages flow to (and from) the individual can be identified, and then the predictability of use of these channels can be determined; the more predictable the flow, the more certainty in determining which channels will be used, and thus the easier it is to deal with them. Similarly, the content of the messages can be examined for their predictability—how many involve relatively routine retransmissions of messages, and how many require the transmission of "new" messages?

Thus load can be measured as a function of (a) decisions or judgments to be made, (b) relative speed or effort given to processing message inputs, by type, (c) quality of processing, (d) predictability of inputs by channel, and (e) predictability of inputs by content. Load is determined by (a) the extent that more judgments must be made in a given time period, (b) the greater the speed or effort in processing, (c) the higher the quality of processing, (d) the less predictable inputs are by channel, and (e) the less predictable inputs are by content category. Each of these factors can be evaluated alone or combined with others to provide an overall appraisal of the load for a given individual (or for a higher level part of the system).

In addition, a subjective appraisal of the amount and nature of the load conditions under which the person operates is needed—is it, for example, "too much or too little," "too easy or too hard," "too ordinary or too changing"? By linking this information with the initial appraisal of load, it becomes easier to decide whether any imbalance is present.

In this section we have shown that information load has been measured, at least in relatively simple situations, in terms of the processing capacity of individuals—expressed in "bits per second." About seven alternatives (plus or minus two) can be handled if uni-dimensional attributes are being judged, while capacity increases somewhat for multi-dimensional judgments. The translation from these research studies to a brief outline of how to assess the information load in a specific situation is also presented from both the external and subjective participant's viewpoint. Next we will examine some of the effects of existing in an environment where load levels systematically either fall below or exceed an individual's processing capability.

COMMENTS ON THE DETERMINANTS OF LOAD

To carry further the logic of structural-functional analysis, we must do more than simply argue for the importance of "load" as a central concept in analyzing organizational communication. It is also necessary to describe the mechanisms which lead to different levels of load. Ideally, of course, a comprehensive and general theory of load would specify all crucial variables and the exact nature of their relationship to load in the organizational setting.

Unfortunately, such a theory does not exist. It is possible, though, to indicate a number of factors which have been shown, in various circumstances, to have a significant impact on load. Some of these factors have been studied mainly in relationship to individual behavior, while others have been examined at the group, organizational, or higher system-level settings.

Perhaps the easiest way to conceive of the various factors affecting load is to consider three major aspects of load. First, there is the *environment* in which the individual (or higher-level system) exists; as an observer of the environment those factors that are likely to promote greater or lesser amounts of information flow to the individual can be sought out. Next the individual can be studied to determine his or her *processing capacity*. And finally, the individual's *desire* for information processing should be examined, since desire, coupled with environmental conditions and actual processing ability, strongly influences the degree of underload or overload.

Environmental conditions affecting load have an upper limit that is based on the number of channels reaching the individual and the maximum capacity of each of these channels for transmitting information. Thus the greater the number of channels, and/or the greater the channel capacity, the greater the load. Certain organizational roles, for example, can involve much heavier communication flows than others. A manager involved in supervising 30 individuals who require frequent attention will be under a heavier load than a manager with fewer individuals, especially if these subordinates are engaged in work that does not require close supervision. The example of air-traffic controllers can be cited as a clear case of a job involving very high processing levels and very high risks; as aircraft are given guidance in landing and take-off, many factors must be constantly considered (numbers of planes, runway conditions, weather, equipment, etc.).

The degree to which an individual's work requires coordination or interdependence with others in the organization will directly affect the load—the greater the required coordination, the greater the load. Similarly, the more uncertainty there is in the work that an individual does, the greater the processing that must be accomplished to reduce the uncertainty adequately. For example, if the individual faces constantly changing work demands, performance standards, deadlines for completion, etc., then uncertainties increase and the amount of communication needed to resolve the uncertainties increases as well.

Physical factors are also important in determining load. Generally speaking, the greater the opportunity for individuals to communicate, the more likely it is that they will. And while not all of this interaction can necessarily be treated as load (in the sense of responses to requests, orders, demands for information handling), the probability of load rising obviously increases. Spatial proximity is one commonly found predictor of interaction, as are related measures of functional distance, which take into account not only geographical separation but the added effects of doors, hallways, flights of stairs, and other impediments to interaction (Gullahorn, 1952).

Psychological factors can also be included under this general environmental category. For example, one predictor of interaction is the degree of similarity between individuals, where similarity can be measured along several different dimensions. Status similarity, age, sex, or racial similarity, and attitudinal similarity are all likely to be greater among individuals who communicate more often (Rogers and Shoemaker, 1972). Like the other factors mentioned above, similarity acts to increase the probability that communication will take place and by inference makes a higher load more likely. Interpersonal attraction between individuals increases the probability they will interact and hence raises potential load.

The question of individual *capability* in communication processing is an intriguing one. Some writers argue that processing capability can be strongly influenced by the efficiency and thoroughness with which one organizes one's own time and efforts (MacKenzie, 1972). Elsewhere in this chapter it is pointed out that individuals can raise their processing capabilities by undergoing temporary overload experiences that are followed by a reorganization of their energies and efforts. There is extensive research on human information processing that deals with the neurological, psychological, and cognitive components of the brain (e.g., Schroeder, Driver, and Strufert, 1967; Miller, Galanter, and Pribram, 1969; and others) and higher-level systems (Miller, 1971, 1972). Many of the strategies for coping with overload discussed in this chapter have an obvious direct bearing on the processing capability of the individual.

The final determinant of load is the individual's *need* or *desire* to process communication. The greater the individual's perception that increased communication processing is instrumental to retaining his or her position, or advancing in the organization, the greater the processing that will occur. It is a simple matter (although not without consequences) to define one's situation as having low processing requirements by simply refusing to acknowledge the events which others in the organization consider as processing demands. Conversely, by incorporating ever-widening definitions of processing requests into one's view of "the job," it is possible to greatly increase load.

Beyond the work sphere, another important load contributor is the individual's perceived need to communicate with others, whether for affiliative reasons, to enhance self-esteem, to keep up on the latest gossip, or to reduce boredom (the underload phenomenon). Individuals differ in their needs or desires for nonwork as well as work-related interaction, and this can lead to different levels of load. Load can arise, for example, when in the course of a casual conversation with one's supervisor a request for up-to-date details about sports, hobbies, entertainment, or other nonwork topics occurs.

CONSEQUENCES OF UNDERLOAD AND OVERLOAD

A large amount of research has been done on the effects of both underload and overload on various systems, with the individual receiving the greatest amount of attention and higher-level systems receiving somewhat less attention. Regardless of whether underload or overload is present, *stress* on the individual (or system) is a highly predictable correlate. If an individual who has been processing a certain amount of communication suddenly finds this level decreased, stress symptoms usually appear and specific behaviors designed to rectify the situation will emerge. Correspondingly, if the individual finds that far more communication is being presented for processing than is customary, stress symptoms and coping behaviors may also emerge. The basic mechanism that is typically used to explain the "balancing" of load is stress avoidance—the search for relief from discomfort and/or the attainment of a psychologically satisfying state.

The research on underload has primarily been carried out in settings removed from the conventional notion of an organization; this research has been done in conjunction with mistreatment of prisoners-of-war or in specially designed psychological studies of "sensory deprivation." Sensory deprivation is a term that can be taken to be equivalent to severe underload: it involves the systematic constriction or deletion of various sensory channels as routes along which inputs can reach the individual. This can involve placing individuals in unlighted quarters, in completely soundproof chambers, depriving them of food, sleep, and companionship, using various forms of physical or psychological punishment, or other means by which their "normal" communication environment is seriously disrupted. An extensive review of this literature is found in Zubek (1969).

In organizational settings, certain types of jobs are usually linked with underload, particularly those that involve highly routine, simple, monotonous, predictable work tasks, ones with little variety. To the extent that these jobs are simple, repetitive tasks, they require little processing; and if this level consistently falls below the desired level of the particular workers involved, underload results. Assembly-line tasks frequently come under such attack, as do many of the "paper-pushing" jobs found in some organizations. In the organizational setting, the degree of deprivation is typically not as extreme as

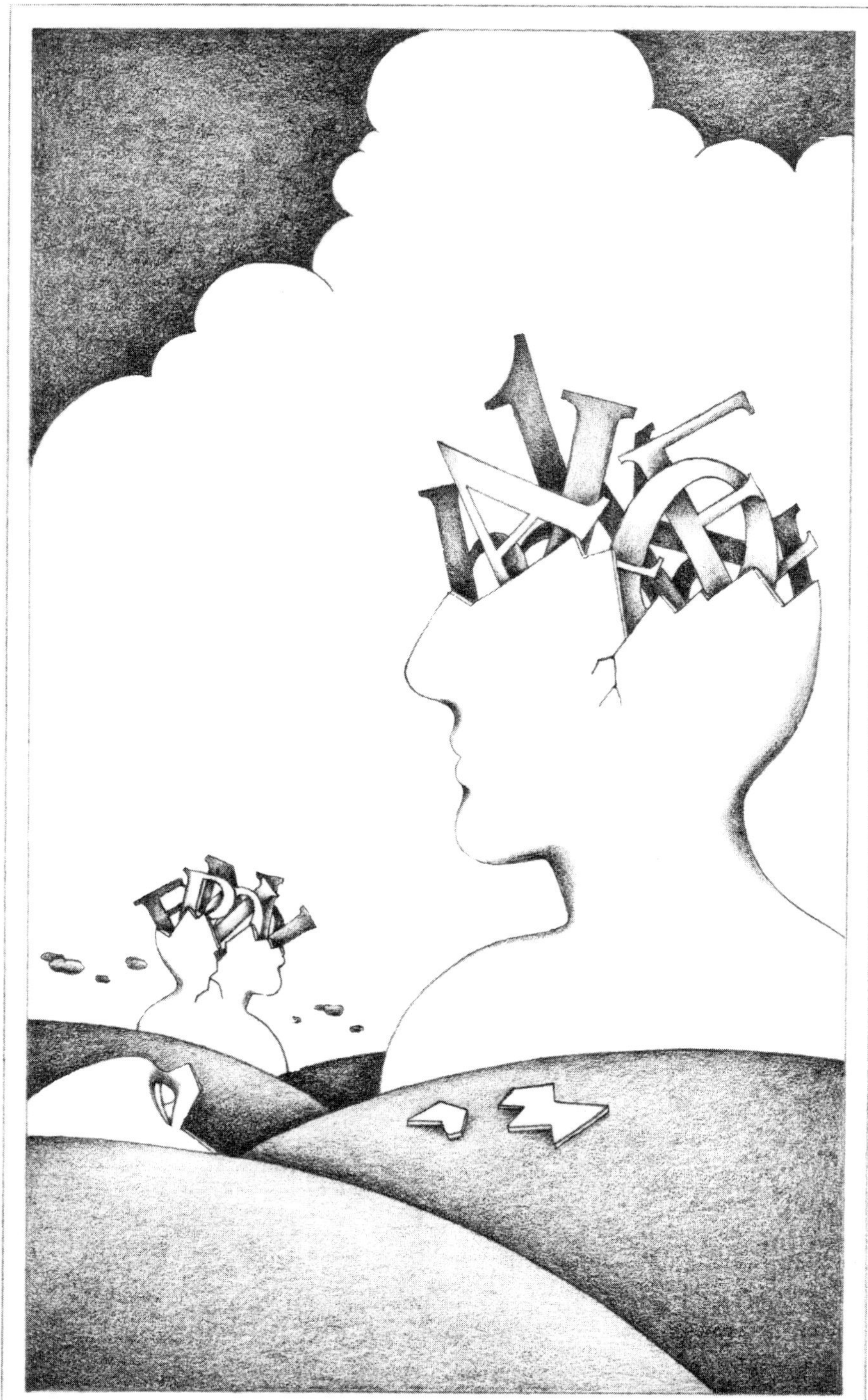

that found in prisoner-of-war settings or in laboratory experiments, but the similarities in the situations are striking.

What happens to people suffering underload? To a considerable extent, their reactions parallel those of individuals who suffer communication *overload*. The conditions of stress are manifested in the form of anxiety, tension, pain, and various physiological changes in body chemistry that accompany stress. Self-esteem may decline, the individual can become psychologically confused and disoriented, hallucinations may occur, etc.

There is a general coping mechanism that often follows communication-underload symptoms—the "creation" of message inputs in the absence of any organizational source of such inputs. There are many reports of workers who describe their jobs as exceedingly dull and boring, and who confess spending their time daydreaming about their life outside the job. Their attention is on their friendships, their hobbies, their debts and worries—a variety of topics that have nothing directly to do with the performance of their work. They compartmentalize the amount of mental effort required to get their job done and use the remainder of their thought processes to create a world that is sufficiently enjoyable so that they remain at their work (Terkel, 1974).

Parallel phenomena have been consistently reported in the prisoner-of-war studies and the laboratory-deprivation studies. Particularly in the former situation, there are numerous reports by returning POW's that they spent their years of imprisonment creating, modifying, and replacing the parts of extremely elaborate physical processes. Entire houses have been planned, constructed, modified, and, eventually, "completed." Intricate stories were "written." Thus, in many cases, in the absence of customary bona fide inputs, the human organism is apt to create sufficient inputs so that the demands for processing are more fully met.

Overload, in contrast to underload, occurs when the individual (or higher system) cannot process incoming communication as rapidly as it arrives, or as rapidly as the person would like it to be processed. Overload produces stress reactions that are similar to the ones described above for underload; in both cases, any appreciable deviation from normal or desired load is an uncomfortable experience.

Research has shown that the relationship between an individual's communication output changes very consistently as the level of input changes (Miller, 1964). Typically, as input rises, the individual is able to process the inputs on a one-to-one basis. Incoming items are disposed of as they arrive. Thus the relationship between input and output at these levels is a straight line.

However, as the processing demands reach the individual's capacity, a state is reached where increases in input fail to result in any further increases in output. The point where input begins to surpass processing capacity is called a "confusional state," a term that reflects the behavior of the individual in this

Consequences of Underload and Overload   111

peak-processing situation. Error rates begin to rise dramatically. It is possible to continue increasing the rate of communication input—you can always give people more work to do, with shorter deadlines—but the output curves show a continuing decline as the input rate continues to climb. The input rate may climb even further, but output will not increase. When inputs fall below the minimum acceptable level, underload occurs and output falls off more steeply. As noted earlier, this condition is also stressful. These relationships are shown in Fig. 5-1.

In sum, then, as information input to a system increases, output increases in a similar fashion. This relationship holds true up to the point where the processing capacity of the system has been reached. At that point, a "confusional state" occurs as the system finds itself unable to deal with the rising inputs. Error rates go up, output declines, and even if inputs continue to rise there will be no further corresponding rate of output per amount of input.

This relationship illustrates one of the striking differences between systems that process matter/energy and those that process communication. Suppose you have just unpacked your new hi-fi system—a stereo AM-FM

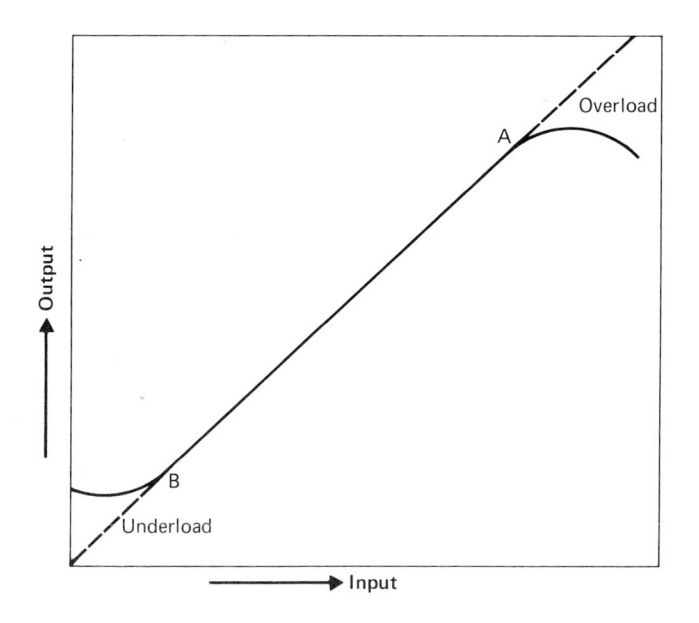

Fig. 5-1. Relation between communication input and output.

receiver with two new speakers. This system is designed to process matter/energy, in the form of electrical current. It is also designed to process information, since it decodes the radio signals and turns them into news programs, music, and other broadcasts. Suppose that a lightning storm comes up just as the system is assembled, and a large pulse of current passes through the system's fuses and other safeguards, into the heart of the receiver. Immediately thereafter, the electrical current input drops to normal levels, but it is too late for the new hi-fi equipment. The overload of energy destroyed the system, and a subsequent reduction of the energy input had no further bearing on the equipment's performance. This is an example of an *irreversible* event.

Communication overload affects a system quite differently than matter/energy does, however. Generally speaking, when the processing capability of an individual or higher-level human system is overloaded, but the input rate subsequently drops back below maximum processing capacity, the individual is able to continue processing as before, with relatively little effect on performance at the former level. In this sense, then, communication overload is much more of a *reversible* process; when a processing system breaks down from communication overload, shifting the input level down to or below maximum processing capability will restore the system's functioning. Humans seem to be fairly resilient in the face of overload; they are more tolerant to being overloaded. However, note that this statement has been qualified by pointing out that overload is *typically* reversible; there are instances where severe or prolonged overload have caused serious damage to individuals, either psychologically or physically.

The fact that a caveat is introduced here actually points to one of the most intriguing aspects of human communication processing: the ability of human systems to *alter* their processing capability over time. This alteration can proceed in both directions. Individuals who find themselves in communication environments that are considerably less complex and less challenging than those they are accustomed to may report a general decline in their own processing capacity. This can happen in situations that fall far short of those described above in the extreme deprivation instances.

The other aspect, of course, is that human systems can reorganize and restructure themselves to process more communication if they are exposed to increasingly challenging environments. Those in many occupations, such as air-traffic control, rely on this principle in selecting and training new personnel. A certified controller, for instance, is expected to be able to process communication at a far higher rate than when he or she first entered school. Similarly, demanding graduate-degree programs often work on the assumption that by systematically overloading the processing capability of entering students, it will be possible to successively increase their capacity during the course of their graduate career. Training programs for aspiring managers often operate on this same principle. Regardless of the setting of such examples, the point is that increases (or decreases) in processing capacity can be brought about by systematically altering the load placed on the human system. And while this will produce stress and coping behaviors in the short run, in many situations it is possible to produce enduring changes in processing capacity.

Earlier, it was noted that human systems can process more information as the attributes they are judging become more complex, although this higher capacity does not increase linearly with the increasing complexity of the judgment task. It is now pertinent to summarize the comparative literature on information processing at a wide range of system levels, beginning with the level of the individual cell, and extending to entire societies. From the cell, higher system levels are the organ, the organism, the group, the organization, and, finally, the society.

A number of studies have worked out the approximate information-processing capacity of the individual cell, pegging the figure at several thousand bits per second. Can we assume this as a starting point and simply add the cell capacities to arrive at the total processing capacity of, say, an entire group? Unfortunately not; there is no simple cumulative process at work. In fact, the results that consistently emerge are that higher-level systems are *less* efficient than the sum of their lower-level component parts would indicate. A group, for example, cannot process communication as rapidly as the capabilities of its members would indicate. An organization, which we can conceive of as a "group of groups," cannot process as fast as the sum of the individual constituent groups. Furthermore, to round off this particular trend, the "fall off" in processing capacities for human systems becomes increasingly pronounced as system size increases.

Two explanations can be offered for this. First, starting with the individual nerve cell, there are clearly delineated response times that are required for the cell to trigger its action, once it has just "fired off." This delay is called a "refractory time," and is the minimum time required for the nerve cell to reactivate itself and be able to transmit information again. If the concept of "refractory time" is extended to higher-level systems, it should be obvious that the *best* that can happen is that all refractory times are equal and minimal. Whenever any one is longer, however, the information flow in the system is slowed. If refractory times vary from cell to cell, or system to system (as they typically do), then not only the times themselves but also the particular *sequence* in which they are activated will determine overall processing capacity. Furthermore, if any "misfiring" occurs, this can only add delay to the processing capacity. Finally, as we move to more and more complex systems, it is easy to see how incredibly complex and limiting these factors can be.

The second explanation centers on the "language" that is used within each system level. To the degree that the larger system does not use the same "language" (and there is ample evidence that this is the case), then recoding or transducing of the lower-level language must take place at each interface with the higher-level system. Recoding takes time, it is fraught with the possibility of error, and it introduces further slowdowns in the system's overall processing capacity.

There are several implications in the notion that higher-level systems become increasingly slow to process communication. First and foremost, there is the need to specify optimum organizational sizes, beyond which the costs and inefficiencies in communication processing outweigh any desired "economies of scale" or other typical reasons for building very large organizations. Optimum size is a matter for research and speculation, but at least one persuasive argument is made for a size limitation of about 500 persons, organized into interlocking groups of about 10–15 each (Jay, 1971).

It is also obvious that the great majority of contemporary organizations far exceed sizes of 500, 1000, or even twice that many personnel. State and federal bureaucracies, and the large corporations of the world have thousands or hundreds of thousands of members. What does this one processing principle have to say about these organizations? The answer, in all likelihood, is that they are not "organizations" in the inter-dependent sense described in Chapter 2. More likely, they consist of a series of organizations within the parent organization. A nonevaluative description of them would be "branches," but often they appear to be personal fiefdoms, satraps, empires, or other enclaves of power that higher-level managers may be very hard-put to direct or guide in any consistent manner.

What we are saying, then, is that the basic communication-processing capacity of human systems is limited, and that larger systems are more vulnerable to these limitations than smaller ones. In many large organizational settings, the membership most likely breaks down into a set of organizations within the larger setting, each of which is largely self-governed, and *capable of maintaining its own boundaries and controlling much of its matter-energy and information flows.* For managers of very large organizations to think that they actually exert much influence more than four or five hierarchical levels away from themselves is, at least in the long run, an exercise in self-delusion.

A second major implication of this principle is that the problems of coding and recoding communication as it moves from level to level within an organization require very careful attention. Major points of distortion can occur when the staff assembles a report, conveys it to their manager, who in turn outines it to a meeting of managers at his level. If that same material is resummarized and conveyed once again to another managerial level, the probability is high that major changes will have crept in. A basic guide should be that communication destined for use by decision makers must travel through the least number of intermediaries; in addition, the persons who originally assembled it are in the best position to remember the process they went through in gathering it and the thought processes involved in assembling conclusions out of their original work.

COPING WITH OVERLOAD

In contemporary society, overload is the more common problem (partly because its impact tends to be more visible than underload), and consequently we will summarize various strategies that offer help in dealing with overload. It should be noted, however, that the notion of "dealing effectively" with overload must be treated with caution, because strategies that seem ideal at one system level may wreak havoc at other system levels. For example, reducing the expected performance levels of employees in a certain unit may make their work more efficient, yet leave unresolved the issue of how the *un*completed work is to be handled by other parts of the organization.

Not all organizations, of course, are equally susceptible to overload. High vulnerability is primarily found in organizations which receive a large flow of communication inputs from the environment, and which must expend a major portion of their resources in coping with the inflow (institutions that process stock and bond transactions come to mind). Also vulnerable are organizations which provide services whose demand level and/or timing are unpredicted, if not unpredictable (the sudden impact of implementing wage-price controls at the national level is said to have seriously disrupted the on-going programs of the agencies which were given these tasks). A third susceptible group includes those that have constraints imposed on them by regulatory agencies, professional standards for the members, or fixed equipment capacity (in general, the attempts by universities in the sixties to expand the facilities to meet rising enrollments exemplify this). In general, organizations that are most susceptible to overload include health services, agencies, the military, school systems at all levels, commodities or securities markets, clerical-stenographic pools, executive offices, and transportation terminals. (Meier, 1972).

It also needs to be mentioned that human systems are often capable of performing at much higher information-processing levels than the preceding discussion may have implied. There are many instances of organizations whose members "pitch-in" and operate under conditions of overload for appreciable periods of time. The members simply accept the stresses and strains of doing this.

Furthermore, there are several mechanisms by which human systems can raise their processing capabilities. These include the use of (1) successive judgments, (2) memory, (3) precision of judgments, and (4) chunking. One way to simplify the processing task is to make frequent use of successive judgments among stimuli, rather than complex simultaneous ones. Memory plays a crucial role in processing, by providing both short-term and long-term storage capacity so that on-going processing activities can be integrated into larger and more complex decisions. Memory also aids in collating and synthesizing communication. The precision of judgment processes can also be manipulated. For example, by making cruder, more simplified judgments, the overall task of processing can be speeded up.

And finally, perhaps the most widely used and most potentially efficient technique for increasing processing capacity is chunking, the label used when individuals extract minimal cues from a larger "bundle" to decide how to process the bundle. For example, highly complex sorting decisions can be treated by chunking if color codes and package shapes are associated with particular sorting routes that packages should take. Given these minimal cues, it is no longer necessary to engage in more refined judgmental processes to decide on the appropriate sorting behaviors. The use of ZIP codes for mail is an example of chunking, since they allow the routing of mail to specific postal offices more easily than by associating street addresses with particular postal stations.

There are numerous strategies open to organizations faced with overload problems, ranging from a "do nothing" approach to highly involved reorganizational and restructuring efforts to improve processing. It is important to realize that no given solution is necessarily "best" nor even always useful in dealing with specific situations.

Among the frequently neglected aspects of decision processes aimed at improving processing capabilities are the *costs* of such actions. These costs can be in dollar terms, in morale or turnover terms, or in other forms of the currencies used to judge organizational actions. The reason that cost factors are often given short shrift is that changes in processing behaviors usually have ramifications for the larger system in which "the problem" is embedded, and these larger concerns may not be taken into account when any changes are made.

Strategies for coping with overload can be broken down into three general classifications, depending on a rough assessment of the amount of effort involved in implementing them. This kind of classification scheme provides some of the details needed to assess how to cope with overload; the question of which solution will be most effective in relation to its cost must be left to an examination of individual cases. It is possible, however, to describe some of the implications of these strategies, which will be of some assistance in evaluating their potential merit.*

---

*These strategies are adapted from Campbell (1958), Meier (1972), Weick (1970), Miller, J.G. (1960), Galbraith (1973), Prince (1970) and Dearden, McFarlan, and Zani (1971).

Minimal-Effort Strategies

1. *Ignore the situation, make no changes, await the passing of the problem.* This is not meant to be a facetious suggestion; in fact, it is probably the one most commonly used. It is always possible that the organization and its members possess a degree of flexibility and hidden capabilities that have not yet surfaced, which are capable of handling the situation. Changes may not result in any improvement, or they may even create new problems that are worse than the present ones. The new problems could be irreversible, whereas the present problems may be ephemeral. Obviously, the whole key to the success of this strategy is whether serious problems do in fact exist which, if left untouched, will eventually bring about permanent harm to the organization. The option of *consciously* deciding to do nothing should, however, be a viable one.

2. *"Work to Standards," adhering closely to formalized, codified performance goals that are not affected by perceived overload conditions.* Here the strategy is to follow detailed rules and procedures, independently of the load or of any backlog of work. In (1) above, the organization's members continue "business as usual" in the hopes that the problem will either fail to be confirmed or will disappear; in this approach formal rule systems are followed that enable the organization to argue that it *is* operating efficiently according to the standards under which it was set up. This strategy is often seen in bureaucratic organizations that are not directly responsive to the marketplace or to an audience or public whose demands can be easily articulated and input to the organization. In this situation, the organization operates in an environment which usually buffers it from the possible ill effects of not processing more efficiently. "The problem" tends to be defined by only certain members of the organization (often, in bureaucracies, the politically appointed leadership) or in citizen's groups representing the class of individuals to be served by the organization. Organizations that adopt this approach and which exist in this type of environment are very effectively buffered from outside influences.

3. *Allow waiting lines—queues—to build up whenever demand exceeds handling capacity.* In the first example, the overload condition—if one existed—was allowed to express itself in whatever form it happened to occur. In (2), it was generally ignored. Now, however, the emphasis shifts to the particular case when the overload is due to what is recognized as an excessively high rate of input of demands on the organization. Allowing queues to take place in effect externalizes the overload problem to the environment that is generating the initial inputs. If the queue consists of persons seeking, for example, medical treatment, then the problem of how to handle their

medical ailments is left to the persons in the queue; in such a case, hospital emergency rooms or standard patient-admission facilities deal with incoming patients in sequence.

One effect of this queueing is to make the rate of input a constant, so long, of course, as the queue exists. If it is expected that demand for the organization's services will almost never tax the capability of the organization to respond, then planning can be done on the basis of highly predictable input volumes. This is a form of uncertainty reduction for the organization's managers.

Over time, however, denial of access to the organization can generate problem solutions by queue members that lead them to go elsewhere. Sufficient ill will may be built up so that when expanded services finally are available, there will be resistance to returning to the organization. It is possible to envision the very unstable situation of an organization which is initially faced by lengthy queues that continue over time; then, by the time this organization expands its service capability, demand for its services does not meet the new capability and hence the organization finds itself with unused resources.

4. *Set message-priority categories, and then select out high-priority messages.* There are some clear-cut cost-benefit potentials to this approach, because it allows the organization to "skim the cream" off the queue and reduce the loss in resources caused by inability to process the queue. The value to the organization of all incoming communication demands is seldom equal, so by identifying the "high-payoff" inputs and attending primarily to them, the organization can expend the minimal amount of its own resources in return for the maximal gain—in this sense, then, this is a potentially cost-beneficial solution. However, there is also an assumption at work here that queue members can be taken out of line without major disruption by other queue members. This is a delicate situation, and the assumption that such a system would work should be examined carefully. Under this solution, all queue members get serviced—eventually.

5. *Destroy or omit servicing the lowest priority messages.* It is possible, of course, simply to refuse to handle low-priority messages, to eliminate them from the set of inputs to be serviced. It may be advisable to discontinue accepting low-priority messages, free the organization of any input or storage costs that would occur if these inputs received any attention, and further increase information-processing efficiency as a result. Customers or clients can be notified that such requests will no longer be honored.

One of the dangers in this approach, however, comes from appraising these situations on a class basis, rather than on an individual basis. It may be that some processing of low-priority messages is imperative in order to retain the goodwill and usage levels of certain clients in the environment. Fractional savings on some low-priority messages may generate a backlash which loses some high-priority business as well.

6. *Allow the clients to self-serve their own needs.* This solution is a popular one in organizations such as libraries or supermarkets, where a significant portion of the burden of communication processing is shifted to the client. In effect, clients contribute their own energies and resources (sometimes a significant amount) to resolving the communication requests, and thus make it possible for the organization to do far more processing than it could do without the client's assistance. The success of this task largely hinges on the degree of sophistication required of the client to carry out the search and processing activities. For example, processing required to shop in a large, complex, multi-department supermarket (with its home and garden section, clothes, household items, and numerous other nonfood products) is certainly nontrivial. If clients cannot handle this task, then the organization cannot externalize this part of the overall communication-processing load.

7. *Reduce performance standards from prior levels.* This approach, like the previous ones, is also a fairly easy one to implement, in the sense that organizational members are allowed greater waste, less rigorous specifications, more errors in handling their work, less sensitivity to the needs of clients, and less coordination with other units in the organization. Reduction in performance standards does not necessarily mean a whole-scale departure from existing performance levels. It can be directed to a selective relaxing of standards in those areas which seem most amenable to cost-beneficial changes. For example, reducing response time for customer complaints may be acceptable in lieu of not being able to attend at all to an important number of complaints. Again, this strategy has many pitfalls, not the least of which is the "image" of the organization to its clients and to its members—who may think that "things are really going downhill" and alter their work performance downward—as well.

Moderate-Effort Strategies
The foregoing seven strategies can be implemented rather easily in an organization, although as noted, ease of implementation is not to be confused with the possible rewards or losses from the results of implementing these strategies. The next set of processing strategies involves appreciably more effort and more expenditure of energy on the part of the organization, but it also carries the promise of a more effective treatment of overload problems.

120 Communication "Load"

8. *Establish performance standards that make it possible to provide adequate resources to meet communication-processing demands.* If overload conditions are to be coped with, then it is imperative that clear knowledge be present as to the magnitude of the overload and the various processing steps that need to be completed to resolve the situation. Gathering this knowledge requires a step-by-step tracing of the routes that inputs take, the precise activities that are performed at each of the transfer points for each request, and an understanding of the strengths and weaknesses of the system that is designed to process them. Where are critical skills missing? Are supplies and equipment needed? Is there sufficient manpower to accomplish the task? Finally, what must the performance of organizational members at each step along the way be in order for the load to be handled?

Given this knowledge, it becomes feasible to provide specifications for acceptable performance standards. In addition, it is possible to make projections to an overall appraisal of the resources needed to deal with the load. Finally, it is critical that these standards be clearly conveyed to organizational members, and that new members be adequately instructed in the performance expected of them. It should be noted that the acquisition of this knowledge, and its use in managerial decision processes, can consume a large amount of resources.

9. *Analyze the communication flow so that rules for "chunking" can be precisely determined and implemented.* As noted earlier, "chunking" involves the use of a small subset of cues from a larger set that permits speedy processing of the communication in the larger set, without a detailed examination of the elements in that set. Chunking is very commonly done in processing settings; what is less common is an explicit study of the rules under which various chunking methods are most efficient.

One critical question concerns the error rate in using chunking: how often are incorrect decisions made because the basis on which the chunking is done fails to reveal genuine internal differences in the overall package being processed? Are the chunking strategies in fact the most efficient, or are there other strategies which could speed processing even more, keeping factors of cost and accuracy in mind? Hence this strategy becomes a moderate-effort one when taken in the light of a positive approach to improving communication processing, something that can be brought under managerial control as well as left to the individual discretion of members of the organization; it is an extension of (8) above.

10. *Encourage middlemen by turning some work over to subcontractors.* Subcontractors, by definition, are independent of the parent organization, and

serve two purposes. First, they provide a specific product to the parent organization; second, they relieve the parent organization of the communication processing associated with the task area under subcontract. The parent organization is primarily responsible for specifying what it wants, negotiating an acceptable exchange of resources, monitoring the completed work, and incorporating it into the basic flow of activity in the organization. In many instances, it is more efficient in terms of both resources and communication processing to subcontract task areas, because the subcontractor may be operating at levels where scale economies are far higher than the single parent organization could achieve.

A certain degree of control is lost by turning tasks over to subcontractors, and it is possible that profit potential is also foregone. Furthermore, the health and continuity of the subcontractor may be independent of the parent organization, yet still be vitally linked with the success of the parent. So subcontracting has powerful advantages that can accrue from it, but it has fairly substantial risks as well.

11. *Create additional branch offices to enlarge processing capability.* To a considerable extent, this strategy is the reverse of (10); the decision is made to expand the organization's ability to process certain types of communication by adding new units within the organization. This presumes that there is sufficient volume of processing for the branch offices to warrant their operation, along with the extra managerial, overhead, capital, and other costs that are associated with a branch. This requires a careful assessment of the minimum volume the branch must perform to be viable, and since new resource-consuming items (such as capital expenditures) may be required, it is likely that a *very* sizable jump in communication processing may be dictated before the addition of a branch can be justified.

12. *Creation of "slack resources" to handle peak loads.* Clerical and stenographic pools are perhaps the most common example of slack resources that organizations can maintain in order to meet changes in processing loads. As the needs arises, members of the pool are deployed to different parts of the organization and then returned to the pool to await further demand.

But the concept of "slack resources" need not be restricted to lower-level personnel. It can also be applied at higher levels, both to managers and technical personnel, where a pool of available talent and energy is maintained in the event of need. This allows an organization to gear up quickly for a "crash project," without, for example, going through the time and trouble involved in seeking out and acquiring new personnel. Furthermore, in addition to reducing response time in handling rapid changes in load, the prior experiences of these individuals in working in the organization can minimize the need for socializing them into the larger organization. Such issues as supervision, reporting, pay, and benefits should be more familiar to them than to newly hired personnel, thus lowering their processing needs and increasing their contribution to organizational needs.

The cost of this strategy is also obvious, because the organization is sustaining personnel for whom there may be sizable periods of idle time. Whether this is a prudent move depends largely on whether need for such available resources is likely. If the expectation of need is high—and if the rewards for being able to meet it in an efficient, orderly, and timely fashion are also high—then the strategy appears justifiable. On the other hand, in the face of limited evidence of need, the costs may be excessive. This is in part due to the fact that having personnel of varying skill levels available but unused can lead to deterioration of morale, interest, and performance. The personnel must be used in meaningful ways during those periods when they are not providing a pool of slack resources.

Major-Effort Strategies

The first set of strategies involved essentially minor alterations in the behavior of organizational members in such a way that the organization's ability to process communication could increase. Considerably more effort and resources are required to use one or more of the second set of strategies, but they carry the possibility of considerably greater leverage on overload problems. A significantly higher level of energy and effort is required to implement the final set of strategies, with a correspondingly greater amount of potential influence available to be exerted. Each of these strategies involves the deliberate *restructuring* or reorganization of the activities that members of the organization perform.

13. *Creation of lateral relations in the organizational structure.* Most organizations have clear hierarchies, and quite often information flow is guided or mandated along these vertical lines. Yet there arise many instances when transmitting communication and requests "through channels" creates excessive distortion, requires too long a time, and generally contributes to slow progress toward a goal. For this reason, it is possible to create *horizontal* or lateral relations throughout the organization, in which personnel who possess knowledge that others need become readily accessible to one another, without the rigid requirements that strict "chain-of-command" hierarchies be followed. Even if the person in another part of the organization is at a different status level, lateral relationships can ignore this factor and permit better communication flow to occur.

The main problem this strategy can create arises from the greater use of communication links; the volume of messages can rise to the level where the main work activities in the various linked divisions are impaired. In other words, if the message-traffic rate between divisions reaches a level sufficient to disrupt the main work of the division, then the strategy has become dysfunctional. The trade-off is between this occurrence and the improved processing that can result from readier access to people elsewhere who have critical materials. Another problem, of course, is that managers may treat this as undesirable "bypassing" and create strain within the organization as a result.

14. *Creation of self-contained task forces with specific assignments.* By departing from the existing organizational structure, which typically involves segmentation of the organization into different functional divisions (e.g., sales, research, production, etc.) and moving to a *product-oriented* or task-oriented structure, it is possible to effect significant reductions in the communication processing of the overall organization while accomplishing certain important goals as well.

The concept of a self-contained task force involves the assembly of the personnel and material required to accomplish a specific task. *All* the resources that are needed are included within the task force. The task force has its own management, and there will be a minimum of interface between the task force and the larger organization. If a statistician is needed by the task force, it gets one; if normal organizational rules and procedures are impediments to the speedy completion of the task force's efforts, then these are bypassed or waived. In short, the "self-contained task force" becomes an organization within the overall organization, and largely autonomous from it.

Clearly there are dangers here. The personnel and management of the task force must be carefully chosen because in actual fact the task force does not exist in isolation from the parent organization, and this must be dealt with realistically. Furthermore, there are many inefficiencies that are possible. Perhaps the task force doesn't need the statistician on a full-time basis; an inefficient use of the person is created. The fact that there are established policies and procedures in the parent organization does not automatically mean that they are "bad"; in fact, they may be highly efficient. To rapidly bypass them may be quite wasteful and even unnecessary for the task force's speedy progress.

15. *Implementation of management-information systems.* All organizations, of course, have management-information systems by the very fact that managerial processes are at work. Beyond this simplistic statement lies a wide range of formalization and mechanization of information systems that can assist managers in their activities. A well-designed and maintained file system

in one manager's office can be an indispensable "management-information system." More commonly, however, the term has come to refer to large-scale, often computerized systems for the acquisition, storage, retrieval, and dissemination of information about various aspects of the organization's activities. This can range from inventory control (no simple task) to large-scale simulations and predictions of future market demand for the organization's products and services (an incredibly complex task). Investment in management-communication systems can easily run into the millions of dollars, and there are numerous pitfalls involved in the establishment and use of such systems. The literature on management-communication systems is very extensive (see Prince, 1970, and Dearden, McFarlan, and Zani, 1971).

16. *Reorganization, restructuring, fundamental change of the organization.* This is the most drastic of all strategies for altering information-processing capabilities, since it gets at the very basic design features of the organization itself. In federal bureaucracies, one way this is accomplished is to dissolve an agency and create a new one in its stead. In the private sector, large-scale changes of a similar nature are also not uncommon. The decision process that is involved in this is an inordinately complex one, and requires the weighting of many factors, of which information processing is but a part. However, the critical point from our perspective is that in such situations it is as important to pay specific attention to the information-processing implications of reorganization as it is to other factors, such as personnel, environment, and financing.

SUMMARY

In this chapter, we have reviewed one of the core traits of any organization's communication system—its load. We defined load in terms of the rate and complexity of processing placed on individuals in the organization and higher-level units as well. The difference between input and capacity was pointed out so that we could draw an operational distinction between underload (input falls below capacity), load, and overload (input exceeds capacity).

Two main points were made about load. First, as load increases, output increases, up to the point where the capacity of the individual or system is reached; at that point, further increases in load are not accompanied by increased output. Second, the larger and more complex the system, the less efficient in processing it becomes: differences in reaction times and the need to "translate" messages between system levels act to make the larger system slower than the sum of the capabilities of the lower-level components.

Finally, 16 strategies for coping with overload are discussed. They are grouped according to the amount of organizational resources they require to be implemented (ranging from minimal to major) and their degree of probable impact (negative, neutral, or positive).

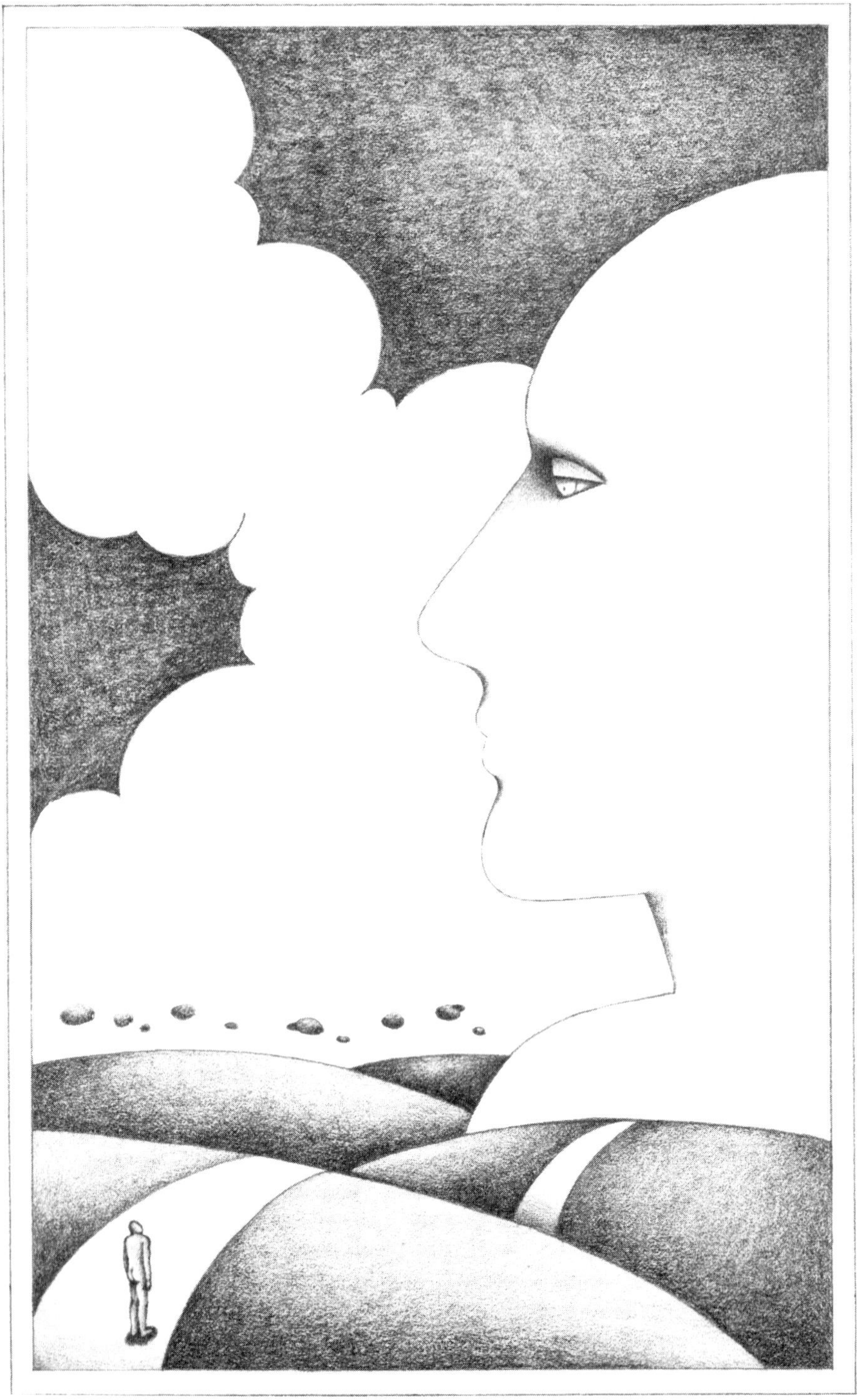

6
Communication "Rules" in the Organizational Hierarchy

In the previous chapter we treated the concept of communication "load"—how to evaluate it, what some of its consequences were, and how to cope with the most endemic, related problem, overload. Much of that discussion centered on the individual, and on the interplay between load at the individual and organizational levels. In the present chapter, the discussion shifts from the individual, treated largely as an isolated entity operating in the larger organization, to the minimum organizational "building block"—the two-person system, or *dyad*.

To say that the dyad is the minimum building block is in no way intended to diminish its importance. It is perhaps better called the *fundamental* unit, because of the critical role it plays in developing the web of interconnections among organizational members—the web that permits all control and coordination activities to occur. A key feature of organizational dyads is that their members can perform overlapping roles. A and B can be a dyad, and so can B and C. Thus a two-step chain from A to B to C is established by the two overlapping dyads, AB and BC. The presence of AB and BC represents the first step in developing longer and more complex chains of dyads; these chains represent the transformation of a set of independent individuals into an integrated, organizing body.

Dyads arise on the basis of single relationships (such as shared work flow, power, and communication) or multiple relationships. The hierarchy of authority in organizations is a common example of one type of relationship by which dyads are formed; and social exchange or friendship is another example, one which can be independent of authority relationships. In organizations, authority relationships are extremely important because they are the typical means for giving orders and directions and receiving subsequent reports. This interchange makes possible both the control and the coordination of organizational activities.

In Chapters 7 and 8, these overlapping dyads (AB and BC) will be extended to larger and more complex configurations, such as groups or organizations. First, however, some of the major communication properties of organizational dyads need to be examined; not until this is done will the implications of dyadic communication in larger contexts be more apparent. Furthermore, the two-person interaction is one of the most frequent, if not *the* most frequent, forms of communication exchange that take place in an organization.

There are many types of dyads to be found in organizations, as noted above. The two-person unit of primary importance in the present chapter is that which is built on hierarchical *authority* relationships; it is this type of dyad that provides the basic "chain of command" along which orders and numerous other messages flow.

Starting at the top of an organization, the first such dyad links the chief executive officer (or the president, the "head") to his or her immediate subordinates. In turn, these subordinates are likely to have subordinates of their own, so a given organizational member can be a subordinate in one dyad and a manager in another. These overlapping manager-subordinate relationships continue to occur as one moves downward through the organization to the lowest level where supervision takes place. The members below this level are not included in the managerial hierarchy; they are subordinates only.

One point bears repeating: as one examines any organization, the person at the top fills only one role. This person is a manager only and does not operate in the organization as a subordinate. All other personnel at the managerial level, however, occupy both supervisory and subordinate roles, and hence are involved in a wider variety of intra-organizational relationships than either the person heading the organization or those who are subordinates only. Finally, it should be noted that the term "supervisor" can, in many settings, be replaced by the term "manager." It is common to refer to persons who fulfill the organization's needs for control and coordination at the first level of the authority hierarchy as "supervisors," or "foremen," while individuals of higher rank are called managers. However, in this book we will use the term manager to refer to individuals at all authority levels, unless otherwise indicated.

The importance of these points, particularly the fact that most managers exist in supervisory roles in some instances and subordinate roles in others, will become clearer as the concept of communication "rules" is explored and it is shown how these rules influence (if not govern) the basic supervisor-subordinate relationship.

THE CONCEPT OF COMMUNICATION RULES

The concept of "rules" of communication in the managerial hierarchy can best be introduced by first giving a few examples:

> *Manager:*
> Well, Gerry, I'm glad to have you on-board here. It's going to take you a while to learn the ropes, but there's one thing I want to make clear—my door is always open to you if you've got a problem with your work, or even some other problem, for that matter. Feel free to stop in and see me, anytime you want. Victor here will take you around and show you the rest of the place.
>
> (Victor and Gerry go off.)
>
> *Gerry:*
> Is he serious about that...is he really that open...that available, usually?
>
> *Victor:*
> Well, I might as well tell you now, before you find out the hard way. He thinks he's open to us, and he tells everybody that, but nine times out of ten if you take him up on it you'll find he gets impatient and cuts you off. Most of us don't think he's accessible at all. And we don't really *want* him to be...otherwise he'd be nosing into our work and personal life too much.

What can be concluded from this situation? From the boss's point of view, it seems clear that he is (at least verbally) stating a communication rule that he would like followed: "Feel free to stop in and see me with a problem—my door is always open." From Victor's point of view, however, quite the opposite perception of the rule prevails. Instead, in Victor's opinion, the boss operates more of a closed-door policy than an open-door policy. And Victor, at least, is not at all sure he wants the situation changed.

130   Communication "Rules" in the Organizational Hierarchy

Let's consider a different example:

Gerry:
Say, Victor, I've been looking through my copy of the *Supervisor's Personnel Policy Guide,* and it says here that if one of my subordinates has a problem or complaint that can't be worked out with me, they're to go to the Personnel Office. I'm not sure I like that idea. Any malcontent could get me in a lot of trouble by going over there and blabbing stuff without me knowing about it. I'm going to let it be known that nobody better be found going over there unless they clear it with me first.

Victor:
Gerry, that policy is about nine months behind the times. We used to operate that way here—no subordinate would dare take Personnel up on their word to help out and look like they were going around our authority. But times have changed. The people higher up decided we shouldn't have that much authority anymore—it was causing too many problems, too much turnover. The people who come to work here today don't listen like they used to. So now it's not a very wise policy to interfere with somebody who thinks they have a problem. You'll cause yourself more grief trying to block it than letting Personnel handle it. Let it ride, Gerry.

Here a classic conflict exists between the formal communication rules, as laid out in part of the *Supervisor's Personnel Policy Guide,* and the informal procedures desired by the managers. To avoid communication problems, if not more severe problems, both managers and subordinates need to know the nature of the rules, understand them, and agree, if reasonable harmony is to prevail.

Another example will show the operation of communication rules in a different light. Martha has just returned home from her job, the first day after moving into a new "office-landscape" environment. Previously, desks, chairs, tables, and whole offices had been laid out in neat, long, orderly rows. Secretaries sat outside their bosses' offices. The place was rather dreary, predictable, and common—just like most other offices.

But in the new setting, many things had changed. Movable walls, some just waist high, separated different work areas. Color had returned in abundance, on walls, chairs, desks, everywhere. Potted plants served as partial screens, yet one could still see through them to people at their desks. Work spaces had lots of new gadgets that looked like they might be of help in doing the work.

The Concept of Communication Rules   131

Martha's comments, for our purposes, are restricted to some observations on the communication in which she took part.

Martha:
You know, the hardest thing to deal with was the loss of privacy. I felt like people were staring at me, or at least we had a lot of trouble avoiding eye contact. I haven't got my own work space organized very well yet, so when I get asked for something sometimes it takes a while to find it. And I can't find other people very easily—they're off hidden behind some big plant on the other side of the room. But the thing I really found uncomfortable was dealing with the managers. Now, if someone doesn't want to see me, there is no hiding it—secretaries can't say anything about not being in the office, or tied up with other people, or things like that. So I don't know a graceful way to approach someone that I need to see.

This situation will no doubt change as time passes and the organization's members make an adjustment to the new working conditions. But it does show how dramatically reorganization and changes in office layout can affect the rules according to which people conduct their communication and the degree to which uncertainty and confusion can temporarily disrupt the previous, ongoing communication practices and procedures.

To illustrate further the notion of communication rules, consider a manager going about the daily job routine. The manager may enter the work area and give minimal "good mornings" or other greetings. Longer discussions may be held with some subordinates, to inquire about the progress of their work or about personal matters. Some subordinates may seek out the manager for answers to questions. It is likely that a stack of memos, letters, phone messages, and other communication demands awaits the manager. There may be a meeting scheduled later in the day, at which strong criticism may be encountered about a recent decision that was made without first securing the appropriate approval.

The results of a number of research studies (e.g., Burns, 1954) indicate that managers spend about two-thirds of their time each day in communication activities, and that a fairly large portion of this time goes to direct interaction with subordinates or other managers. Thus anyone accompanying a manager during the day is likely to observe a great deal of interaction taking place.

Suppose that the study of this manager extends over several days, for as much as a week or two. During that period of time it is quite likely that one will find a number of common features, a number of consistent *patterns of be-*

havior, with respect to the communication activities in which the manager participates. *To the extent that regular, habitual patterns of behavior are noted in the communication activities for this manager, we say that certain "rules" (norms, expectations, expressions of "proper" behavior) are in effect.* At a broader level, to the degree that certain communication rules are found to occur extensively throughout the organization, communication "policy" exists, especially if the policy is formally written out and approved at top management levels.

These rules, or their aggregated form as policy, are sometimes found in statute books within the organization, in company policy and procedures manuals, or in other expressions of appropriate organizational etiquette. A straightforward example of communication policy is: "If you have a question about benefits, see your supervisor; if he or she cannot help you, then contact Staff Benefits." But more common than such formalized communication rules are the *informal* rules that exist within the organization, e.g., rules governing when to meet face-to-face rather than send a memo, or which topics are appropriate and which are not. Acquiring these informal communication rules is a time-consuming and formidable task faced by new members of the organization, who need to "learn the ropes" before a serious breach of rules and/or policy is committed.

Most of the communication rules learned by new members of an organization are acquired informally—by trial and error, from discussion with other organizational members—or informal training provided by the organization or by existing documents. The key here, however, is to recognize that much of this knowledge is acquired informally, and over a period of time as repetition of similar events occurs. Ultimately, these behavioral norms or rules become the expected behavior in the relevant situation.

Provided that (1) there is a close mesh between the individual's goals and the organization's goals, and (2) the individual is exposed to the expected behaviors, and (3) the individual implements these behaviors, there will be very smooth and harmonious integration of the new member. *But any breakdown in this series of logical prerequisites can lead to breakdowns in effective interaction.* Statements such as "I didn't know she dislikes interruptions when she's talking with someone else," or "Where was I supposed to find out that these are the proper forms for submitting an equipment request?" are indications of breakdowns in communication where the rules or norms are at least part of the overall problem.

There is basically no alternative to using rules for communication in an organization. If there were no rules, then every situation would have to be treated as unique, and the costs and inefficiencies of such behavior would be enormous. So the issue is not whether there will be rules, but rather what kinds of rules are in effect, and how to ensure that these rules are widely shared and used in such a fashion as to achieve the goals of both the organization and its members.

THE INEVITABILITY OF DIFFERENT RULE EXPECTATIONS

A critical premise in the conceptualization of communication presented earlier is the idea that the "meanings" for symbols are unique to individuals. Where individuals have had very similar associations between the symbols (words) and their referents, the meanings should be quite similar. Each person develops his or her own referents for particular symbols on the basis of past experiences. This same process of meaning assignment also occurs with rules of behavior, since from childhood a person is placed in different situations and sees the success or failure of many types of behaviors. Parents, teachers, and friends have reinforced or praised some of our behaviors, and discouraged others. This usually produces a pattern of behavior that basically fits into the society and class in which a person lives.

Most individuals have been exposed to a variety of organizations, beginning with schools, and perhaps including church, children's programs, informal friendship groups, the military, and groups that last into later life. In these organizations, certain ways of doing things will be observed and adopted. Some group members may have been shown certain ways to behave and may have been required to behave in specific ways.

Over the years, the acquisition of rules may be gradual and uneventful, leading the child into adolescence and from there to work in the same organization that has employed the father or brother for many years. In such a situation, the additional learning required when work with the organization begins may be minimal. But in an increasing number of situations, this smooth, easy progression is not found; college may intervene, and perhaps graduate school, and a different career path may be selected. This path may cut across several organizations during the course of the individual's working career, and even within any one organization different jobs require learning quite different sets of rules.

In this context, then, it should be clear that people come into a given work situation with a wide variety of background experiences, and with quite different repertoires of behaviors to handle different aspects of the work. Communication as a means for establishing appropriate rules under a given situation becomes far more important (and subject to greater breakdowns), and the specific problem of learning the communication rules to be followed (independent of other rules governing task accomplishment) assumes a far greater level of importance. Unless communication is used properly to establish both the work *and* communication rules to be followed, and unless both of these behavior sets are directly instrumental to successful task completion, then serious problems are likely to emerge. The concept of communication rules is discussed in more detail in the section below.

COMMUNICATION RULES: CONTENT RULES AND PROCEDURAL RULES

As already noted, human communication is governed by rules if successful interaction is to have a reasonable chance of occurring. Cushman and Whiting (1972) distinguish between two classes of rules—content and procedural. Content rules govern standard usage or consensus on the name of a concept, the attributes of a concept or the function of a concept. In other words, content rules relate to the symbols that will be used in the organizational context to represent some aspect of the environment. Procedural rules govern the ways people will communicate or interact in the system. Procedural rules guide the ways in which interaction can come about, its location, duration, and other factors. Thus, content rules deal with the meanings that people will attribute to symbols or *what* a word will count for, while procedural rules deal with *how* they will carry out the actual communication event. Content rules grow from agreement among at least two members as to what the use of a particular symbol will count as, in the particular organizational context. As Cushman and Whiting note, families and small cohesive groups frequently develop special consensual meanings for symbols which emphasize the identity of the group and facilitate communication within it. So it is also in organizations, where particular communication rules develop that are somewhat unique to the particular organization. These unique meanings represent a large measure of the task of learning the ropes in a new organization or a new context.

"Proper" language usage also is included under this heading. Profanity may be acceptable only with one's peers, not with one's manager; it may be unacceptable in print but permitted orally. Poor grammar or esoteric words may be unacceptable.

One aspect of some content rules is that they increase the efficiency of communication within a dyad, even though to an outsider the interaction being observed may make no sense whatsoever. In many organizations, abbreviations, concepts, and various symbols may take on quite special meanings of their own. For example, PRS may "mean" the Principal Research Scientist, the Personnel Report Schedule, the Pastoral Research Station, the Potomac Regional Service, or the Primary Rating Scheme. The Personnel Inventory may "mean" a stack of computer printout, a section within the Staff Training Division, a file on each officer, or a new sales promotion program.

It would be virtually impossible to catalogue all the rules that are developed in an organization, particularly if the organization is changing in structure or function over time. Just as language itself changes over time, the particular content rules in any dyad will gradually change. Cushman and Whiting state as a necessary condition for rule-governed communication:

> The parties involved need sufficient assurance that they have the requisite degree of consensus on the meanings of the symbols and the situation involved in their communication. (p. 27)

The second set of rules, *procedural* ones, deals with the ways that actual interaction (whether face-to-face or through other means) will take place. For communication to occur between the two members of a dyad, there must be at least some minimal set of rules about such issues as who will communicate first, how much communication may occur, where it is appropriate or permissible to communicate, who will control the interaction, and how it will be terminated.

As with content rules, there are various levels of acceptance or standardization of procedural rules. Some apply to all members of an organization, while others are unique to a particular part of an organization. Along with the content rules, procedural rules are sometimes spelled out in staff manuals, although usually most such rules are not collected and codified to this extent. Formalized procedural rules often deal with such matters as who should initiate what kinds of content and what channels should be used. But as these formalized procedures seldom cover all the standard ways of communicating, there will be numerous ad hoc rules that are in effect, including those that indicate exactly how "the boss wants things done."

For example, informal rules may develop about what sorts of things should be referred to the Division Heads, and which things can be taken directly to the Training Officer. Does the Branch Head in the main office want to see copies of all correspondence passing out of the branch? Should you make annual, quarterly, or other reports? What is the best procedure for applying for benefits, holiday leave, or sick pay, independent of what the formal procedures may specify? Who is to initiate budget requests for the following year? Is the telephone readily usable as a means of arriving at decisions, or must face-to-face interaction always (or almost always) take place? Will a phone call suffice, or must it be followed by a memorandum? What letters can be sent out under your own signature, and which require your boss's signature? In each of these instances, it is the procedural aspects of the communication, rather than the content itself, that is of interest.

The use of communication rules in both the content and procedural aspects of dyadic interaction is closely related to the clinically-based work on relational control by Watzlawick, *et al.* (1967); these ideas are briefly described in Chapter 3. They use the term "relational control" to refer to the process of seeking and accepting control that occurs during dyadic interaction;

the control process can be complementary (one person accepts control), symmetrical (neither accepts control), or equal. In simplest terms, relational communication deals with the issue of whether either member of a dyad is "one-up" (has control), "one-down" (accepts control), or "equal" in an interaction. Control may be constant during an interaction, or it may change back and forth in the dyad from moment to moment, topic to topic, or exchange to exchange.

Sometimes two individuals are found heatedly discussing a topic, arguing against one another's views. Their argument may not reflect true differences in viewpoints, but instead may arise from a more basic disagreement on who is in charge of the situation— who is to be in control. Formally, control may be designated as the responsibility of the manager, with appropriate communication rules to indicate when "enough" disagreement from the subordinate has been voiced. The subordinate may not know—or may choose to ignore—these rules, and a struggle for control of the relationship may occur. Wholesale violation of communication rules by manager and subordinate may lead to escalating conflict and an unpleasant situation for both parties.

Problems can also occur when rules and actions (both the content and relational aspects) are in conflict. A manager may claim to be always open to discussion of subordinates' problems, but if they leave a meeting feeling put down or silly they will learn very quickly that their boss expects them to fend for themselves. If an offer of openness is contradicted by actual behavior when someone brings a sensitive problem for resolution, significant relational problems can arise. Thus the question "What on earth did I say that was so offending?" may have little to do with the actual referents of the words that were used, but a lot to do with the way the interaction control was handled. The relationship can be affected more by *how* something is said than merely by *what* is being said.

The essential feature in relational control is that at least two sequential messages are considered, one from each member of the dyad. The communication behavior of one dyad member in response to the other must be noted before one can start to analyze the relationship. Relational analysis depends on message sequences. Each time a person communicates, the response can be described in terms of the message preceding it as one-up (where the individual moves toward gaining or maintaining control), one-down (where an individual moves toward yielding control), or one-across (where an individual moves toward neutralizing control). Acceptance of the control by the other confirms the first person's definition, while rejection refutes this definition. The control pattern can thus show whether one person is "putting down" the other, whether there is a balance of control, or whether one is attempting to define the relationship in a particular way that is not accepted by the other. As more and more transactions are reviewed, major patterns can be distinguished and the overall relationship more clearly understood. Rogers and Farace

(1975) present ways in which the relational aspect of dyadic interaction can be measured.

An example may help to show some of the different states that the relational aspect of an interaction can take:

Manager:
Jones, this report should be expanded. (one-up)

Subordinate:
I thought that it was long enough. (one-up)

Manager:
No, it fails to justify the budget increase. (one-up)

Subordinate:
I will try to put more in it, then. (one-down)

Manager:
You need more output, you know. (one-up)

Subordinate:
I am working flat out now. (one-up)

Manager:
Could you do with an assistant? (one-down)

Subordinate:
Yes, that would help. (one-down)

Manager:
I will see what I can do. (one-across)

Subordinate:
This report will take some time. (one-up)

Manager:
You had better get going then. (one-up)

This is illustrated graphically in Fig. 6-1 to show how the control changes.

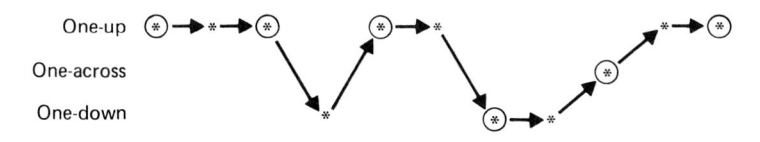

Fig. 6-1. Illustration of relational control patterns. ⊛ represents the manager, * the subordinate. Arrows indicate changes in control as conversation proceeds.

It becomes clear that the manager and Jones are not having a friendly discussion about the report, although ostensibly the report is their subject. The subordinate is not completely accepting a one-down position. Although the manager might feel that all that had happened was that some constructive advice had been given, the analysis shows that at the same time the relationship is clearly being controlled and that the manager is in charge. Jones, the subordinate, does not accept the one-down role and may leave feeling rather frustrated.

Patterns of relational control can reflect potentially large discrepancies in the self-designation of "manager" or "subordinate" in a given situation. Over 20 years ago, Burns (1954) documented the now popular observation that utterances managers believe are commands or orders are often responded to as suggestions or advice by subordinates. In Burns' study, *half* the comments that managers felt were orders were perceived as suggestions, not orders, by subordinates. This should reinforce the point that *managers "manage" only to the extent that others are willing to respond in a subordinate capacity.*

COMMUNICATION RULES: SOME SPECIFIC EXAMPLES

Communication can be effectively managed by adopting a specific, behavioral perspective; one which moves communication phenomena out of the realm of global, ambiguous considerations and into an arena where concrete steps can be taken to diagnose communication problems and attempt to alleviate them. In the present section, a rather ordinary discussion between manager and subordinate is presented to highlight some rules that are in use. In addition, a model describing some of the common interaction rule topics is presented. The goal of this section is to provide enough illustration of different types of communication rules so that readers can then use this same approach in their own situations. In the subsequent section, we will outline methods by which these rules can be analyzed, once they have been identified and studied.

The hypothetical interaction takes place between a manager and one subordinate. In the logical flow of events from the beginning of the interaction to its eventual conclusion, what is one of the first rule topics that must be dealt with? It is the initiation of the interaction—who seeks it out, under what conditions. For example, many managers maintain an "open-door" policy; they want any of their subordinates who wish to communicate with them to simply drop by. Others want contact by telephone, or by appointment only. The manager may either feel that his or her rank gives unlimited rights of access to subordinates—or may, instead, consider it appropriate to ask about the possibility of interaction while allowing the subordinate a graceful exit if conditions warrant. The desired policy for initiation obviously may vary from manager to manager, and subordinate to subordinate.

In most organizations, the rules for access become much more stringent as the discrepancy between managerial levels increases. It is often not proper form—if not outright dangerous—to drop in unannounced on a manager three levels above you in the hierarchy. Yet in other organizations, the only necessary preface might be a comment to the effect "I know it's a little unusual to stop by like this, but I really thought you ought to know..."

Not all conversations that are initiated actually take place, right away or even shortly thereafter. A delay in meeting may occur. Who can propose a delay, and for what reasons? How long can the delay last without the "relational" message clearly being that of a "put-down"? How many delays can occur between two individuals before a serious strain is put on their relationship? What are the appropriate words to use in smoothing over the fact that a delay in conversation must take place when one of the two has just made a clear overture to initiate? For this rule topic, as in the others, there is no clear-cut answer, but it should be apparent that the rule one uses ought to be clarified and the implications of it thought through.

Perhaps one of the single greatest rule considerations in any conversation is the decision concerning what topics are to be discussed. Is the manager (or subordinate) really the correct person to raise the topic with at all? Is it considered appropriate that the topic even be discussed? What are the preliminary topics that provide an easy transition to the major topics to be discussed? Are any transitions necessary, or is it possible to "get right to the point"? What is the appropriate ratio of task-related and social communication to the total communication that occurs?

In conjunction with deciding what topics are to be discussed, it is also important to decide whose topics get priority. Most interactions are of limited duration, and both persons may have things they wish to cover. Will the supervisor dictate which topics are discussed—always, sometimes, or only on occasion? What are the clues each person can use to signify that, on a specific occasion, it is felt that his or her topics warrant priority treatment, regardless of what the norm of discussion has been between the two?

While a conversation is proceeding, the participants will be making decisions about when one particular topic is to be concluded and another one introduced. Who decides when topic changes are to occur, and how does the other person indicate approval or agreement with the topic shift? It may be the case that one partner is in a rush to get to important matters, while the other remains unsatisfied with the outcome of the conversation.

Another routine occurrence in conversations, particularly in the organizational setting, is outside interruptions. The telephone may ring, someone else may drop in, mail may arrive, etc. Each of these other communication events presents a demand for the attention of one individual or the other. Some response is required (including ignoring the demand), and the way that response is expressed can have a marked influence on one person's evaluation of the other. For example, if conversations are always broken off in midthought when another claimant for one partner's attention appears, the other is likely to interpret this as conveying low status, a "put-down." On the other hand, if outside interruptions are allowed to break into a conversation only on occasion, and with appropriate explanation, then this may prove no burden to the conversants' relationship.

Obviously, someone must terminate an interaction, and this provides another rule area. What are the clues by which one individual signals the desire to end the conversation? These can range from outright dismissal, walking out, to less extreme and more subtle "concluding remarks" or bodily movements. It may be necessary to break off the conversation, with both partners recognizing that it is incomplete, and hence procedures need to be established by which it can be resumed.

One of the most important general communication rule topics is the amount of communication—the frequency and/or duration of interaction. A minimum frequency is usually necessary to impart work information to subordinates, and to maintain good working relations with them. That frequency may vary from once or twice a month to several times a day, depending on such factors as the nature of the task, the experience of the person involved, and the basic need for communication on the part of both persons. Frequency is thus highly variable and close monitoring is needed in order to assure that an adequate amount is taking place.

In addition to rules such as those above, the extra dimension of *satisfaction* must also be taken into account. By themselves, the way that these rules are expressed represents a considerable learning task for new employees, and a problem of maintaining their continuing relevance to the manager: but this gives only an incomplete view of the rule system. What is needed in addition is knowledge of the degree of satisfaction of the two dyad members about each of the rules. If both manager and subordinate agree that they communicate but once a week (and higher-level management considers this appropriate), and both are satisfied, then there is little chance of a communication problem existing on this dimension of their interaction. On the other hand, if one or the other is not satisfied with the frequency of interaction, then a definite problem exists, one which may seriously impair their efficiency as individuals and as an organizational dyad.

In Fig. 6-2, these rule topics are shown in graphic form. Obviously, this is not a complete set of all topics, but it does cover some of the more important ones. Others could be added, or some of these deleted; the important point is that in a given organizational setting, such rules do operate and need to be clearly presented to new members and widely accepted by older members.

If the rules are found lacking, then they should be changed. And there is little need to create confusion, embarrassment, and more serious mistakes in

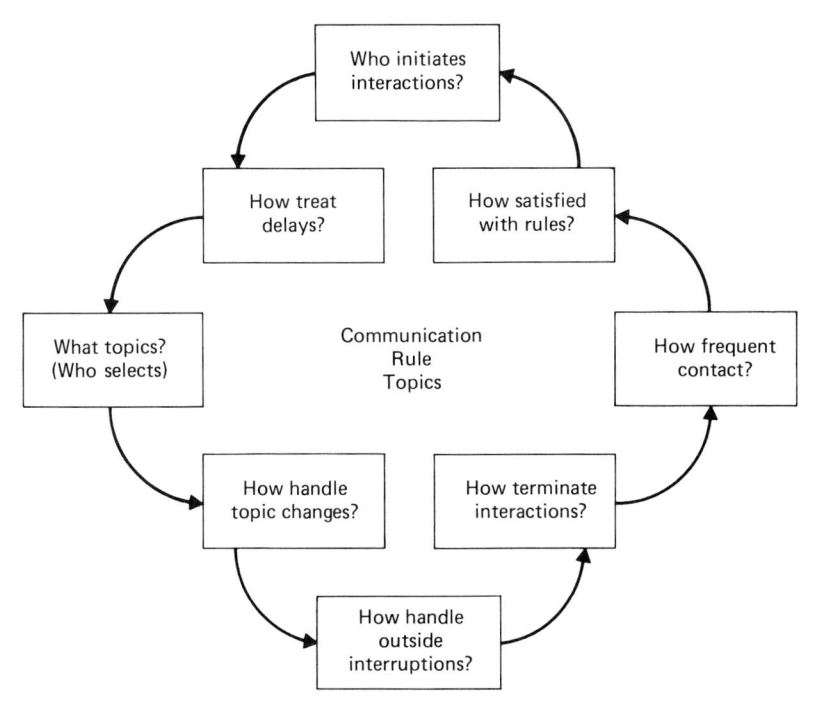

Fig. 6-2. Communication rule topics. Boxes contain example topic headings. Arrows indicate approximate sequence in interaction where topics become important.

the communication functioning of the organization by having the rule system ambiguous, capriciously applied, or unknown in certain portions of the organization. The rules need not be rigidly codified, however, as a solution to all communication problems, because it is likely that conditions in the organization will change sufficiently to warrant fairly frequent change in the formal rule system. What is needed is a continuing dialogue among managers and subordinates about the state of their communication rules and their general satisfaction levels with the rules.

"COORIENTATION" ON COMMUNICATION RULES

Thus far in the present chapter, the reader will have undoubtedly noted that communication rules have been discussed only in the situation where the subordinate (or manager) is describing the interaction from his or her own point of view. This is just half of the knowledge required to engage in an analysis of the manager and subordinate as a *dyad*. If analysis is restricted to single members of dyadic pairs, then the responses can be aggregated into general, broad statements about how managers (as a group) and subordinates (as a group) describe their communication. However, these sweeping appraisals of communication do not yield the specific, detailed insights that can be of such great utility in understanding the behavior of hierarchically related dyads. For a detailed analysis of managerial dyads, both the manager *and* subordinate must provide a combined report on their communication relationship.

By juxtaposing these two reports, it is possible to show the extent to which the manager and subordinate *agree* on their description of their interaction. Agreement about interaction can obviously be an important part of the overall relationship between manager and subordinate (and between co-workers as well, although the present discussion is restricted to supervisory dyads). In addition, if the manager and subordinate predict how the other will evaluate their communication relationship, this enables an analysis of the *accuracy* with which each person views the relationship. From these four items of data—the two direct evaluations and the two predictions—it will be possible to derive several new measures of the "health" of the communication relations among the dyads. In particular, it will be possible to pinpoint rather closely just where certain types of communication problems are likely to occur.

To generate these new dimensions, we turn to one of the oldest and most established models in the social sciences, the *coorientation* model arising from the work of Newcomb (1953), as modified by Chaffee, McLeod, and Guerrero (1969). This is a model which describes how a person views an object (or event) and some other person at the same time. For example, the model can describe how a manager and subordinate view the whole organization, their own work unit, the work itself, their communication relationship, or some other mutually known set of phenomena.

The first coorientational concept noted above is agreement; i.e., the similarity between the way the manager describes a communication rule and the way the subordinate describes the same rule. For example, to the extent the manager's view of "satisfaction with communication frequency" is identical to the subordinate's, then perfect agreement is obtained. Complete disagreement occurs when the two persons hold diametrically opposed views.

Agreement is sometimes distinguished from understanding on the basis of the rule being considered; if the rule is an evaluative one (such as a "satisfaction" topic), it is called *agreement*. If it is not evaluative (such as "frequency of contact"), then it is called *understanding*. Agreement will refer to both possibilities in the present chapter.

Accuracy, in contrast to agreement/understanding, is based on the prediction or estimate of the other's view of a communication rule, versus the

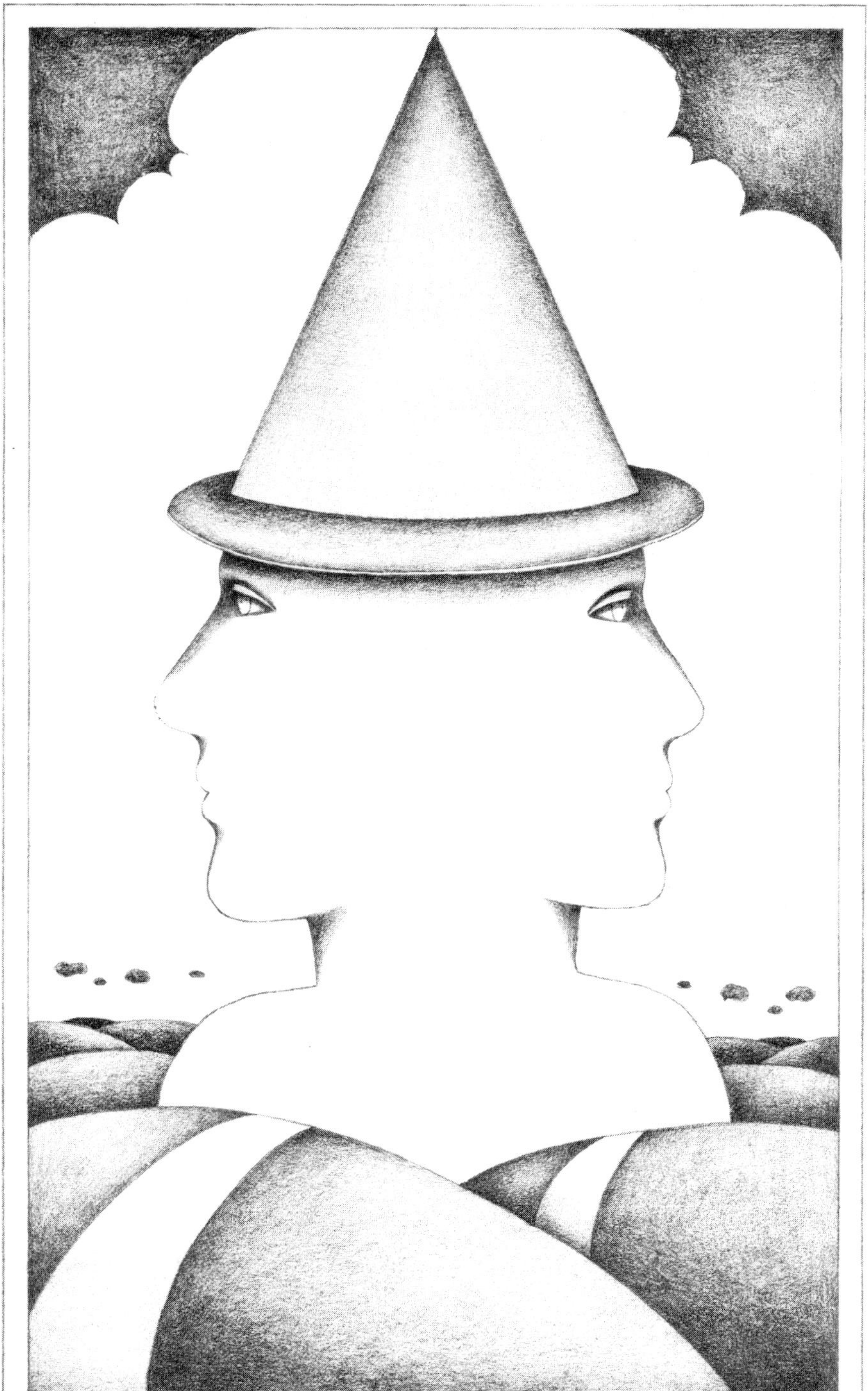

actual description of that rule given by the other. For example, if the manager's point of view is used as a basis for comparison, accuracy is achieved when the manager predicts that the subordinate likes free access to the manager...and the subordinate does in fact desire free access.

A measure of accuracy based on the subordinate's prediction of the manager's response compared with the manager's actual response can also be constructed. To the extent the subordinate makes good predictions, accuracy is achieved.

Accuracy (or agreement) are not just "present" or "absent." It is quite possible to measure them in such a way as to indicate different degrees or amounts of them. Changes in accuracy or agreement can be shown by taking repeated measures at different points in time for the same set of dyads.

In Fig. 6-3, a model of coorientation is presented. It should be emphasized once again that agreement and accuracy emerge only when *both* members of a supervisory dyad indicate their views of a specific communication rule *in relation to each other*.

While it is possible to generate a precise measure of accuracy and of agreement, it is also useful to reduce the results into two groups, one labeled "high"

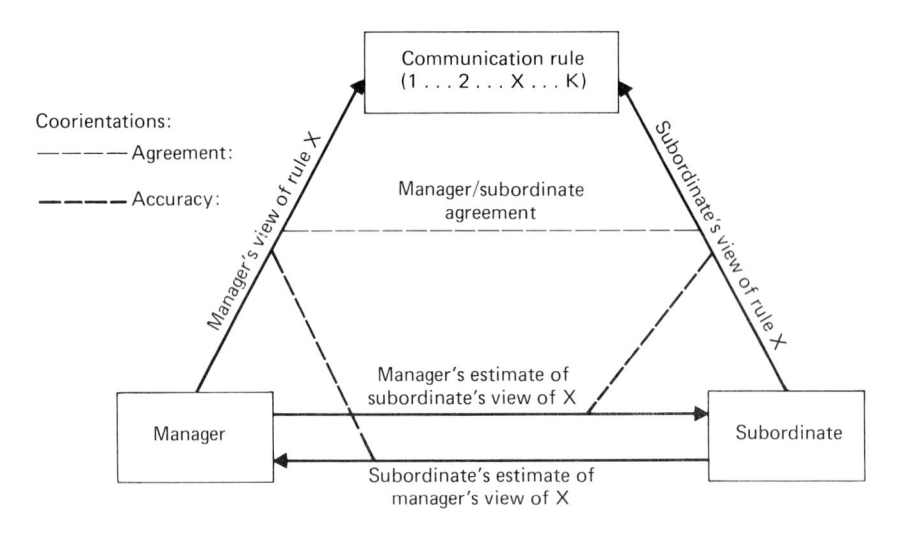

Fig. 6-3. The coorientation model, adapted from Chaffee, McLeod, and Guerrero (1969). Solid lines indicate perceptions of communication rules and prediction of the other's views. Light dashed line shows comparisons for agreement measure; heavy dashed lines indicate comparison for accuracy.

	Accuracy	
	Low	High
High Agreement	Pluralistic ignorance	Monolithic consensus
Low	False consensus	Dissensus

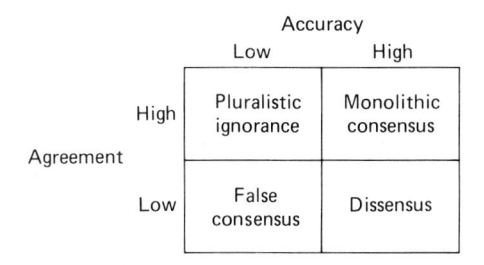

Fig. 6-4. Accuracy and agreement on communication rules. Table entries show terms representing four possible combinations of accuracy (high and low) and agreement (high and low).

and the other labeled "low." This yields a 2 × 2 table of four cells, in which each cell represents one level of accuracy and one level of agreement. This is shown in Fig. 6-4, and is taken from the work of Scheff (1967). The labels in each cell are Scheff's terms for the particular combination of accuracy and agreement.

Perhaps the clearest and most explicable cell is where both agreement and accuracy are high—*monolithic consensus*. In other words, both the manager and the subordinate hold the same viewpoint, and, furthermore, each accurately perceives the other person's viewpoint. Monolithic consensus has some potentially appealing qualities to it, but it has some potentially negative implications as well. At first glance, it would seem to be the "ideal" case, since not only do dyads of this nature fully agree on a communication rule, they also perceive the other person's view accurately.

But a new manager—say a new political appointee in a civil-service bureaucracy—may find that there exists monolithic consensus at all supervisory levels below him. Furthermore, the personnel at these levels are resistant to any attempted changes (after all, the appointee's term in office is apt to be much shorter than theirs). In such a situation, change is going to be slow and difficult.

A quite different situation exists in the cell labeled *dissensus*. This represents the situation where a managerial dyad shows low agreement about a particular rule, but high accuracy about their disagreement. In most instances this is probably a healthy situation, because it allows both individuals to express different points of view while at the same time knowing what the view of the other happens to be. This condition enables alternative viewpoints to enter a discussion without creating interpersonal friction at the same time.

The third situation exists where agreement is high but accuracy is low. This is the situation where both parties actually agree, but for some reason each person believes that the other disagrees. In Scheff's terms, this is *pluralistic ignorance*. This situation represents a frequent error in much of the communication taking place in organizations. For example, a manager may believe that a particular worker is interested only in a wage increase and not in the quality of the work being turned out. The manager values high-quality work. At the same time, however, the worker is dissatisfied and wants to take pride in doing a good job, but feels that the boss is only interested in squeezing out as many units of work per day as possible. Consequently, both persons agree on the importance of good work, but each believes the other does not hold this view.

Pluralistic ignorance sets the stage for what can be bitter discussions—yet at the same time provides a setting wherein intervention through communication can have dramatic effects. Inaccuracy can be corrected, thus altering the situation to one of monolithic consensus, without having to deal with fundamental *disagreements* over issues.

The final cell in the table, *false consensus*, occurs where agreement is low and accuracy is low as well. Not only do the two individuals disagree, they are not even accurate in their estimate of the position taken by the other person. For example, suppose the subordinate believes that the manager wants work to be started only after the manager has given the go-ahead. This position is acceptable to the subordinate. In fact, the manager wants the subordinate to show initiative in finding work to do, and believes that the subordinate fully understands this expectation. Here we have low agreement about how work is to be initiated, and low accuracy about how the other views the situation.

In this situation the subordinate is likely to be punished for doing what the manager supposedly wants, rather than praised or otherwise rewarded for any efforts. If this confusion persists, then the two are apt to continue to apply quite different criteria to the situation and the strain and strife between them are likely to continue as well.

One of the main results of this presentation should be to underscore the importance of accuracy in relation to agreement. Perhaps the weakest position for a manager to hold is one where considerable inaccuracy is present in the communication relationships with subordinates. Where inacurracy is found, it is likely that serious interpersonal strife will occur. Furthermore this strife can be quite elusive since its basis is hidden in a series of misperceptions one person has about the other. Low accuracy can make either person's behavior seem unpredictable or capricious, since it doesn't "make sense" from the other person's view.

If a manager finds a high proportion of subordinates in the low-accuracy cells—pluralistic ignorance or false consensus—then it seems clear that action should be taken to remedy these conditions. Perhaps discussions in an open and informal setting will enable the subordinates to indicate the rules of the "game" that they feel the manager is following, while they indicate the criteria that they are using. It may be necessary to implement these discussions by first using personnel from outside the group, working separately with both parties. New areas of inaccuracy may well be uncovered, areas that were not recognized before. This type of exercise should provide a much clearer basis for establishing the communication expectations on the part of both manager and subordinate.

BEYOND AGREEMENT AND ACCURACY: "REALIZATION"

To promote improved communication at the dyadic level, the potential power of learning whether a manager and subordinate both agree on a given communication rule, and whether they are accurate in their perception of the other's position, has been shown. In short, the questions "Is your position the same as mine?" (agreement) and "Do I know your position?" (accuracy) have been raised. It has also been stressed that this type of analysis can only stem from the knowledge of how both dyad members view their communication; it cannot be learned by studying either member alone.

There are still more refined, more complex "levels of understanding" which can be analyzed in the dyadic setting. Yet another question can be asked: "Do you know that I know your position on (this rule)?" Or, adding a further dimension of complexity: "Do you know that I know...that you know...that I know your view?" This sequence can be continued, step by step, with each new level providing additional insight into the way the dyad members perceive their relationship.

Scheff uses the term *realization* to describe these added levels of complexity in interpersonal relations. The term realization is mentioned to show that the original shift from "individual-difference" or single-person analysis to dyadic "rules" analysis opens up substantial new power to the analytic and practical skills of the communication scholar and/or practitioner. But this shift is merely the first of many that can be undertaken as the bonds of communication in dyadic relationships are examined. With an increase in the number of levels of relationship studied, the ability to uncover meaningful aids and impediments to effective communication is enhanced. This area should be a fruitful, high-priority topic for subsequent study.

SOME EMPIRICAL FINDINGS

A review of some of the results from studies using the communication-rules paradigm provides some illuminating insights into organizational communication at the dyadic level. Boyd and Jensen (1972) mailed questionnaires to a sample of nearly 1,000 manufacturing firms employing 50 or more persons. Overall, only one firm in seven replied, although about one in four of the firms with 1,000 or more employees responded. The results, while not readily generalizable to the original 1,000 firms, provide some interesting insights.

First and second-level managers were asked to state whether the lower-level manager had the authority to perform work-related tasks in nine different areas. Overall, the supervisory pairs agreed only about half the time on whether the subordinate had the authority. The percent of disagreements ranged from 44 percent for material purchasing to 59 percent for maintenance. These data suggest that a fundamental rules topic in a manufacturing organization—the specification of who has authority for what—can exhibit sizable amounts of disagreement. The authors also cite other research indicating that service organizations are susceptible to large amounts of disagreement on basic rule-related areas.

Burke and Wilcox (1969) studied one central communication rule—the "openness" between manager and subordinate regarding communication of feelings and ideas, about the job and the relationship. Their study was conducted by mail survey in six offices of a public-utility company; about half of the respondents completed the instruments, 323 in all. Unlike the study described above, in this instance respondents both supplied an evaluation of their manager's openness and predicted what the manager would provide as a description of the relationship. Note that this does not satisfy the core requirement for dyadic analysis, since no independently generated data by the manager are used to determine agreement or accuracy. The comparisons here are between the subordinate's perceptions of his or her openness and perceptions of the manager as well.

In the main, the respondents were likely to see their manager as someone who was as open as they saw themselves; managers were less likely to be seen as more open or less open than subordinates considered themselves. For most respondents, then, their own openness ratings were equated with that of their manager. But what of the respondents who saw their manager as either more or less open than they viewed themselves? Here the data indicate that the more agreement on openness the subordinate perceived with the manager, the more satisfied the subordinate was: more satisfied with the company, the job, supervision, climate for growth during performance and appraisal reviews, and climate for growth in supervisory interaction.

The reader will note that these findings reflect agreement on openness, without any reference to the absolute level of openness. When amount of openness is related to satisfaction on the same five topics, the greater the openness, the greater the satisfaction. Taken together, these two findings suggest that agreement regarding openness has an important bearing on selected aspects of job satisfaction, and the amount of openness does as well.

A third study provides yet a different perspective on analysis of communication rules. Hunt and Lichtman (1970) examined the independent perceptions of workers, first-line supervisors, and managers on eleven job-related areas. Each set of individuals was asked to describe whether the first-line supervisors performed each of these eleven functions. Again, these data do not meet the strict requirements for a relational analysis, since they do not reflect the specific appraisal of the relationship between given pairs of supervisory dyads; instead, they represent aggregated appraisals not tied to specific dyads.

The data, collected in a federal agency, provide some intriguing glimpses into the difference in communication behaviors perceived by the three groups. For example, where 36 percent of the managers say the supervisors provide downward communication, 15 percent of the supervisors say they do and 9 percent of the workers say they do. In terms of communication rules, then, these data suggest that managers are more likely than supervisors or workers to think that downward communication is taking place.

For upward communication, a different pattern emerges. No managers say supervisors communicate upwardly; 3 percent of supervisors and 8 percent of the workers report upward communication. Thus, although the percentages are small, workers are more inclined to believe they are participating in upward communication than are either of their two immediate supervisory levels.

Two other topic areas included in this study also bear on communication rules, although indirectly. What about leading and/or motivating employees? For managers, 82 percent say supervisors do this; and for workers, 50 percent say supervisors do. But for the supervisor—the one in the middle who is ostensibly performing the behavior—27 percent say they lead and/or motivate employees. Clearly this represents rather sizable areas of discrepancy in agreement and accuracy across the three organizational levels.

And in coordinating group operations? Supervisors (58 percent) are more likely than workers (20 percent) to say they do this, and more likely than managers (36 percent) to say it as well. What data such as these illustrate, then, is a constant pattern of misperception on the part of workers, supervisors, and managers about the state of their relationships. These misperceptions exist, of course, independently of any formally established policies or procedures as to what supervisors *ought* to be doing, are receiving any *rewards* for doing, and are receiving any *training* for doing.

This section will be concluded with some illustrative data gathered by Russell (1972). In his study, specific communication rules were generated; they were grouped into four major categories, and then analyzed in terms of the Scheff model presented earlier.

One hundred field staff and their managers in a state agency were involved in the study. Both members of each supervisory pair completed a questionnaire in which they described their communication. The pairs were identified so that it was possible to compare supervisors with subordinates as a group, and also to look at the independent responses from both members of a particular pair and determine the extent to which they shared similar points of view or understanding of their communication.

The questionnaire included sections on how they viewed their current communication, what they felt was the ideal communication between people in their positions, and how they felt the other member of their pair would describe their communication.

Using an initial set of 60 communication rules, four independent categories of rules were identified. These dimensions focus on different aspects of sharing (or interdependence) between a manager and a subordinate. They are:

1. innovation—involvement in bringing up new ideas and modifying programs to meet particular situations.

2. maintenance—bringing nonwork and family matters into discussions.

3. sequencing—involvement and responsibility for seeing things through to completion.

4. initiation—responsibility for seeing that tasks are actually undertaken.

When managers as a group were compared with their subordinates as a group, certain relatively consistent differences were found. Managers tended to report that their communication was less frequent than the subordinates felt it was, and the managers were also less satisfied with the overall amount of communication that they had. Many more managers than subordinates would have liked more communication. Each group tended to feel that they shared the responsibility for communication. While the managers felt they initiated communication equally with their subordinates, however, the subordinates saw a much greater amount of communication being imposed on them by their managers.

Subordinates tended to feel that a greater proportion of the communication initiated by their supervisors was related to getting the current program done than their managers did. Each group saw the other as more concerned with getting the job done while they saw themselves as having a more balanced interest in nonwork communication and communication about new ideas as well.

These differences in perceptions suggest that the subordinates generally saw their communication with the managers in a different light than the managers themselves did. In general, there was a tendency for the subordinates to view their supervisory communication in a narrower way than their managers. Given their different roles within the organization, this difference would seem understandable; the managers' main role is to communicate with subordinates, but the converse is less often true.

The managers and subordinates in this study had worked together for at least a year, and in most cases for considerably longer periods. Despite quite limited amounts of communication in some cases, most pairs were able to achieve a high level of understanding. However, although over half of the responses were classified as consensual (the members of the pair agreed on the procedural rule, and each individual was able to predict the other's viewpoint accurately), between one-third and one-half of the responses showed *some type of misunderstanding*. It is this group that gives some cause for concern. Approximately 20 percent were classified as having false consensus (the individual thinks that they agree but in fact they disagree). There were about 10 percent classified as dissensual and another 10 percent as pluralistically ignorant. A similar trend occurred for each of the sets of communication rules, for both managers and subordinates.

False consensus is the most frequent type of misunderstanding in this illustration; monolithic consensus is the most common result of all, indicating relatively strong agreement about communication rules and substantial accuracy about the perceptions of others. In some cases, where there were differences, some persons were unaware of the differences. These are the cases that cause most concern. If two persons disagree and both recognize it, each can make allowances for the other's point of view. But if one person is inaccurate about the other person's viewpoint, and expects it to be the same as his or her own, then the stage is set for some potentially serious misunderstanding. These results are summarized in Fig. 6-5.

One purpose of Russell's study was to test the theoretical relationship between understanding and other facets of the relationship between members of a supervisory pair. In general, coorientation theory would lead to the ex-

	Accuracy	
Agreement	Low	High
High	Pluralistic ignorance (10%)	Monolithic consensus (60%)
Low	False consensus (20%)	Dissensus (10%)

Fig. 6-5. Results of accuracy/agreement analysis (from Russell, 1972). Percents in boxes show distribution of dyads into four coorientation types.

pectation that understanding of rules and broader aspects of a relationship would be positively associated with each other. Levels of understanding about the procedural aspects of communication were in fact significantly associated with subordinate morale, evaluations by managers, and the informality of the relationship. Pairs with high understanding had better evaluations and viewed their relationship in a more social and informal way than did those with lower understanding.

COMMENTS ON APPLICATIONS

The data that were presented in the previous section indicate that significant amounts of disagreement and inaccuracy in the perception of communication rules can occur in organizations. This can be prevalent even in organizations whose members have known one another for long periods of time, although one would expect the problem to be less severe in such situations.

It seems likely that in instances where problems of rules arise, individuals may well be penalized in one form or another, with an accompanying decrease in their self-esteem and organizational performance. They may truly become victims of "the system"; i.e., victims of the operation of a rules system where both manager and subordinate may be unaware of what is happening.

One thrust of this argument is to reinforce the importance of basic introductory training for new employees, training designed to provide an understanding of the expectations that their managers will have for them. Such training is preferable to a presentation of generalized and diffuse managerial expectations. Specific "rules" training may require face-to-face discussions between managers and new subordinates, accurate and updated policy guides, or brochures or video cassettes originating from the manager.

A second outcome of this approach to communication analysis is a significantly increased emphasis on improved agreement and accuracy between manager and subordinate (particularly longer-term subordinates) about the expectations each has for the other. This should not consist simply of general statements and formalized rules, but should include detailed discussions of how communication is to be initiated, what topics are to be encouraged, and what cues signal availability or nonavailability for interaction.

An important reminder in this discussion, as we have noted earlier, is the strong tendency for individuals to assume that their way of perceiving the world is identical to that of their managers or subordinates. This tendency must constantly be fought, because it is clear that when there are age, sex, racial, ethnic, and other differences between the members of supervisory dyads, it is likely that the perceptions of each of the members will differ substantially. Assuming that the other person always "thinks like me" could prove a major source of embarrassment, difficulty, and trouble.

Finally, to the extent that new employees frequently join an organization, a given manager or subordinate must keep in mind that the entire rules concept must be enacted afresh. The slow and sometimes painful process of achieving agreement and accuracy must be renewed each time a new dyadic relationship is formed; failure to adequately do so can render the dyad an ineffective unit.

Of the two concepts—agreement and accuracy—it is perhaps too easy, from the supervisor's point of view, to stress the former over the latter. This is not necessarily a wise course. Complete agreement produces only "yes" answers, and all managers need subordinates, peers, and supervisors who have their own independent views of many topics. Perhaps accuracy is the more important goal to strive for initially, because with accuracy, employees "know where they stand" with respect to one another's views.

SUMMARY

This chapter was devoted to the analysis of communication within an organization's basic supervisory unit, the hierarchical dyad. Although the discussion was oriented to the management hierarchy, the concepts and procedures are also applicable to other dyads in the organization, e.g., coworkers. The concept of communication rules—the norms and procedures that govern the interaction between manager and subordinate—is of central importance in a rules analysis. We distinguished between rules concerning the content of communication and rules concerning the procedural aspects of communication. The discussion of rules was interlaced with the key notion of rule satisfaction as the primary mechanism for evaluating the state of the rule system in a dyad.

Considerable emphasis was given to a model of communication rules based on the respective orientations (coorientation) of the manager and subordinate toward their communication rules. By gathering reports about their communication from the manager and subordinate, measures of agreement and accuracy concerning their rules were developed.

Then, combining both agreement and accuracy, an analytic scheme was outlined that has considerable power for unlocking, in a precise manner, the state of communication in a given supervisory dyad. With this information, it is possible to uncover a wide array of potential communication strengths and communication weaknesses; and by couching the rules in terms of specific behaviors, it is possible to intervene in the relationship and improve overall communication effectiveness. The chapter concludes with some comments on the applications of this information in the organizational setting.

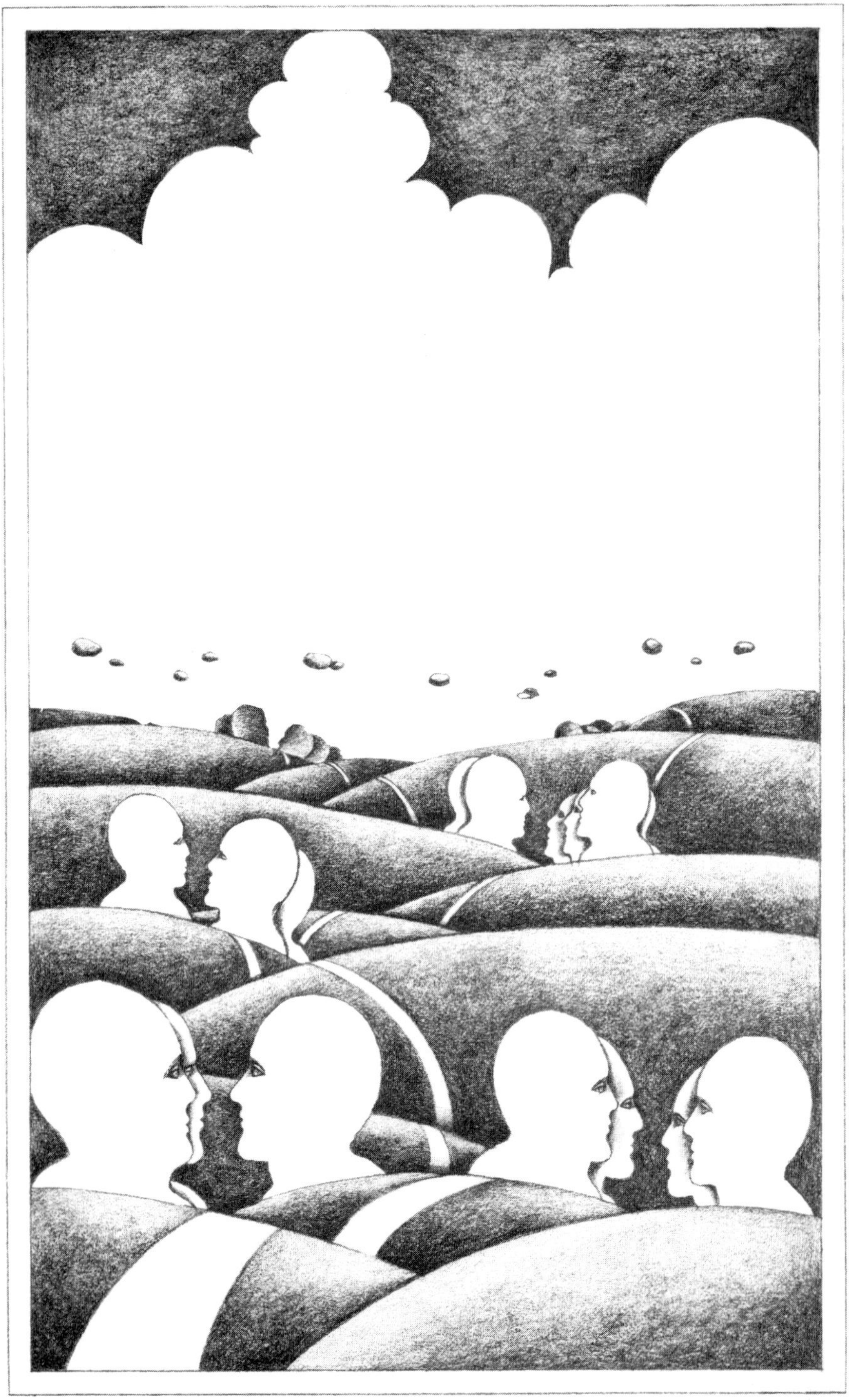

7
Communication in Organizational "Groups"

People who live and work in organizations or, for that matter, who live and work almost anywhere in modern society, experience groups as one of the most pervasive of social phenomena. Even as these comments are being written, there is the continuing awareness present among the authors that, as members of several organizations, it will soon be necessary to meet and work with other members in those units. In each meeting, it will be necessary to engage in a number of different activities, some decisional, some ceremonial, some social. Much of what gets done will be routine, cut and dried, probably of little lasting import. Occasionally, the results of these group activities have repercussions in other departments, or in the organizations themselves.

Sometimes each group functions well together: decisions are made quickly and efficiently, and people feel kindly towards one another. More often than not, however, a group will divide into subgroups to argue, debate, and struggle over major or even minor differences of opinion. Decisions will often be made with agonizing slowness, and feelings and emotions will mount to critical levels.

On rare occasions tensions will reach the point where one or more of the members—out of anger or frustration or discouragement—feels compelled to leave the group for the remainder of the session. This usually requires some mending of fences in smaller private groups after the larger group has concluded its business. But through it all, the group remains a viable, functioning unit.

At another time, colleagues or clients located outside our main organizations provide new opportunities for group membership. Much of this time will be spent in meetings, usually with four or five but perhaps as many as eight or nine people. Some of the group meetings are on a regular basis; others are for the first and perhaps only time. Yet despite this diversity, each group is made up of organizational people brought together by some organizational decision-making process to accomplish some organizationally related task or goal. This is the case with most organizational groups.

In this chapter the focus shifts to the communication behaviors which people engage in as they participate in small groups embedded in a larger organizational system. Nonhuman groups, formed among certain animals or insects, or human groups that exist outside of organizations, such as families or town councils, will not be dealt with here.

A separate chapter devoted to the topic of groups carries the assumption that group communication behavior differs from communication in the larger organizational context, or in the individual "load" or dyadic "rules" contexts. To some extent this is true, but the differences are often those of degree rather than kind. Much of what has been said about individuals and dyads (and about organizations as a whole in Chapter 8) is applicable to communication in small groups; however, the size of groups, the presence of direct face-to-face interaction, clear task responsibility, and other factors sometimes create communication patterns that are sufficiently different to be worth specific scrutiny.

The wealth of group research that exists makes it possible to discuss groups from a structural-functional framework much more readily than is possible at other system levels. Following the approach adopted in this book, the discussion will focus primarily on the communication aspects of small-group behavior. First, three dimensions of *structure* in small groups are reviewed: communication networks, power structure, and leadership structure. Then attention is given to the *functions* which must be maintained in a small-group system to insure its continued operation. These include group cohesiveness, productivity, and satisfaction. The process of interaction—the *mechanism* whereby the communication, power, and leadership structures operate to maintain the small-group system—is described. And finally, several important perspectives on small-group behavior are presented.

WHAT CONSTITUTES A GROUP?

What constitutes a group? Were we to ask that question of a mathematician we might learn that "any number of entities that contains some well-defined common characteristic constitutes a group." Furthermore, a mathematician would say that there are two ways to form a group. First, every object which has the specific characteristic that we are interested in could be clearly identified and enumerated. Thus, a group consists of all those objects which are specifically named by the enumeration process.

Second, the group could be formed by establishing a rule which indicates the conditions under which an object qualifies for group membership. If the first method was used to form an ad hoc work group in an organization, it would require listing the people who were to become a part of that group, e.g., Shari, Georg, Ken,...Janie. Were the second alternative to be used, a rule such as "all first-line supervisors in Division 3," or "supervisors with less than three years' experience," would be needed.

This, of course, is not the type of answer that psychologists have typically given to the question. As Shaw (1971) points out, some have studied groups without ever attempting to define them, while...

> Others have defined groups in terms of one or more of the following characteristics: (1) perceptions and cognitions of group members, (2) motivation and need satisfaction, (3) group goals, (4) group organization, (5) interdependency of group members, and (6) interaction.*

All of these characteristics are plausible candidates to enter into a definition of "group," but for our purposes we wish to define an organizational group as a subset of a larger organizational structure which is obtained by arranging human resources so that people can work, interact, and communicate together on a regular basis. Detailed procedures for identifying the communication groups in an organization are presented in Chapter 8.

THE STRUCTURE OF SMALL GROUPS

In our earlier analysis of structure, it was noted that structure reflects the predictability or patterning of relations among people. Since groups are a component of organizational structure it follows that groups are formed by relations among people. If the relations are based on communication, then communication groups emerge; if a different kind of relation is examined, a different kind of structure or different groups are found. Obviously, the *same* people in an organization may be simultaneously involved in several relations. This leads directly to the notion that a complete analysis of small-group behavior may require an examination of multiple relations among group members and, therefore, multiple structures.

---

*From M.E. Shaw, *Group Dynamics: The Psychology of Small Group Behavior*, 1971, p. 5, McGraw-Hill, New York. Used with permission of McGraw-Hill Book Company.

The philosopher Bertrand Russell (1948) illustrates the point well:

> Take, for instance, a piece of music. One note may be earlier or later than another, or higher in pitch, or differing through a wealth or poverty of harmonics. All of these relations must be included in a thorough analysis of the music. Further, any reproduction of the music, whether broadcast or recording, must also reflect all of the relevant relations. Failure to accurately reproduce one or more of the many relations that define music creates what audio engineers commonly call distortion. So, too, in our analysis of small groups the examination of single relations may be simplistic and naive, or by analogy, with the above example, distorted. Rather, a complete analysis of any given group may require the consideration of several simultaneous or at least contiguous relations.*

This, of course, raises the question as to which relations and structures are important in the study of small groups in organizations. Research by Oeser and Harary (1962, 1964) provides one excellent set of alternatives. They analyzed an organizational group into three classes of elements: tasks, positions, and persons. A role was defined as persons assigned to positions which have specified tasks. They then defined five relations on the three sets of objects: (1) personnel assignment, which matched persons to positions, (2) task specification, which assigned positions to tasks, (3) power relations, the formal authority lines, (4) liking relations, and (5) communication relations. As can be seen, the analysis is much more complex than any single-valued relation such as "communicates with," and as such, it is much more powerful.

Other types of structures could, of course, be added or used as alternatives for those offered by Oeser and Harary. We will examine three: communication, power, and leadership. These three have been studied frequently in small-group research, and they deal with basic processes of group activity.

Communication in Micro-networks

When people in social systems talk with one another on a regular basis, the patterns created by the messages they exchange are called communication networks. If the communication occurs in small groups the resultant patterns are called "micro-networks." If the communication patterns occur in large organizations they are called "macro-networks." This distinction is important because books on communication frequently discuss communication networks, but almost exclusively in terms of micro-networks. Large organizational macro-networks receive scant attention.

---

*From B. Russell, *Human Knowledge: Its Scope and Limits,* 1948, p. 255, Simon and Schuster, New York. Reprinted by permission.

Knowledge about micro-networks developed out of research on whether different kinds of communication networks affected group performance. The question makes sense from an organizational viewpoint because organizations can exercise some degree of control over how members are organized and who may talk to whom. Some of the theoretical views on this topic were given in Chapter 4.

The initial work that described micro-networks was published by Bavelas (1948, 1950) and Leavitt (1951), who developed procedures for studying communication networks in the small-group laboratory. Using a laboratory setting the researchers positioned people (initially five) around a table that was partitioned off so that each person was physically isolated. The only way group members could communicate was by sending messages through slots in the partition walls. The group was then assigned a task which required the participation of all group members. The specific network was imposed upon the group by controlling the slots each member could use to transmit messages. Some slots were open and some were closed, depending upon the network pattern.

Several types of networks were studied, utilizing both symmetrical (two-way) and asymmetrical (one-way) channels. Leavitt employed the circle, chain, Y, and wheel patterns. These four, as well as other networks that have been studied, are presented in Fig. 7-1.

The theoretical position articulated by Bavelas suggested that two kinds of descriptors should be developed for networks: (1) those for individual positions within a network, and (2) those for the network as a whole. In general, indices for the network as a whole are simple sums of the individual measures. Leavitt (1951) argued that two concepts, centrality and peripherality, were of prime interest in the study of networks; he presented metrics for each.

Subsequent investigation has examined the influence of several other variables. Shaw (1964) organizes these under three categories:

1. *Network-related variables:* group size, changes in network, opportunity to organize;

2. *Information-input variables:* noise, information distribution, reinforcement; and

3. *Group-composition variables:* ascendance, authoritarianism, leadership style, and popularity.

These variables have been studied in relation to their effects on problem-solving efficiency, communication activity, organizational activity, and member satisfaction. They are typically measured by observational or questionnaire techniques.

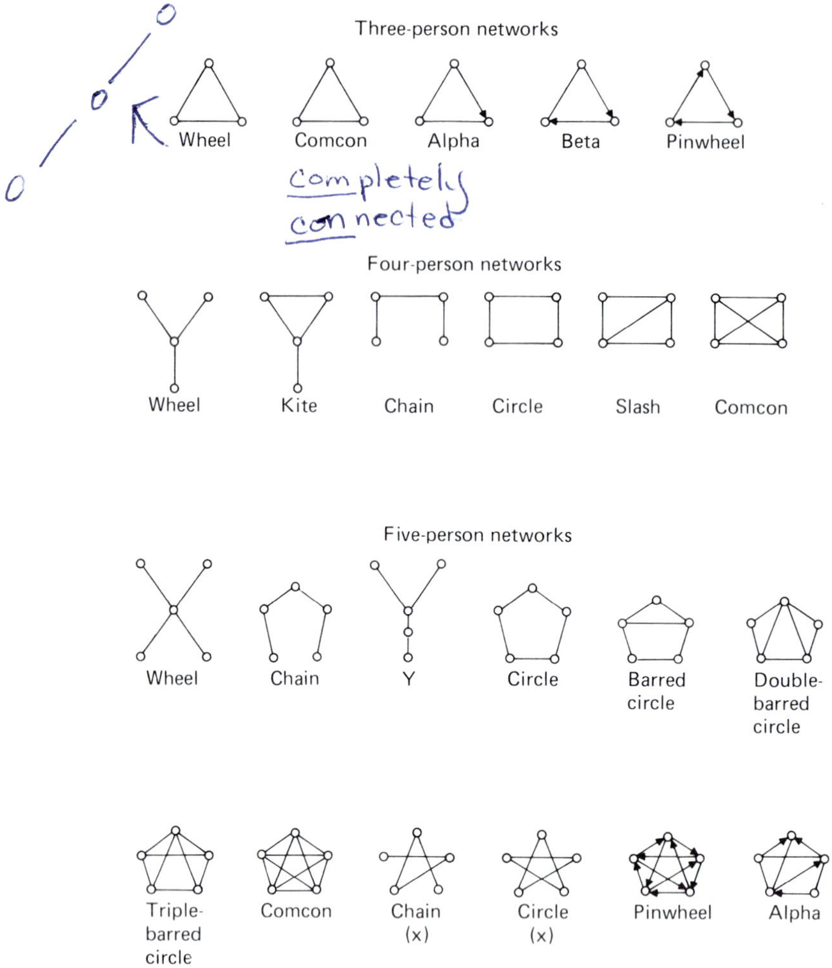

160   Communication in Organizational "Groups"

Fig. 7-1. Communication networks used in experimental investigation. Dots represent positions, lines represent communication channels, and arrows indicate one-way channels. [From M.E. Shaw, "Communication Networks," in L. Berkowitz (ed.), *Advances in Experimental Social Psychology*, Vol. I, 1964, p. 113. New York: Academic. Used with permission.]

Of the several dozen studies that have been conducted over the past two decades, only one consistent finding has emerged; it pertains to the concept of centrality. Centralized nets (e.g., wheel, Y) are more efficient—they permit faster problem solution with fewer errors—when dealing with simple tasks. Decentralized nets (e.g., circle, comcon) are more efficient when the task is complex. Decentralized nets, however, are more satisfying to group members, regardless of whether the task is simple or complex. The effects of other variables listed above have been reviewed, summarized, and tabled by Glanzer and Glaser (1961), Shaw (1964), and Collins and Raven (1969).

Unfortunately, there are several problems in attempting to apply the findings from small-group studies to larger organizations. First, the findings of the various studies are inconsistent and often contradictory. Nearly a quarter of a century of research has produced surprisingly little agreement among scientists as to the role that networks play in group processes.

Second, it is difficult to generalize the findings to small groups actually existing in large organizations, because the behavior of groups in the laboratory differs considerably from groups *embedded* in an organizational setting (e.g., Cohen, Robinson, and Edwards, 1969). The point that Cohen and his associates make is that groups in an organization usually have a history, are clearly aware of power and status relations, and operate within the norms of the organizational context. Most small-group laboratory research, on the other hand, has used ad hoc, randomly formed groups without histories or a normative operating context.

Third, it is difficult to generalize the findings to groups larger in size than that used in the experimental design, since the findings seem to change as group size changes. Differences occur in the performance of three-, four-, and five-person groups, a fact which makes it unsafe to extend the findings to larger groups. This problem is all the more important if one considers that many if not most of the groups which operate within large organizations are larger than, say, the typical laboratory small group.

A fourth problem stems from the fact that virtually all studies have been designed to examine networks as a causal variable; i.e., they examine the effects that networks have on some aspect of group performance. Because virtually no research has been conducted to determine those factors which produce alternative network formations, little is known about the conditions which lead to the development of a circle or chain or Y or wheel network, or even to a more centralized (versus decentralized) network.

This problem of the evolution, or emergence, of group networks focuses not on the end-state of network formation, but on the process itself. The issue is change in communication patterns—how fast, through what intermediate states, and to what stabilization points? This point is well illustrated in a chapter on group structure and performance by Davis (1969). He says:

> One strategy for the study of group structure under controlled conditions is to *impose* a structure upon a small group. Structure is thus treated as an independent variable, and the consequences of a particular structure may be observed with regard to group performance, interpersonal responses, and the personal reactions of members. A second strategy is to regard group structure as an

emergent phenomenon—the interpersonal consequence of a set of persons' interaction over a period of time. Group structure is thus regarded as a dependent variable.*

While Davis's chapter, like the other available literature, does treat imposed structures, it does *not* deal with emergent structure.

Fifth, it is apparent that the micro-networks (such as the circle, chain, wheel, and Y) are highly atypical networks for real groups. Granted that an organization could arrange its work groups in one or more of these particular configurations, the fact remains that they are not "typical" organizational networks. Other arrangements are possible, occur more frequently, and are perhaps even more desirable.

Finally, previous micro-network research differentiates networks by creating discrete, private links between people. But differentiated patterns of interaction also exist in small groups where everyone talks *openly* in front of everyone else (called the *completely connected* micro-network, or comcon). Even though everyone could talk to everyone else, not everyone does. Discussion typically centers around one or two persons; several may say almost nothing at all; others may maintain their own private dialogue (perhaps under their breath) throughout the entire discussion. Thus, people are not equally connected and a more highly differentiated structure would appear to exist.

Recognition of these problems forces us to raise serious questions regarding the usefulness of the entire network concept, at least as studied in the laboratory, for organizational analysis. Were our knowledge of networks limited to what has been provided by the micro-network research, the conclusion would most likely be that little is known and even less is useful. Here is where the distinction between micro- and macro-network becomes helpful, however, for as we shall show in Chapter 8, macro-network analysis can and has been a highly useful tool for organizational analysis even though micro-network research has not.

Power Structure

The term "power" or "social power" is one among many in the behavioral sciences used to describe the same general phenomenon: the potential effect of one person on another, in which the effect is some form of change of behavior, cognitions, attitudes, or emotions. Several terms which tend to be interchangeable with power are authority, influence, control, dominance, status, prestige,

---

*From J.H. Davis, *Group Performance*, 1969, p. 88, Addison-Wesley, Reading, Mass. Reprinted by permission.

and rank. For the sake of simplicity, we shall consistently use the term power to refer to the phenomenon defined above.

Raven (1965) developed a six-part typology that is useful for classifying power according to its source or base. The six categories are: (1) reward power; (2) coercion power; (3) referent power; (4) expert power; (5) legitimate power; and (6) communication power. For ease in discussion we shall use "A" to refer to the person with the power and "B" to refer to the person being influenced.

Reward power is the control that A exercises over B because A can supply something that B wants. *Coercive power* is that exercised by A to punish B for not conforming to A's wishes. There are many examples of these two types of power, as anyone who has sought political power, an undeserved promotion, or true love can attest. Note, however, that both forms of power are dependent upon the ability of A to monitor B's behavior in order to determine whether to exercise the reward or punishment function.

Referent power is that exercised by A over B by virtue of the fact that B desires to identify with or imitate A. People often compare themselves with a selected A; the extent to which B desires to be like A may be taken as a measure of A's power over B. For example, the extent to which Manager Anne Jones compares herself with and desires to be like Executive Vice President Stan Clarke can be used as an index of one type of power which Stan has over Anne. Obviously, referent power requires neither the surveillance of B by A nor even A's knowledge.

Legitimate power is that which derives from the general norms that a person learns about his or her place in the social structure of society. Associated with these norms is a whole set of role relations and expectations about who may exercise control over whom under what circumstances. As Collins and Raven (1969) say, "Legitimate influence, then, is based on B's acceptance of a relationship in the power structure such that A is permitted or obliged to prescribe behaviors for him and B is legitimately required to accept such influence" (p. 167). Parents, teachers, employers, and law officers are all examples of people who ordinarily exercise legitimate power.

Expert power is that power that A maintains over B because B perceives A as superior in knowledge or ability along some relevant dimension. Thus, Vida Blue has expert power with respect to the authors on the subject of baseball pitching, but probably not with Catfish Hunter or Mike Marshall. However, they would all no doubt maintain expert power over us. With respect to the subject of organizational communication, the authors would exert some degree of expert power over these three gentlemen. If the topic were the role of the black man in American society, then Vida Blue would probably have expert power when talking with Catfish Hunter, or Mike Marshall, but might not have expert power when talking with other black men.

Communication power (Raven calls this information power) is derived from a message, regardless of its source. Communication power, then, is independent of A even though a relevant A may be the one to send the message to B. For example, a reliable message that Company X is about to make a three-for-one stock split is power regardless of whether it came from the company president, your broker, or a fellow shareholder.

Raven's typology, which we have presented and illustrated, is applicable to a wide range of human behavior. The reason that we have presented it here is that it is a particularly useful framework within which to analyze the power phenomenon in small groups. First, the typology shows us that power is not a univariate phenomenon. Rather, it consists of a number of components, each of which may separately be identified as an element of power and all of which must be taken together if the power variable in organizations is to be explained.

A second point which emerges from this analysis is that power exists only in relationships. There must be a B in order that A may exercise power. Since there are many B's and A's in an organization, the power structure will depend upon the pattern of relationships between B's and A's. Weick (1969) makes this point when he says that "...control is made possible by the pattern of alliances that exists in the group. It is the pattern of relationships, *not* the traits of the individual *per se*, that makes it possible for influence to be concentrated" (p. 5).

It should be apparent that many power relationships need not be overt or recognized by those who enter into them. For example, A may not know that B uses her as a referent and consequently A will not know that she has power over B. An important implication of this point is that power relations should be sought out and studied even if the people who enter into them are unaware that they exist. Of course, the relations specified more publicly by organizational authority charts are important as well.

There is a third point which arises from partitioning the power variable. By definition, all people in an organization enter into relationships with other people; they are interdependent in terms of power, work flow, and communication. Consequently all members of an organization can exercise some power over others, although the magnitude of power can vary widely. Everyone in an organization is an A in relation to another B along some power dimension.

As pointed out above, this will occur even when the people involved are unaware of the power relation. For example, each A probably has expert power in relation to some subject matter and to some other B's in the group. Given these relations, it is important to learn how much of each type of power a person exercises in his or her relationships with other people. Thus, as many wise white-collar workers know, janitorial, maintenance, and other support workers often exercise considerable power over organizational affairs even though they are usually at the bottom of (or excluded from) traditional organizational authority charts.

A number of other points might also be made. First, coercive and reward types of power are the traditional views of power. It is interesting to note, however, that because they require surveillance they are two of the most expensive forms of power. It might be useful for organizations to consider emphasizing other forms of power. Second, note that expert power is a relatively unstable phenomenon; it shifts and changes from person to person and probably from day to day. This, as will be discussed shortly, is consistent with our view of leadership in a group. Third, types of power can be combined to yield a higher total power. A person may have one or any combination of types of power, and the greater the number of types of power (as well as the amount of each type) the greater the person's total power.

It seems reasonable that the typology of power just outlined can have great utility in the analysis of the power relations in small groups within organizations. As described, power is a variable that is multidimensional, centered in relationships, and observed in contexts that other frameworks often ignore.

Leadership

Considerable energy has been expended by theorists and scholars in an effort to determine the nature of leadership. The results, for the most part, have been less than satisfactory. In this section we present what seems to be the most viable current conceptualization of leadership.

Gibb (1969) has indicated that the concept of leader has had a plethora of definitions, e.g., someone who assumes a particular office who influences others, or is most emulated by others in a group. Leadership has been defined in terms of centrality among sociometric choices (Bales, 1953). Hemphill (1952) suggested that the leader is one who engages in leadership behaviors; this circular definition, of course, still leaves undefined the notion of leadership behaviors, but at least it has the advantage of focusing on behavior rather than persons.

Early studies on leadership attempted to isolate personality traits which produce leadership; though some personality variables (like intelligence, self-confidence, and extroversion) have been shown to be slightly correlated with leadership, two decades of research have yielded little fruitful result. Likewise, attempts at finding clusters of personality traits, commonly known as the "Great Man" phenomenon, have been abortive.

In the past decade theorists have begun to focus their efforts on the notion of interaction. The interaction theory of leadership attempts to account for a wide range of phenomena which seem to affect the complex concept of leadership: individual personality variables, group structure, group needs and goals, role differentiation, and the situation in which the group operates. Gibb lists the essential features of interaction theory:

1. Groups are mechanisms for achieving individual satisfactions.

2. Any group is a system of interactions within which a structure emerges by the development of relatively stable expectations for the behavior of each member. Such expectations are an expression of each member's interactional relations with all other members and are, of course, determined by the other members' perceptions of his personal attributes and his performance on earlier occasions.

3. This role differentiation is a characteristic of all groups, and some role patterns appear to be universal. However, the nature of the group-task situation, the size of the group, and a great variety of other variables determine the role needs of the group-in-situation.

4. The association of a particular individual member with the performance of a role or pattern of roles is largely determined by the particular attributes of personality, ability, and skill which differentiate him perceptually from other members of the group.

5. Leadership is but one facet, though perhaps the most readily visible facet, of this larger process of role differentiation. Leadership is simply this concept applied to the situation obtaining in a group when the differentiation of roles results in one or some of the parties to the interaction influencing the actions of others in a shared approach to common or compatible goals.

6. Leadership, like any other role behavior, is a function of personal attributes and social system in dynamic interaction. Both leadership structure and individual leader behavior are determined in large part by the nature of the organization in which they occur. Leadership structure is relative, also, to the population characteristics of the group or, in other words, to the attitudes and needs of the followers (p. 270).*

This notion of leadership significantly departs from previous formulations. First, the leader is not someone who is in possession of "leadership traits" and, therefore, leadership is not an individual property. Who leads depends on the needs and constitution of the group. Further, this orientation suggests that leadership is distributed in varying amounts among those group members most able to solve group needs. As needs change, the leadership

---

*This and the quote on page 167 are from C. A. Gibb, "Leadership," in G. Lindzey and E. Aronson (eds.), 1969, Reading, Mass., Addison-Wesley. Reprinted by permission.

distribution within the group changes. Collins and Guetzkow (1964) illustrate this when they say that

> Leadership is a scattered activity—one member being influential at one time because of a particular combination of environmental demands and personal characteristics, and another being influential at another time because of a different congruence of demand and trait (pp. 214–215).

Third, leadership can seldom be effectively imposed from outside the group; rather, it must emerge from within.

This last notion requires elaboration. Gibb provides a meaningful distinction between "leadership" and "headship." Leadership, he says, is applicable only when there is voluntary acceptance of influence without coercion or threat of punishment. Otherwise, the person in charge might better be called a head, exercising authority derived from the formal position. To differentiate the two concepts Gibb says:

1. Domination or headship is maintained through an organized system and not by the spontaneous recognition, by fellow group members, of the individual's contribution to group locomotion.

2. The group goal is chosen by the head man in line with his interests and is not internally determined by the group itself.

3. In the domination or headship relation there is little or no sense of shared feeling or joint action in the pursuit of the given goal.

4. There is in the dominance relation a wide social gap between the group members and the head, who strives to maintain this social distance as an aid to his coercion of the group.

5. Most basically, these two forms of influence differ with respect to the source of the authority which is exercised. The leader's authority is spontaneously accorded him by his fellow group members, and particularly by the followers. The authority of the head derives from some extragroup power which he has over the members of the group, who cannot meaningfully be called his followers. They accept his domination, on pain of punishment, rather than follow (p. 213).

When the notions of headship and leadership are applied to organizations, an interesting parallel emerges with the concepts of formal and informal organizations. The heads of the organization are the persons of primary influence and responsibility in the formal structure. The leaders are the ones who emerge as best able to fulfill the needs of the organization's informal structure. These two concepts are not, of course, mutually exclusive. In fact, they merge into the idea of legitimacy of leadership: the delegation by the group of a leadership role on someone who already possesses headship (*cf.*, Gibb, p. 213).

Though far from fully formalized, interaction theory, which shifts the locus of interest from individual traits to a distributed role-differentiated group property, seems superior to earlier conceptualizations of leadership. Also, the distinction between leadership and headship permits a more refined analysis when application is made to formal organizations. Taken together these concepts can provide a more adequate conceptual framework for the analysis of leadership in small groups within organizations.

SMALL-GROUP TRAITS

So far we have identified three major dimensions of group structure. But structures, by themselves, tell very little about the behavior of any system. Once the parts are known, it is necessary to learn how they work together and what they produce. It is a little like knowing that a car has pistons, a drive shaft, wheels, etc., and then learning how these parts operate in relation to one another to make the car run.

As indicated earlier, functional analysis requires the identification of system traits or characteristics which must be maintained if the system is to continue in operation. For example, the mixture of gasoline and air in the carburetor (a trait) must be maintained within a specific range in order for combustion to occur in the engine's cylinders. If the gas and air mixture is either too rich or too lean (i.e., the value of the trait exceeds the acceptable range), then the engine will not function. Thus, the various parts of the carburetor operate together to maintain an appropriate gas/air mixture so that the engine can be operated.

Organizational groups also have traits which need to be maintained for proper functioning. Like the previous example of the car and its engine, should key group traits be either too high or too low, the group will cease to function. Sheperd (1964) identifies four major problems with which a small group must cope in order to maintain its own existence:

> These problems are, respectively, *adaptation* to factors outside the group (for example, control by a large organization of which the group is a member, or necessity to cooperate with another group); *instrumental control* over those things in the group which are relevant to performing its work (for example, assigning tasks, making decisions, or performing activities); the *expression and management of feelings* of the members (for example, expressing dissatisfaction or pleasure, resolving interpersonal antagonisms, or relieving tensions); and the development and maintenance of *integration* of the members with each

other and of the group as a whole (for example, willingness to do things, satisfaction with the group, or a sense of comradeship). (p. 28)*

Each of these four characteristics is critical for the survival of the group. Failure to achieve any of the four can lead to the dissolution and demise of the group.

Adaptation to organizational constraints is fundamental. Groups which are embedded in organizations typically owe their existence to a management decision. If management assigns a task but the group insists on working a different problem, management may well decide to disband the group. If the group is required to interact with another group in the organization and it refuses to do so, or interacts only in a disruptive and uncooperative manner, management will likely take corrective measures: perhaps, first a reprimand, then replacement of group members, and finally dissolution of the group. Organizations tend to have little patience with rebellious and uncooperative groups and tend to react to deviant groups in the same way that groups react to deviant members. As Schachter (1951) demonstrated, group members tend to orient towards an unconventional member, increasing their communication with him or her in an attempt to get the person to conform to the group's norms. If unsuccessful, the group eventually ceases interacting with the member and the deviant is rejected from the group.

A group must also maintain control over itself and its resources. Each member has a different set of abilities and potential contributions to make to the group, but they must be harnessed and organized into an effective and coordinated effort. Like the individuals of which it is composed, and the organization in which it is embedded, a small group which has tremendous resources but lacks the ability to control them will soon become dysfunctional.

The expression and management of feelings is a major problem for most groups. As in the case of the meeting described at the outset of this chapter, a group can quickly disintegrate if it does not cope with this aspect of group life. Bales (1950), whose work we will discuss shortly, described this as the socioemotional task facing the group.

From a commonsense view there are a number of obvious emotions which must be managed, among which are anger, frustration, anxiety, insecurity, pride, and satisfaction. Other primary emotions that groups experience are *fight, flight, pairing,* and *dependency*. As Sheperd (1964) indicates:

At any point in the life of a group one of these emotions is dominant—the group may be in a fighting mood, for example, and almost every comment, no

---

*This and the quote ending on page 170 are from C.R. Sheperd, *Small Groups: Some Sociological Perspectives*, 1964, Scranton, Pennsylvania, Chandler. Reprinted by permission.

matter how innocuous, seems to call for a hostile reply; or it may be in a flight mood and unable to deal with any issue, evading or ignoring things with which it should deal; or it may be in a pairing mood, in which one or more pairs of members are carrying on personal conversations with the unspoken approval of the others; or it may be in a dependent mood, in which the group, rather than tackle its problem, tries to get someone or something to solve it. (p. 52-53)

All of the categories described above are pathological and unproductive, and certainly any complete framework for analyzing group moods should include at least one (and probably more) *productive* categories. A category called *coping*, in which the group mood consists of mutual, cooperative effort to accomplish the group task, is an obvious, productive example.

The final, and perhaps most important trait, is the development and maintenance of *integration of members*. This aspect of group functioning is synonymous with or at least similar to the concept of cohesiveness, which is typically defined as the degree to which people are attracted to one another and are motivated to remain in the group. Its importance is emphasized by Shaw (1971) who says:

> According to most theories...the first demand that must be met by a group is the resolution of internal problems. Indeed, unless it solves these problems the group will cease to exist. Therefore, there must be some minimum degree of cohesiveness if the group is to continue to function as a group (p. 193-194).*

Furthermore, in summarizing the research literature, Shaw indicates that compared to low-cohesive groups,

> ...high cohesive groups engage in more social interaction, engage in more positive interactions (friendly, cooperative, democratic, etc.), exert greater influence over their members, are more effective in achieving goals they set for themselves, and have higher member satisfaction (p. 205).*

These, then, are the four traits of small groups which must be maintained by the group to preserve its own functioning—adaptation, instrumental control, expression and management of feelings, and development and management of integration. But several additional comments are in order. First, a group may maintain these traits and still dissolve or be dissolved, as might happen to all groups within an organization that went bankrupt. Maintaining these traits does not ensure continued group functioning, but failure to maintain the traits does imply that the group will cease to exist. The relationship

---

*From M.E. Shaw, *Group Dynamics: The Psychology of Small Group Behavior*, 1971, McGraw-Hill, New York. Used with permission of McGraw-Hill Book Company.

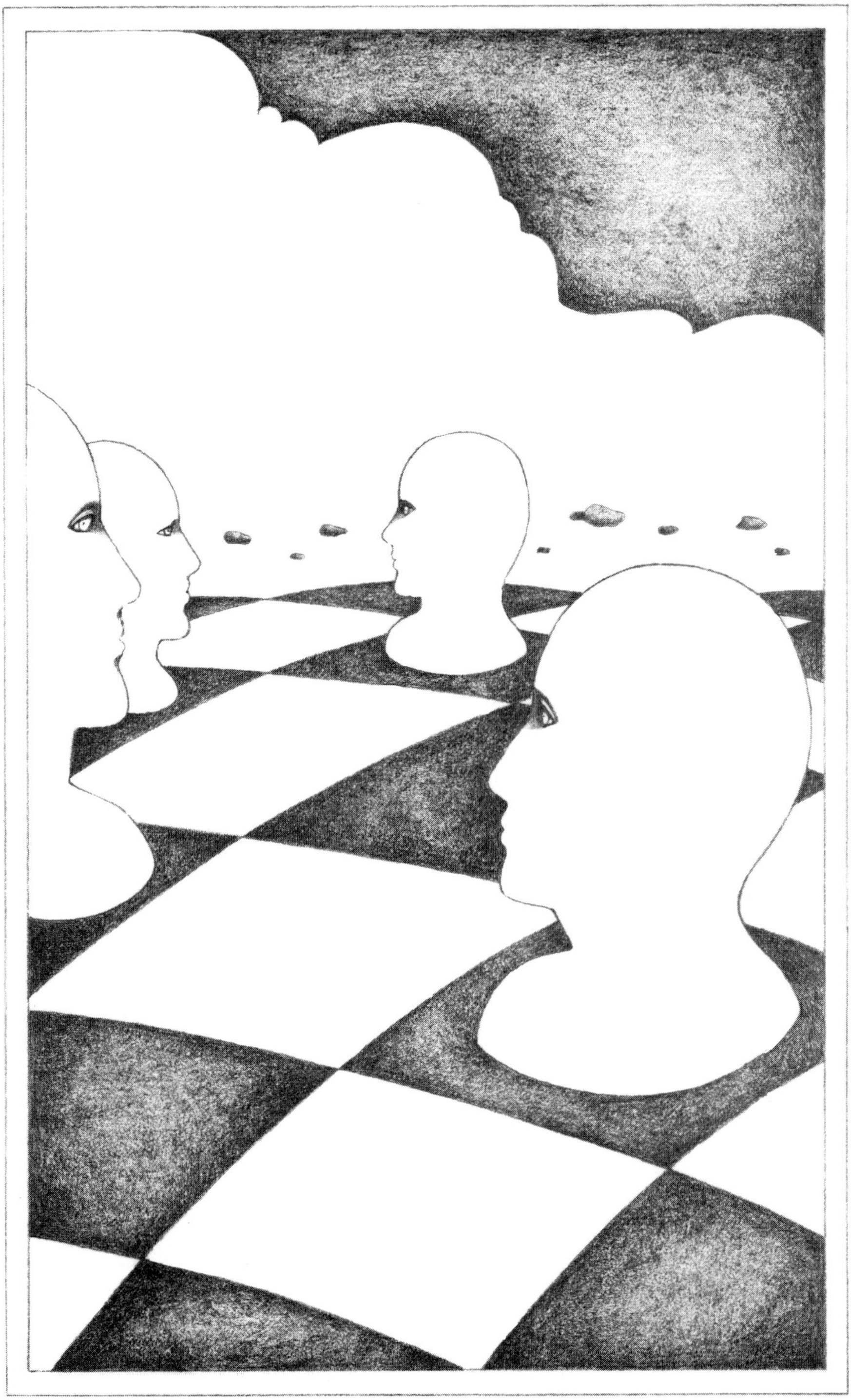

between life and the temperature of the body provides a good example. If the temperature of the body (a trait of the human system) is within the range required for life, say 90°–108° F, it does not necessarily mean that the body is alive; on the other hand, if the body temperature falls outside of that range it means, except under the most extraordinary conditions, that the body is no longer living.

Second, these group traits must be maintained within a proper range, although precisely what that range should be has not been indicated. The reason for this is simple: we don't, except in the most general terms, know. For example, it is theoretically possible for the group trait cohesiveness (or integration) to vary from none to completely. For all practical purposes, if a group has no cohesiveness, it doesn't exist or won't exist for long. Yet because a completely cohesive group is unknown to us, cohesiveness is considered to fall within a range from "low" to "high."

But how low can cohesiveness drop before the group begins to disintegrate? How high can cohesiveness range before it again becomes dysfunctional because group members are unwilling to leave when it is appropriate, or to admit new members to their tightly knit work group or circle of friends? It will require considerable research energy and effort over the next few decades to answer that question, but at least the parameters of the problem have been identified—and that is often the first step to its solution.

For now, it must suffice to identify the requisite traits, to specify approximate relative ranges (such as low to high), and to affirm our belief that the sensitive communication manager can, despite its limitations, effectively utilize the system we are detailing to manage small-group communication processes in the organization.

THE MECHANISM: COMMUNICATIVE INTERACTION

In the earlier discussion of functional systems, three perspectives from which any particular aspect of the system could be analyzed were described. First, communication could be analyzed as a system which has certain traits (e.g., noise) which must be maintained within appropriate levels for the system to function. Or, communication could be a trait of another system (e.g., democracy) which must be maintained by other mechanisms, such as "freedom of speech" laws. Finally, communication could be viewed as the mechanism in a system (e.g., an educational system) whereby one of its traits, authority, is maintained. In our analysis of small-group communication we have taken the small group as the system and identified four traits which must be maintained for its continued operation. Now we turn to an examination of the mechanism which maintains the small-group system: *communicative interaction*.

Let us define interaction as a sequence of events (i.e., a process) where each action of each person in the system (in this case, a small group) is contingent upon the preceding actions of others in the group. Thus, the focus of interaction is on the sequencing of constrained, behavioral responses. There are many forms of interaction, including physical, emotional, and verbal. We have attached the modifier "communicative" to the term interaction to indicate that we are interested in that aspect of interaction that is based upon communication processes. Some authors use the term interaction interchangeably with the concept of communication while others use it more broadly, referring to any behavior a person makes in response to some other person. We have adopted the latter viewpoint, and therefore should note that the concept of communicative interaction implies two things: first, that communication is not the only form of interaction which might affect group behavior; and second, that interaction does not, as we have explicated the concept, constitute the sum total of the communication process.

Analyzing Communicative Interaction
Interaction analysis is a set of procedures for analyzing the content of interaction. It generally requires the creation of categories for classifying the content of interaction and sometimes includes procedures for identifying the author and/or recipient of each act. These data are then analyzed to determine the nature of the communication process occurring in the group.

There are three important aspects to any interaction analysis: (1) choosing the categories, (2) selecting the unit of measurement, and (3) selecting the unit of analysis. We will discuss them in that order.

One of the first issues that must be faced in analyzing interaction is the set of categories to be used. Bales' (1950) system, which was one of the earliest developed, is called Interaction Process Analysis, or IPA. It consists of 12 categories which are equally divided between two major areas: the task area and the socio-emotional area. Further subdivision is achieved by virtue of the fact that the categories are really pairs of opposites: asks for information, gives information; agrees, disagrees; etc. The result is 12 categories which show three task problems—orientation, evaluation, and control—and three socio-emotional problems—decision, tension-management, and integration.

Though probably the most widely used, Bales' IPA is certainly not the only one available. Longabaugh (1963) and Fisher (1974) developed a scheme based upon functional communication acts in decision making. Fisher's scheme consisted of categories of interpretation, substantiation, clarification, modification, agreement, and disagreement (Fisher, 1974, pp. 238–243). Flanders developed a system particularly appropriate to student-teacher interaction, which has significant potential for application to personnel training in the business environment (see Amidon and Hough, 1967).

The unit of measurement refers to the basic elements which are to be counted by the observer and recorded into the category scheme. In selecting the unit of measurement there are, as in the selection of categories, several alternatives. Bales (1950), for example, uses the expression of a single thought or idea as the basic unit. Fisher (1974) and Valentine (1972) used functional discussion units. Others—for example, Hawes (1972a, 1972b) and Amidon and Flanders (1967)—have used time as the basic unit; every three to five seconds, depending upon the study, observers coded the particular behavior that was occurring at that moment.

The third aspect of analyzing interaction is the selection of the unit of analysis. Bales (1950), whose analytic scheme we have already briefly reviewed, defined his basic unit as the "act," i.e., one complete phrase, sentence, or thought that is communicated to another person. When an entire discussion is analyzed on the basis of "acts" the result is an enumeration of the number of times each of the categories was utilized in the discussion. Comparisons can, of course, be made between the various categories, as for example when the ratio of the frequency of use of two categories is made, but this method of analysis will not permit statements to be made regarding the sequencing of behavior, i.e., acts of one kind *followed by* acts of another kind. That requires that the basic unit of analysis be the "interact."

To analyze interacts it is customary to code the entire sequence of interaction so as to maintain the order in which the various elements of the interaction occurred. Then successive overlapping pairs are identified and entered into a matrix where the rows represent the antecedent or first action and the columns represent the subsequent or second action; thus, each entry represents two actions, i.e., an interact. This type of analysis will show us the extent to which one kind of act is *followed by* another kind of act throughout the course of the discussion. Thus, analyzing the interaction provides a more complete picture of the overall interaction process than simply analyzing the number of different kinds of acts.

Obviously, this kind of reasoning could be extended *ad infinitum*. If two acts are analyzed together as an interact, why not analyze three together, or four? As a matter of fact, Weick (1969) suggests that three acts together be taken as the basic unit of analysis. He calls it the double interact:

> Given that interdependence is the crucial element from which a theory of organization is built, *interacts* rather than acts are the crucial observables that must be specified. The unit of analysis is contingent response patterns, patterns in which an action by actor A evokes a specific response in actor B which is then responded to by actor A. This is the pattern designated a "double interact"...(p. 33).

HOW THE MECHANISM OPERATES

We have identified several major small-group structures, four critical traits, and the mechanism of interaction. Though by no means complete, this functional analysis is sufficiently detailed to provide insights into the complete operation. The theory is simple: the structures operate together in the communicative interaction process to maintain the traits within the range required for group functioning. A work structure is imposed by a manager on a small group, and that influences who will communicate with whom.

Productivity or outcome expectations are established and the group must interact if it is to achieve its goals. While interacting, status will play a part in determining what each person says. The group will need to discover who has the requisite resources and, as leadership is distributed, control will begin to be exercised over others in the group through the content of the interaction.

As the group works together, its own emergent communication structure will develop and relative status will be conferred upon those members who show themselves able to meet the group's needs. The leader(s) will utilize various channels in the micro-networks, sending selective messages to exercise control over various activities. Status will enable some members to express feelings supportive of group goals and designed to manage and sustain the group mood. And all the structures will be employed in an effort to maintain group cohesiveness. Finally, if the status structure, or the micro-network or leadership structure, does not interact effectively, then the group is likely to be headed for trouble.

SUMMARY

In this chapter, a structural-functional framework is used again to analyze another aspect of organizational communication—in this case, the communication that occurs in the small groups that exist within organizations. The analysis requires that the major structures that constitute a small group be specified. Next, the traits to be maintained for adequate group functioning must be identified, along with the ranges appropriate for each trait. Then, the mechanism of interaction which integrates the various structures into an operating process for maintaining the group is described. And, finally, a brief look is given at how the whole system fits together: structure and function in process.

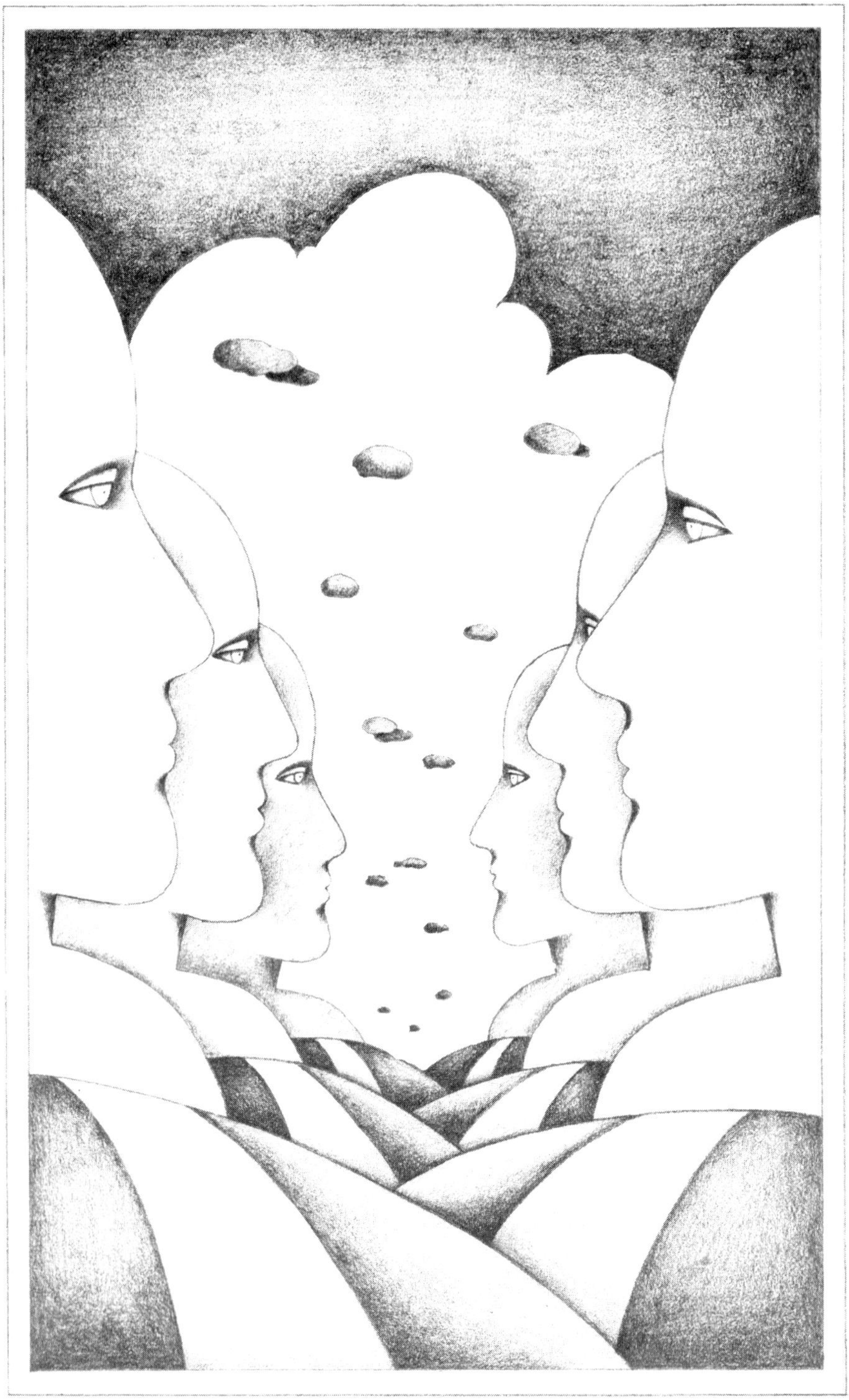

Communication Patterns in Organizations— "Macro-networks"* 8

When managers talk about some of the communication problems they encounter in their day-to-day endeavors, one of the frequent "themes" that arises is often described as follows:

> You know...we've got real problems with our lines of communication. I send out information, but I don't know for sure where it goes, or who gets it, or what people really do with it if it does reach them.

Or:

> Larry, you've been appointed as a liaison between those three work groups for the past six months. But here I find out that you haven't been meeting with them like you should...and they tell me you aren't updated on what's going on in their groups. You're supposed to *coordinate* them, Larry, and it sure looks to me like you're falling down on the job.

Or even:

> Gentlemen, we've invested quite a bit of time and money in reorganizing our operations. The new organization chart shows quite

---

*The authors wish to thank Georg Lindsey for his assistance in writing this chapter.

clearly how each of you, and your work groups, is to relate to one another. To make sure that everyone follows through on the new organization, I'm sending down the word: no one is to talk to anyone in another area or part of the company if the authority to do so isn't clearly specified. Exceptions have to be cleared by me, personally. If we follow this system, the new organization will have a real chance to work. Otherwise, we'll have the same madhouse we had before.

From our viewpoint, these incidents refer to the *communication networks* —the patterns of communication—that occur in all organizations. In the first case, the speaker was expressing his or her unfamiliarity with the nature of the communication networks in the organization. Such a lack of acquaintance with the nature of one's own organizational communication networks is quite common, as many managers will attest, particularly if they work in an organization of 100 or more persons and cannot know each coworker very closely.

In the second example, Larry was chastised for failing to fulfill his duties in a particular communication role, in this case, that of liaison or "linkpin" between three specific work groups. The final example reflects at least one person's desire to ensure that the newly completed organization chart and the behaviors of the organization's members correspond very closely.

The concept of communication network can be illustrated by drawing an analogy to the human nervous system. The nervous system perceives aspects of the environment through the sensory system, translates these perceptions into messages, and carries these messages to various parts of the body. As the messages move from part to part within the body, control and coordination of bodily activities takes place. Message content may be stored in memory for later use. A particular message may be changed in form as it moves from part to part so as to improve its usefulness to the receiving part.

Breakdowns are common. Appropriate messages about the environment may be incomplete or inadequate; they may not be put in suitable form for use by the body's parts, or they may not get to the right part at the right time. Breakdowns can be costly, perhaps even fatal, to the continuance of the body as a living organism.

Organizations, too, acquire information from the environment and convert it into communicative messages. Within the organization, communication moves from unit to unit through the repetitive, recurrent contacts between organizational members, face-to-face, by written means, by telephone, or by other communication modes. An organization's communication network emerges from the accumulation of member-to-member interactions, some of which are routinized and highly predictable. Other instances of message exchange may occur more randomly, and are often as important (if not more so) for the organization's functioning as the routinized exchanges are.

For most organizations, the organization chart depicts the authority hierarchy, the basic pattern of command and control. A major presumption of an organization chart is that it also shows the main network for task or job-related communication in the organization. At a minimum, commands and orders move down the hierarchy, while reports of compliance move up. Thus an organization chart (see Fig. 8-1 for a simple example of a hypothetical "Company X") describes the basic communication network in an organization. While organization charts are often criticized (for failing to show recent personnel changes or the reality of organizational linkages), they nevertheless provide a foundation for depicting the major, formal communication network.

But in most organizations, communication is not restricted to formal communication only. In fact, many people believe that most organizations would cease to act if their members were constrained solely to formally prescribed interaction. Hence the widely known "informal" network, the grapevine, the "inner circles," i.e., the network of interaction that can (and does) range broadly across different content areas, use various communication modes, and perform much broader functions than the formal network.

Organizational networks provide the mechanism by which communication can move from member to member; they permit the control and coordination of individuals, groups, and larger components within the organization. Networks make the achievement of output goals (such as production) possible. They provide the means by which new ideas and practices can be incorporated into organizational behavior from sources inside and outside the

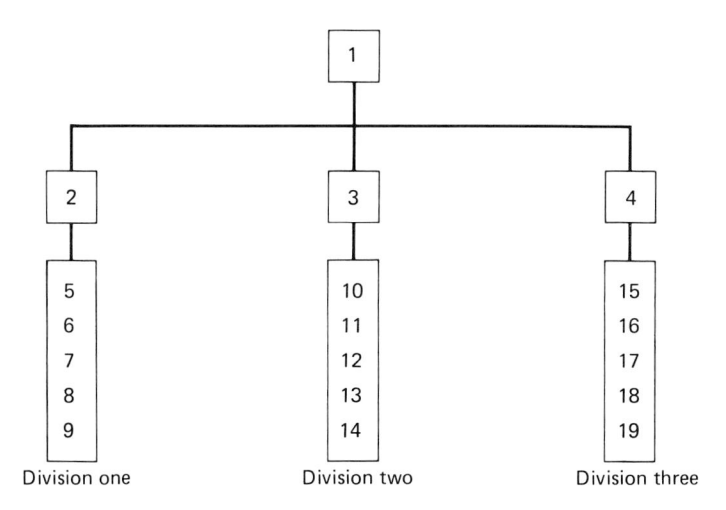

Fig. 8-1. The organizational hierarchy of Company X. Person 1 is the top manager, and Persons 2, 3, and 4 are division managers.

organization. Networks make possible the socialization and maintenance of members. Without networks, organizing would be impossible.

During the past several years, a significant amount of research has been conducted on communication networks in large organizations: how to describe and analyze them, and how to use communication network results both for research and applied problems. The present chapter contains a discussion of the main concepts and principles required to understand organizational communication networks, or "macro-networks," in contrast to small group micro-networks. This chapter also includes a brief review of the historical bases for network analysis.

COMMUNICATION NETWORKS: BASIC CONCEPTS

Network Members and their Links

Communication networks have already been described as "repetitive patterns of interaction among the members." To describe and analyze networks, there are initially two concepts to review: (1) members, and (2) the links among members.

Network analysis is conducted within the framework of a set of rules or criteria which determine the organizational members to be included in the analysis. These criteria define the boundary of the system to be examined. Often the rules are simple: include all members, everyone. More often, however, some smaller portion of the overall organization is specified. This might be all members of a particular plant, or of a division or unit within a facility. Or it might be all individuals who work on a certain product (or service) from point A to point B in the relevant work sequence. More detailed information is required to precisely indicate the members to be studied: what are their names (are the personnel lists fully up to date?) and where are their work stations located?

Why is an obvious point like this emphasized? Because network analysis examines the actual and potential patterns of relationships among a set of people simultaneously, and anyone who is omitted will not be part of the resultant networks. So if someone who actually links two work groups is not included in the analysis, then that linkage will not appear in the final results and the groups will appear relatively less connected than they are. Thus, it is extremely important in any network analysis to fully and completely identify those persons who will be members of the study.

Let's assume that the members to be studied have been clearly and unambiguously identified. Let's also assume that a large number of people —several hundred or even several thousand individuals—are to be studied. Smaller sets of people are also amenable to analysis, but where 100, 200, or more individuals are involved, there is less likelihood that anyone on-site will have a systematic and comprehensive knowledge of the networks in operation; in small organizations, this knowledge is sometimes present and the larger-scale techniques less necessary. Regardless of the number of persons, however, the next problem is to identify the communication links that bind some of these members together, and that do not bind other members of the organization.

There are three general properties of communication links that need to be examined. The results of this examination, in conjunction with other preliminary information needed in a network analysis, will guide the specific research procedures to be followed and will determine the kinds of questions—theoretic and/or applied—that can be answered at completion of the study. The three general communication-link properties are *symmetry*, *strength*, and *reciprocity*.

Each member has potential communication links with *all* other members in the study, although it is very unlikely that he or she will have that number of links (load capacity, task demands, spatial separation, and other factors will inhibit the total number of links that are established). But whenever links exist, they can be symmetric or not. A symmetric link occurs when two persons interact on an equal basis, such as when people meet to share information, giving and taking equally on both sides. An asymmetric link is found when there is inequality in the exchange—as when, for example, one person primarily seeks information and the other primarily provides it.

We can show how this link property is important by comparing the phrasing of two questions, each of which would show a communication link. In the first case, the question is: "Who do you talk with about X?" This question carries the assumption that the interaction is equivalent, or symmetric, and the final network will assume equality of exchange in information flow. On the other hand, if we ask "From whom do you seek information about X?" then we have posed an asymmetric question and are on our way to producing a network that will reveal patterns of information seeking and information giving.

The most obvious example of asymmetric links occurs in the work-related net, where orders or commands are directed to subordinates, but are not received from them. The most common example of symmetric links in organizations is the informal, social or maintenance communication about politics, sports, weather, and other topics that are not part of the work process. When links are asymmetric, specific paths of communication movement can be traced from person to person, and these paths are one-way only (non-reversible). Symmetric links show paths that are two-way, i.e., that are reversible.

The second link property is *strength*, which is used to differentiate links with high frequencies of interaction and/or lengthy time-periods of interaction from links with lesser amounts of interaction. By determining the range of link strengths that occur among members of an organization, it is easier to determine which members communicate together most strongly, in contrast to those who are bonded more weakly to one another. If the only knowledge obtained about link strength is a measure of the simple presence or absence of a link, then the process of aggregating members into the network is much more difficult, and valuable information about differences in the "bondedness" of network members is lost.

The third link property, reciprocity, deals with the question of the *agreement* between the two individuals over the nature of their link. This can range from outright denial of the linkage (one person reports that the two communicate, while the other says they do not), to complete agreement (both parties reply identically to a question about their interaction). The burden on the investigator here is to decide how much agreement is required before the link can be said to exist. If the criteria are too stringent, then links that actually exist will not be counted and the network will suffer accordingly; if too lenient criteria are used, erroneous links will be included in the analysis—another undesirable outcome. Consequently, a considerable amount of care and attention must initially go into deciding what will and will not constitute a communication link.

Thus far the set of individuals who are to be members of the network analysis has been identified and three important link properties—symmetry, strength, and reciprocity—have been reviewed. The product of this activity is a "map" of each member's links with the other persons in the study. A pictorial representation of this for member "1" is shown in Fig. 8-2. The varying widths of the solid lines (to Persons 2,3, and 4) show different levels of communication-link strength, while the presence of the solid lines shows that the links are reciprocal. The relationship is symmetrical with Persons 3 and 4, as shown by the double arrowheads for each dyad. Asymmetry with Person 2 is shown by the single arrowhead. The dotted lines indicate links to Person 1 that are perceived by 5 and 6 (but not reciprocated by 1).

There are other link properties, tied more directly to communication, that are also important for network analysis. The first of these is the content basis of the network, and the second is the mode of communication used by network members. While much of the previous discussion has referred to the work-related communication network, it is quite feasible to study networks for other types of content areas as well. All that is required is an appropriate shift in the question that is posed to the members: who do you talk with about new ideas and practices (innovation)?...or about gossip and rumors?...or about any other topic of importance? If the network study has a functional orientation (see Chapter 3), then the network questions should tap the functions under study.

A second important communication property is mode: whether the interaction is face-to-face, in group meetings, or by memo, letter, or other written means. In many organizations, considerable resources are devoted to estab-

Communication Networks: Basic Concepts   183

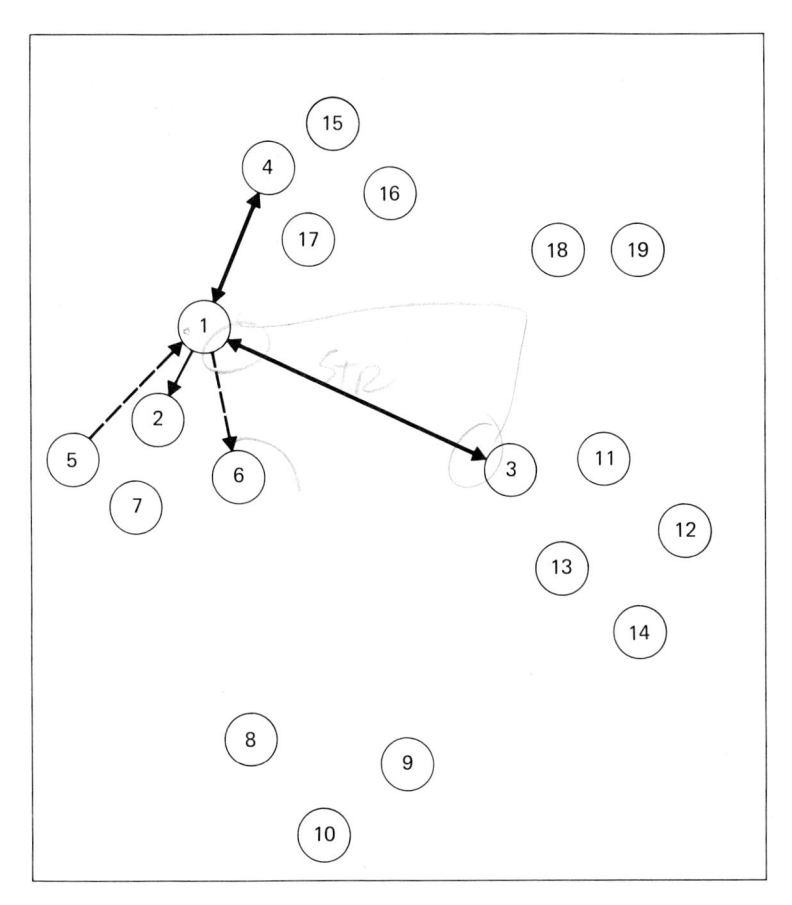

Fig. 8-2. The communication contacts possessed by Person 1 to other employees of Company X. Wider lines connecting Person 1 to others represent stronger links. Arrow heads show direction of link.

lishing and maintaining a memo-distribution system, or a teleconferencing system, or a series of overlapping group meetings. Each of these communication modes can be studied separately or combined in various ways by asking organizational members to report which communication modes they use.

From the preceding discussion, it should be clear that, conceptually, the number and types of communication networks in an organization are extensive. Furthermore, these networks can be—and must be—precisely defined in any given study. Which network is most appropriate depends on the purpose of the study being conducted; however, some of the alternatives available to an investigator have been illustrated. Next the problem of actually identifying the network itself will be reviewed, using the two basic elements—members and their communication links—as the starting points.

Communication Network Roles

In network analysis, particularly when several hundreds or thousands of people may be included, it is unlikely that the patterns of communication links among all these persons can be comprehended without the aid of procedures that simplify and reduce the links to manageable proportions. It is also important that any reductionist or classification scheme have clearly delineated rules of operation, and that as little as possible of the information originally present be altered or lost. For the past 25 years, a series of communication roles have been developed by a variety of researchers that provide such a system. Each role represents a different type of communication

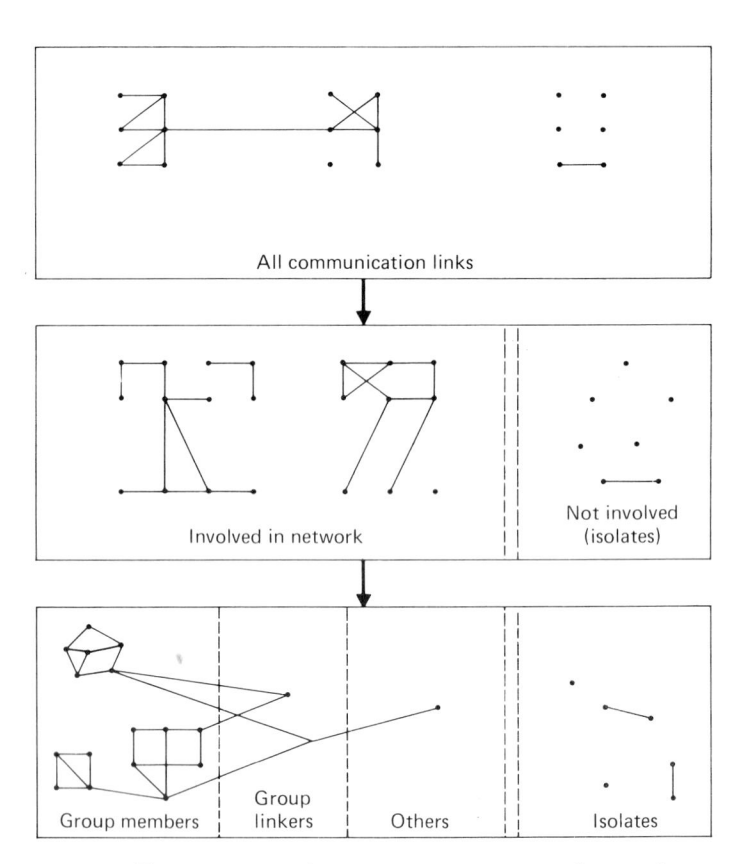

Fig. 8-3. The emergence of a communication network. Top figure shows unordered links, middle shows isolates separate from network participants, and bottom shows specific network role assignments.

behavior, and when these roles are linked together, they make it possible to construct a communication network. In Fig. 8-3, the results of this classification process are shown in three separate stages.

The first partitioning of members is into two categories—those who are involved in the network, and those who are not. The latter category contains the network isolates. Isolates are individuals who have no communication links with anyone else in the network.

It may seem difficult to conceive of anyone in an organization who has no links whatsoever. Note, however, that the distinction between involvement and noninvolvement in the network is a relative one, specified in each study. In a study of a total communication network (all content and all modes), the investigator might arbitrarily specify that only those persons who communicate once a month or more often will be considered to be "involved" in the network; all others, by this definition, are isolates.

Furthermore, if links must be reciprocated before inclusion in the analysis, then individuals with no reciprocal links will be classed as isolates. Finally, if the analysis shifts from a total, combined communication network to networks that are much more specific (e.g., a network based on links that occur monthly or more often, are all reciprocal, involve only discussion of innovation topics, and take place only in face-to-face settings), then the number of persons involved in this network will be small and the number of isolates large. The number of isolates will therefore vary as a function of the way the network is defined; the important point here is that the analysis procedure requires a clear specification of this definition, which can be altered if different purposes or assumptions are made about the communication behavior of organizational members.

It is equally important to note that the number of isolates can vary widely from organization to organization, even if all other aspects of the classification criteria are held constant. For example, in a study of three women's religious communities (Jacob, 1972), the members interacted frequently and at length across five separate functional areas, and thus contained very few isolates. In contrast, the combined network for work, innovation, and maintenance-related conversations in a large Eastern commercial banking division had two out of five isolates (N of 960) when reciprocal interactions occurring weekly or more often were analyzed (Farace and Pacanowsky, 1974).

Let's return to the other major type of roles—those individuals who participate in the network. There are two major classes of these individuals: group members, and intergroup linkers. Briefly, groups are composed of members whose communication is devoted more to each other than to persons outside the group, and group linkers who serve the function of uniting or binding two or more groups, thus moving messages from group to group.

The identification of group boundaries and the membership of groups is a complex and intricate problem that has long been a formidable barrier to the study of network analysis in large organizations. However, some recently developed procedures seem to have overcome this problem; these procedures provide the basis of the following discussion (Richards, 1971; Richards, Farace, and Danowski, 1974).

One criterion for group composition has already been noted: that all the members must have some *minimum portion* of their total communication with other members of the group. If more than half of each group member's communication is with others in the group, then it should be clear that an individual can belong to one and only one group. If only half, or less than half, of the person's communication is within a group, then multiple-group membership is possible.

A second criterion for constituting a group is the presence of pathways or routes from member to member within the group, such that all members can be reached, even though indirectly, by the others. An individual who cannot communicate with all other members of the group on a direct or indirect basis would not be considered a group member.

Two other criteria reflect the ease with which a set of individuals can be subdivided into smaller groups by eliminating either (a) a small number of links, or (b) a small number of members. In the simplest case, no single link nor individual can be removed and cause the group to dissolve into smaller groups; this indicates additional support for the intact nature of the group.

Thus, four criteria can determine when a set of individuals will constitute a group: when more than half of their communication is with each other, when each member is linked to all other members, and when no single link nor member can be eliminated and have the group break apart. The fifth and final criterion is that each group should consist of at least three members.

Given a set of groups isolated from among a set of network participants, the roles that serve to join two or more groups can be isolated. The two main inter-group linking roles are bridges and liaisons. Bridges are group members who, in addition to having a predominance of within-group communication, also have one or more links with members in one or more other groups in the network. Liaisons are individuals who do *not* meet membership criteria for groups, yet have links in two or more groups.

The distinction between bridges and liaisons is an important one, as Fig. 8-4 indicates. When examining communication flow throughout an organization, there is a greater likelihood that distortion will occur when the linkages for a set of groups are provided largely by bridges rather than liaisons.

In Network A, a message introduced into the organization must pass through each group and then travel on to the next group. There are many links in the "chain" through which the message passes, thus increasing the likelihood of distortion of its content. There is a greater chance that the details of messages will be dropped out, added, or modified than is found in Network B, where the message reaching the group originates from the same source (the

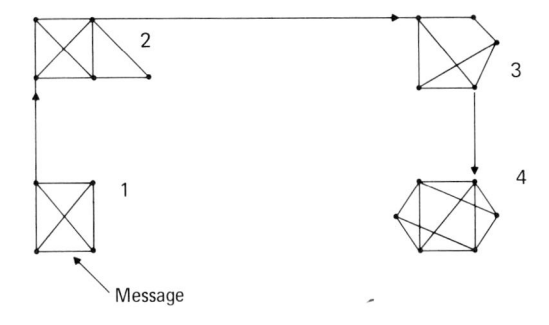

Network A: Bridge-linked

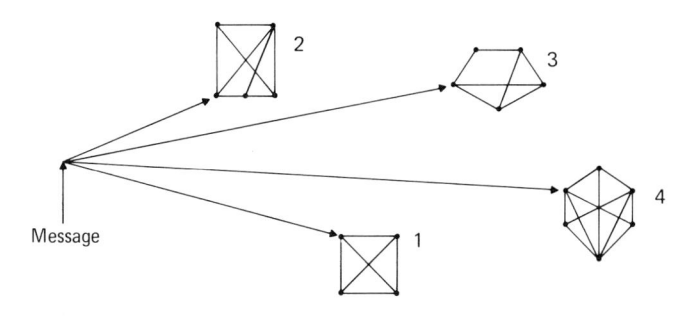

Network B: Liaison-linked

Fig. 8-4. Comparison of probable distortion levels in two networks. Arrows show paths of messages in each network.

liaison) once it is introduced into the organization. If the same message is introduced into each network, and is compared for Groups 1 and 4 in both networks, that the message will probably correspond more closely in Network B—fewer retransmissions of the message means less distortion.

Of all the communication roles that have been studied, it is the liaison which has the longest history of research and the greatest accumulation of findings. Given this history, and the continuing importance attached to the role, a brief review of the concept and a summary of the main findings pertaining to it follows.

The Liaison Role
Managers of organizations have realized, for quite a long period of time, the importance of a role which serves to coordinate the activities of some larger set

of components in the system. Some of the earliest formal organizations in history—military and religious organizations—have employed liaisons in their formal structure to coordinate the operation of various units.

The term liaison denotes a connector, a linker, a coordinator. Within the social sciences there have been a number of terms which have some degree of overlap with the concept of the liaison communication role. Some examples are: Likert's (1961) "linking pin" notion, which specifies that organizational groups ought to have overlapping membership; Walton's (1963) notion of "magnetic centers" in organizations, who draw people to them for information and advice; Katz and Lazarsfeld's (1955) notion of "opinion leaders," who serve as interfaces between the mass media and groups of people, and provide interpretation and advice concerning mass-media information; and Merton's (1957) "cosmopolite," designating someone who links the local village to the more advanced urban/technological world on the outside. Common to all these concepts is an underlying notion of a role in some type of *social structure* which is important in relating in various ways the components or members of the social system.

As noted earlier, in communication-network analysis the concept of liaison refers to the component or role position in the network which does not share a majority of communication contacts with the members of a single group, but which links two or more groups together. The concept was developed in the organizational context by Jacobson and Seashore (1951) when they found in their investigation of communication patterns in the Office of Naval Research that:

> ...some individuals appear to function as "liaison" persons between groups, and characteristically have many, frequent, reciprocated, and important contacts which cut across the contact group structure.

This early work was instrumental in explicating the liaison-communication role with respect to the nature of the communication contacts of organizational members. The way was now open for the examination of whether these individuals are distinguishable from other organizational members on a variety of dimensions. What relationships exist between the nature of their communication contacts and other variables? Are these individuals different from nonliaisons with respect to other communication variables...their control of information flow...their influence in the organization...their personal characteristics? How do liaisons perceive themselves on these kinds of dimensions? How do nonliaisons perceive them?

These questions received little further attention until the late 1960's. Nearly two decades passed after Jacobson and Seashore's work before further exploration of the liaison-communication role was made. Schwartz (1968)

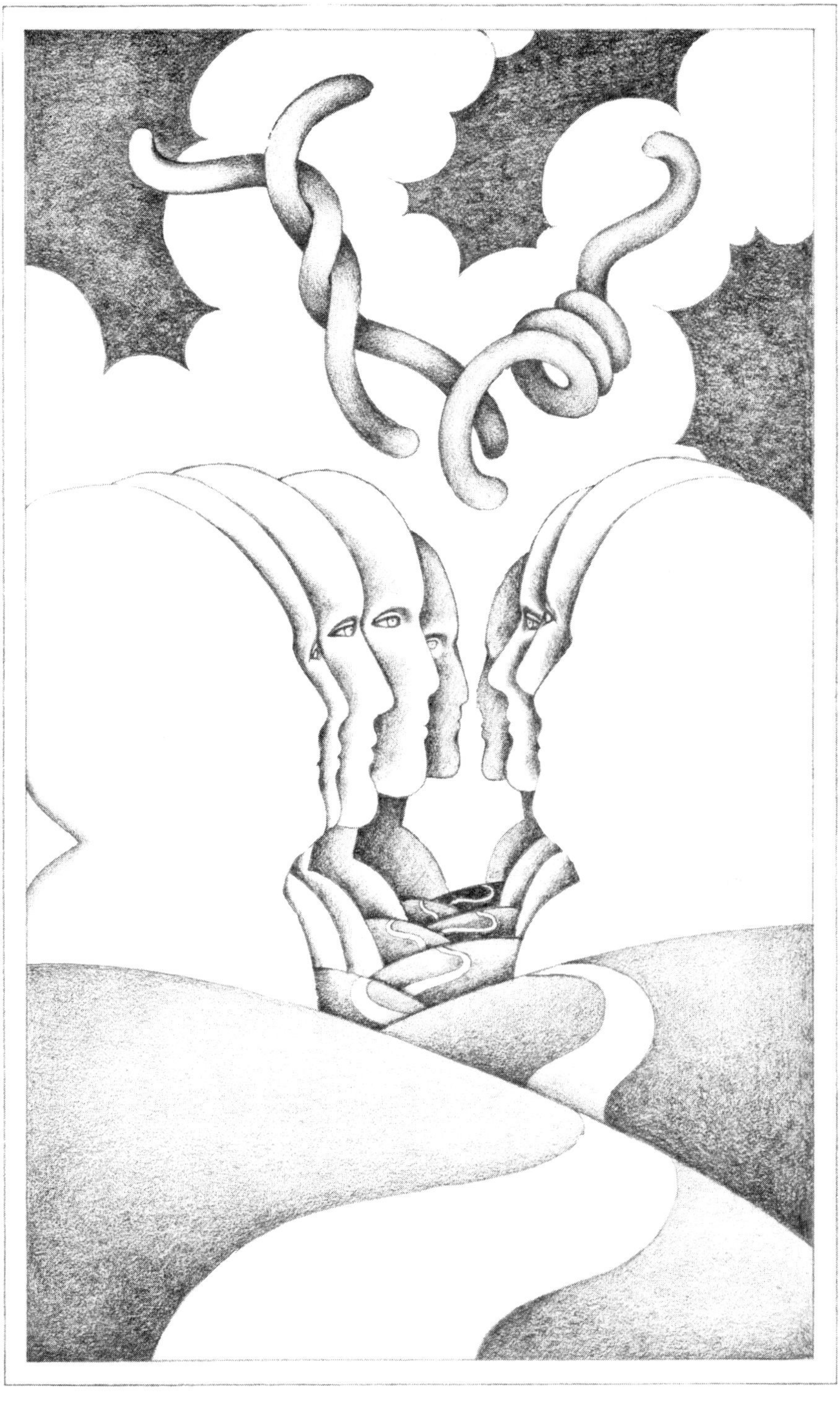

conducted a network analysis in a midwestern university college containing 142 members. The communication content upon which the network was defined was not differentiated into subcategories—all communication messages were treated the same. Then, MacDonald (1970) defined three different content networks in the headquarters of a large, 185-member federal bureaucracy located in the Pentagon. He used content categories for production, maintenance, and innovation communication, which were discussed earlier. Finally, Amend (1971) analyzed the communication network for technical matters in a 50-person research-dissemination organization; in this particular organization technical topics served a task-related or production function.

In discussing the results of these studies, the findings selected appear to be generalizable across specific organizational settings. It should be cautioned that these findings are not to be taken as widely supported knowledge claims, but are tentative generalizations because of a limited empirical base. A review of Table 8-1 will show 15 generalizations about the liaison role. The characteristics of liaisons are described in terms of (a) their actual, objective differences from nonliaisons, (b) differences in how they perceive themselves and the organization, and (c) how nonliaisons perceive liaisons.

In general, there appear to be major differences between liaisons and nonliaisons on a number of dimensions—both in terms of their actual communication behaviors, how they perceive themselves and the organization, and how others perceive them. The liaison-communication role appears to be both a valid and a useful one.

Summary of Communication-Network Roles

In the preceding pages, the major types of communication roles used in network analysis were discussed. Next, all of the various network roles will be summarized and presented in one combined illustration.

First, remember the distinction between members who are involved in the network and those who are not. The latter category, isolates, has several logical subdivisions. First are the "true" isolates, as discussed earlier—individuals with no links to other members. In addition, there are isolated dyads—pairs of members, with one link to the other only. Similarly, there can be isolated groups, i.e., sets of persons who meet the group criteria but who are not connected to the larger network. Obviously, all types of isolates have a considerable potential for being dysfunctional to the organization. Where noted, they should be investigated to determine if they warrant integration into the network.

Among the network participants there are the group members, bridges, and liaisons; they have been discussed previously in this chapter. Finally, there

Table 8-1. Summary of research on the liaison communication role.

Actual

1. Liaisons have higher agreement (between themselves and others they talk with) about the identity of their contacts than do nonliaisons.
2. Liaisons are more likely than others in the organization to serve as first sources of information.
3. Liaisons have higher formal status in the organization than do nonliaisons.
4. Liaisons have been organizational members for longer periods of time than have nonliaisons.
5. The levels of formal education and the ages of liaisons are similar to those of nonliaisons.

Liaisons' perception of themselves

1. Liaisons perceive themselves to have greater numbers of communication contacts in the organization.
2. Liaisons perceive themselves to have greater amounts of information with respect to the content dimensions upon which their role is defined.
3. Liaisons perceive the communication system as more "open"—information is seen as more timely, more believable, and more useful.
4. Liaisons perceive themselves to have greater influence in the organization.

Others' perceptions of liaisons

1. Liaisons are perceived by others to have greater numbers of communication contacts in the organization.
2. Liaisons' communication contacts are seen as having a wider range throughout the organizational structure.
3. Liaisons are perceived as having more information on the content dimensions on which the network is defined.
4. Liaisons are perceived as having more control over the flow of information in the organization.
5. Liaisons are perceived to have more influence over the "power structure" of the organization.
6. Liaisons are perceived to be more competent at their organizational activities.

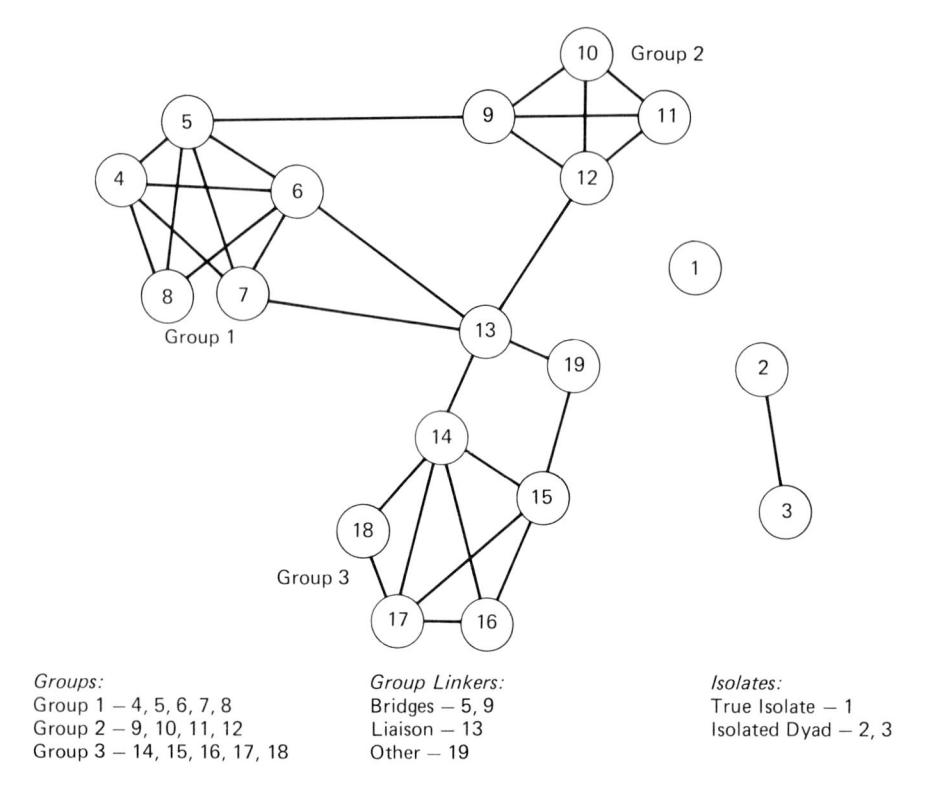

Groups:
Group 1 — 4, 5, 6, 7, 8
Group 2 — 9, 10, 11, 12
Group 3 — 14, 15, 16, 17, 18

Group Linkers:
Bridges — 5, 9
Liaison — 13
Other — 19

Isolates:
True Isolate — 1
Isolated Dyad — 2, 3

Fig. 8-5. Illustration of communication network roles.

is one remaining category, "others," which contains all members not classed into any of the above categories. In Fig. 8-5 there is a graphic example of each of these roles. For simplicity, all the links are assumed to be symmetrical, equal in strength, and reciprocal.

The Historical Basis for Communication-Network Analysis

The primary sources of concepts, propositions, and methods related to communication networks are found in sociology (particularly in some of the sociometric literature), and in the social psychological small-group communication-network studies done in laboratory settings.

The sociometric literature is very extensive, as the review and summary by Lindzey and Byrne (1969) indicates; however, only a relatively small subset of those studies deals with communication flow or networks. Examples of this latter group are Festinger, Schachter, and Back's (1950) study of the linkage between functional distance and interaction probability among residents in a public-housing unit; Gullahorn's (1952) examination of the relationship between spatial separation, interpersonal attraction, and the probability of interaction; and Barnlund and Harland's (1963) study of the impact of propinquity and prestige on interaction.

A particularly rich series of studies on "social networks" (often including information movement, rumor diffusion, or other aspects of communication) is found in the work of Barnes (1969a, b), Bott (1965), and Mitchell (1969). Their studies have been conducted in urban settings, including some in the developing nations, and represent a significant contribution to network theory in "public" (as opposed to organizational) settings. Other sociological studies of long-standing value are exemplified by the Coleman, Katz, and Menzel (1957) investigation of the diffusion of new drugs among a set of physicians, and Loomis and Beegle's (1950) work in rural social systems.

The laboratory network research was described briefly in Chapter 7, and some of the major reviews are mentioned there. Among the many and somewhat diverse findings that various authors have attempted to integrate out of the large body of laboratory network studies, perhaps the most quoted one relates task complexity and network centrality: decentralized networks are more efficient at performing complex tasks, while centralized networks do better when given simpler tasks. However, even this finding has been disputed rather vigorously by Guetzkow and Simon (1955), who argue that if groups are given an "opportunity to organize" and achieve this satisfactorily, then there are no differences in their ability to complete certain tasks. This holds true regardless of whether the network is a "circle," "wheel," or "all-channel."

Laboratory network studies have several distinctive features that become relevant when the concepts and procedures found in them are extended to larger social systems. These studies are typically conducted on groups of seven to nine or fewer respondents, while groups in extant organizational systems may be considerably larger in size. Given that there can be a wide variety of group sizes in an extant social system, the need for measures that are *comparable* across such groups is significant. The laboratory research has, in general, been restricted to a comparison of fairly small groups without using a common measure to numerically express their differences on some property.

Across both the sociological and social psychological literature, there are at least five concepts which are often linked with various communication-network characteristics and thus provide useful direction for further research: (1) *propinquity* (spatial separation or functional distance), (2) *status differ-*

ential (either perceived or system-defined), (3) *interpersonal attraction*, (4) *satisfaction* (or morale), and (5) *nature of task* (e.g., similarity of work duties in an organization).

While these five by no means exhaust the list that is relevant to communication networks, they do occur regularly enough in the literature to have generated some support for their relationship to various network measures. In general, the probability that individuals will interact (and hence form groups) increases as (1) spatial or other physical barriers disappear, (2) status differences decrease, (3) interpersonal attraction increases, (4) satisfaction or morale increases, and (5) task behavior is more similar to that of others.

The communication-network variables per se that appear in the literature are reviewed extensively by Proctor and Loomis (1951), Glanzer and Glaser (1959, 1961), and Guimaraes (1970). Again, the set of indices that deals explicitly with communication (message transfer, information exchange)—rather than with more standard sociometric indices based on power, attraction, friendship, etc.—is relatively small. There are three major types of these variables: *centrality* (which reflects the degree to which an individual is positioned at the "crossroads" of communication flow), *choice status* (the degree to which an individual has links with other system members), and *connectedness* (the degree to which members of a group are interlinked).

In his summary of the concept and use of social networks, Mitchell (1969) distinguishes four additional network concepts that are related to those that have just been mentioned. These are *anchorage* (the point of orientation of the network), *reachability* (the extent to which other system members can be contacted with a minimum of intermediaries), *density* (the degree to which sets of system members are interlinked, i.e., interconnected), and *range* (the degree to which a system member has direct links with other members).

The methodology used to analyze communication networks has emerged from three sources. Some investigators have employed sociograms, where the terminology and selected principles of graph theory have been used. Other investigators have cast communication relations in the form of matrices and used matrix methods to generate networks. Still other investigators have applied multi-dimensional statistical techniques (such as factor analysis or cluster analysis) to matrices of communication relations. These three approaches can perhaps best be summarized by comparing their relative abilities to (a) adequately represent network data and (b) reduce it to meaningful and useful results.

The problem of data representation has been treated in two main ways—in the form of sociograms, and as matrices. The sociogram, developed by Moreno (1934), uses points to represent system members, and lines joining these points to represent communication relations. Figures 8-4 and 8-5 are examples of sociograms. The sociogram is largely a descriptive device, with relatively little formalization of rules for preparing sociograms (see Proctor and Loomis, 1951, for a presentation of such rules). As the size of the system increases, it becomes impossibly cumbersome to draw sociograms; this problem is further aggravated by the lack of systematic rules that lead to replicable outcomes.

Network data have also been represented in the form of matrices, where a row represents the "communicator," a column represents the "communicatee," and the matrix cell entries reflect the communication relation. These entries may be binary, where "1" refers to "presence of contact" and "0" refers to "absence of contact," or higher-level measurement may be used. The relation may reflect type of contact, mode, or other dimension of the communication process. See Fig. 8-6 for an equivalent example of the two approaches.

The critical limiting factor in matrix representations of network data is that as the system's size exceeds about 200 persons, it becomes very costly (if not impossible) to store, manipulate, and access the data. Thus the use of matrices places an important practical limitation on the size of the system that can be studied.

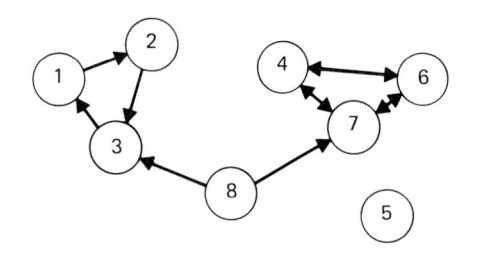

Fig. 8-6. Sociogram and matrix representation of the same communication links among eight persons.

	1	2	3	4	5	6	7	8
1	X	1	0	0	0	0	0	0
2	0	X	1	0	0	0	0	0
3	1	0	X	0	0	0	0	0
4	0	0	0	X	0	1	1	0
5	0	0	0	0	X	0	0	0
6	0	0	0	1	0	X	1	0
7	0	0	0	1	0	1	X	0
8	0	0	1	0	0	0	1	X

Once the communication relations among members of a system are represented, either in sociogram or matrix form, some sort of data-reduction process must be followed that will categorize system members into the communication roles chosen by the investigator. While sociograms can be drawn to reveal such roles in small systems (of about size 50 or smaller), the lack of clearly specified rules and procedures makes this approach infeasible in large systems. Discussions of graph theory and related applications to sociograms can be found in Harary, Norman, and Cartwright (1965), and Coleman (1964). Interest in the potential applications of this area to networks continues to yield new insights (Lorrain and White, 1971).

Reduction of communication-network data by matrix methods has been far more fruitful. The two principal means by which this has been accomplished are matrix multiplication, and matrix manipulation. In matrix multiplication, the investigator first obtains a matrix of the direct (one-step) links among the system's members. Then, by raising the matrix to successive powers, it is possible to identify the two-step, three-step, k-step *indirect* paths linking each pair of individuals in the system. This analysis provides a measure of the integration of an individual into the overall system, since it incorporates both direct and indirect pathways through which other members can be reached.

This approach also provides a general method for detecting cliques or groups of individuals in the system. Unfortunately, the information on path-lengths becomes costly to obtain when large matrices are used, and the clique detection aspects fail to indicate precisely how many cliques are present in the data, which specific individuals belong in which clique, or how cliques are linked together. Luce and Perry (1949), Festinger (1949), and Guimaraes (1970) elaborate on these issues.

Matrix manipulation, in contrast to the multiplication procedure, involves the simultaneous rearrangement of the rows and columns in a matrix to increase the likelihood that individuals who interact with one another will be physically proximate in the matrix. This concept of rearrangement or manipulation of the rows and columns is a particularly important one in our later presentation of contemporary analytic procedures. Conceptually, this procedure requires the investigator to scan the matrix of communication relations in search of groups of system members who share many of their communication contacts with each other. The initial matrix is then reordered so that these "groups" or sets of individuals are clustered as close to one another as possible.

An early description of a method to analyze matrices by manual manipulation is found in Forsyth and Katz (1946). Beum and Brundage (1950) suggested an iterative procedure to reorder matrices, one that uses mathematical weights; this procedure was programmed for computer analysis by

Borgatta and Stolz (1963). An analogous procedure is described by Coleman and MacRae (1960) for groups of up to 1,000 members.

While these methods facilitate the detection of the network structure, none of them provide a systematic set of procedures for drawing group boundaries or locating intergroup linkages. Consequently, when the matrix reordering process is completed, the investigator must then apply a set of specific criteria to the data in order to classify members into selected communication roles. The first such analysis was reported by Jacobson and Seashore (1951), Weiss and Jacobson (1955), and Weiss (1956). They located the members of a federal bureaucracy who occupied the liaison role. The major application of matrix manipulation has been to locate liaisons in various communication networks and to test hypotheses concerning their behavior; these results were given earlier in this chapter.

The major difficulty in using matrix-manipulation procedures is that a very large amount of hand labor is necessary to analyze data from more than 150 persons. About 200 man-hours are required for an organization of this size; the amount of time required increases very rapidly as system size increases. A second problem in following the Weiss (1956) procedures for classifying system members is that the final role-assignment decisions are somewhat judgmental and imprecise.

Earlier in this paper it was noted that a third major analytic technique, multidimensional scaling (e.g., Tryon and Bailey, 1970), has also been used. This approach combines some of the key problems of both matrix multiplication and matrix manipulation, in that it does not seem to offer a unique way to designate the participants in various communication roles. This problem, plus the constraints placed on the techniques by limitations in matrix size, seriously hampers its usefulness in large social systems.

Descriptors of Communication Networks
The product of the efforts described in the preceding sections is a "map" of the communication network among a set of organizational members, i.e., an expanded and specific version of the sample network shown in Fig. 8-5. A map, or network, has a number of properties that can be important to both the scholar interested in the theoretic aspects of network analysis, and/or the practicing manager interested in the application of the technique to his or her particular situation. In the present section, a set of network properties will be reviewed that appear to be theoretically fruitful, either in the literature that has been cited or in our own experience. These same properties, of course, also become useful in applied instances of network analysis as evidence accumulates on the way these properties act under different situations. However, the main discussion of applications of network analysis is presented in Chapter 10.

Network descriptors are "fruitful" when they enter into systematic, scientifically valid relationships with either (a) other network descriptors, or (b) variables that lie outside the domain of communication-network analysis (e.g., personality measures, knowledge levels, attitudes, and behaviors).

Since network analysis is based on the roles to which members are assigned and the links that unite these members, the discussion of descriptors should begin at this point. Given the results of an analysis, what are the relative frequencies and percentages of each type of role? Are the majority of members classed as isolates, group members, intergroup linkers, others, or what? Are any roles absent entirely?

To construct even a rudimentary scientific relationship involving network descriptors, at least one additional variable must be introduced; either another descriptor or a different variable entirely. Suppose that data have been gathered from two different communication functions—task and social communication—and that the percentages of members in each role for each network have been calculated. Are the percentages the same, or, if they differ, do the differences reflect underlying variation in the ways members occupy the communication roles? By using the assumption that the two sets of percentages differ only by random factors, ordinary statistical tests can be used to find out if the role distributions do actually seem to differ. If they do, then the evidence that suggests that the members tend to fill different roles in the two networks—perhaps a group member in one and an isolate in the other, for example.

This same kind of comparison can be made on the same network using the same members, provided that the information is collected at more than one point in time. Suppose an organization adopts a decentralization-of-management program (e.g., the Scanlon plan) and it is important to learn whether there are changes in the task-related network as a result of the new program. By collecting data before and after the program's implementation, it is possible to tell whether any substantial changes have taken place in the communication roles of the individuals involved in the program.

It might also be important to learn how the communication roles are distributed by hierarchical levels in the organization—an example of a relationship between a network descriptor and a nonnetwork variable. In one study (Farace and Pacanowsky, 1974), it was found that communication roles were distributed about equally across nine hierarchical levels in a network based on 960 members. That is, each role was as likely to occur at higher levels of management as at lower levels.

However, when a measure of *relative* status within the hierarchy was used, the results changed. Relative status was defined as the position of a member in his or her own chain of command, in relation to the length of the chain of command (see Fig. 8-7 for an illustration of this concept). The results

Communication Networks: Basic Concepts   199

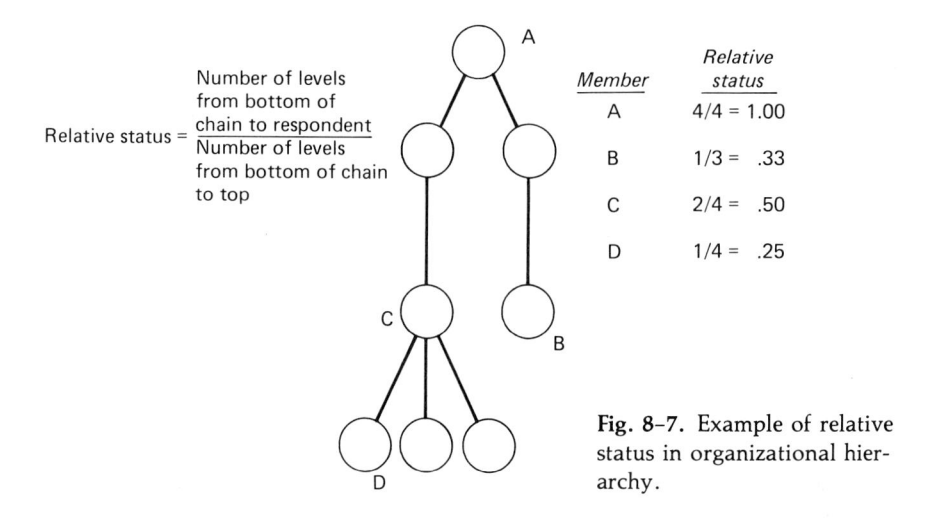

Relative status = $\dfrac{\text{Number of levels from bottom of chain to respondent}}{\text{Number of levels from bottom of chain to top}}$

Member	Relative status
A	4/4 = 1.00
B	1/3 = .33
C	2/4 = .50
D	1/4 = .25

Fig. 8-7. Example of relative status in organizational hierarchy.

suggest that the higher an individual is in his or her own chain of command (regardless of its placement in the total organizational chain), then the more likely the member is to play a central role in the network—to be a liaison or bridge, rather than a group member.

A careful study of the links resulting in a network analysis provides another large source of potential information about the network. What is the average number of links that members have, and what is the range in links they report? What is the average and range in strength of the links? A key descriptor here is the level of reciprocity among the links—to what extent do the members agree on their perceptions of communication relationships with other members?

To what extent do individuals over-report their links—nominate more members than who nominate them in return? Conversely, to what extent do they under-report, i.e., cite fewer individuals than who cite them in return? The literature suggests that one predictor of the way an individual's links will be directed is her or his status in the organization. At lower levels, people tend to over-report contacts on task-related matters with higher-level members, while those at higher levels tend to under-report their links with lower-level members.

Information on the links a person has can be combined with the roles held by the linkers to learn about the individual's importance in the overall network. If, for example, the way group members distribute their links outside the group is examined, the importance of each person to establishing links

200   Communication Patterns in Organizations—"Macro-networks"

between groups can be determined. For example, if Group A has three bridge links with Group B, and these are all provided by one individual, then this indicates the individual's level of importance regarding intergroup linkage.

Another potentially important indicator is zone size, the term used by Barnes (1969b) to reflect the extent of linkages a given member has with others in the network. A first-order zone contains all members with whom the individual has direct contact. A second-order zone extends this to include all individuals who have direct contact with members of the first-order zone, but who are not already in that zone. A third-order zone extends this concept still further to include all individuals having direct contact with members of the third-order zone, without, of course, being in the second- or first-order zone. Zone size can be extended to any number of steps removed from the focal member.

An example is shown in Fig. 8-8. Note that there are three persons in the first-order zone, nine in the second. Member "X" is not counted as part of the second-order zone since contact has already been established at the first-order zone level. The cross-hatched lines indicate that these links do not signify a second-order zone contact.

By obtaining the zone size (of a given order) for a member, the number of persons in the zone can be computed and used as a descriptor. It is also im-

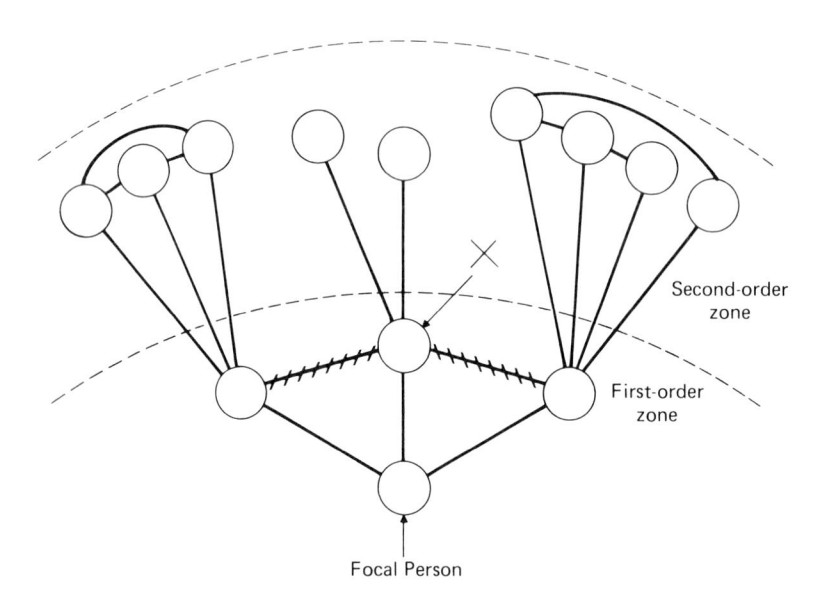

Fig. 8-8. First and second-order network zones for selected focal person.

portant to note that this procedure, in effect, generates an individual "map" for the network of that particular individual. By increasing the orders of the zone, it is possible to chart the expansion of the "sphere of influence" of the member. It is also possible to relate zone size to distortion of message flow, on the assumption that no transmission/retransmission of information has perfect fidelity of meaning established in successive receivers.

It is interesting to note the effects on message fidelity of different distortion levels. If half of the content is lost at each increase in zone, then only one-eighth of the original remains at the third-order zone. If 80 percent is retained (20 percent lost), then about half is left at the third-order zone. If 90 percent is retained, then three-fourths is left at the third-order zone; but if distortion is 50 percent at any one of the zones while 90 percent is retained at the other two, then about half reaches the third-order zone.

These figures show the relationship between zone size and message distortion; they indicate (a) how rapidly distortion rises just a few steps removed from the focal member, and (b) how damaging the effect of one "weak link" is on overall message transaction fidelity. Note also that while zone size and relative distortion levels are important descriptors, the specific location of the zone members (who they are, and where they are in the organization) is obviously of considerable interest in applied situations.

The descriptors presented thus far have been expressed as measures of individuals within the network. This need not be the only type of measure. Network analysis also can be conducted using "groups" as the basic member; the groups can be preidentified or can be derived from preliminary network analysis using individuals as members. Higher-level units can be used—divisions within an organization, organizations within an industry, or even more encompassing "members." So it is important to note that these descriptors are not restricted to single individuals; they can be used on networks whose members are constituted at any of a variety of levels of aggregation or abstraction.

We will continue, however, to assume that the term "group" is used to describe aggregates of members that have been defined by the procedures outlined previously. For the majority of cases, groups will consist of sets of individuals. At the group level, four new descriptors can be determined, each of which taps a new aspect of network functioning. These four are (1) connectedness, (2) reachability, (3) dominance, and (4) openness.

The concept of communication connectedness reflects the amount of one-step, direct within-group communication, in comparison to the total that could occur. In simplest form, it is measured by counting the number of (two-way) communication links that are actually in operation in a group, and then expressing that number as a proportion of the total possible number of links. (The total possible number is easy to compute; it is $N(N-1)/2$, where N is the number of members of the group.) A more refined measure of connectedness would use both presence of links and their relative strength to express the "bondedness" among the members of the group. A highly connected group, then, is one whose members collectively have extensive and strong links with one another, while a group with less connectedness has fewer possible links activated and more of a tendency towards weaker links. Obviously, some minimum amount of connectedness is required for a set of members to be constituted as a group in the first place, but this minimum still leaves a considerable amount of room for variability in actual connectedness.

Reachability or distance is one of the better known properties of groups, and has received systematic and widespread study (Harary, Norman, and Cartwright, 1965). The basic concept refers to the number of steps required to reach one member in a group from some other member. It may take one step, two steps, three steps, or more; the average number of steps required for all members of the group to reach the others is its average distance score. Distance scores take direct and indirect pathways into account. Furthermore, if the communication links are asymmetric, then the distance scores can reflect the paths that must be followed when the "one-way streets" of asymmetric relations are present.

A very different kind of measure—dominance—is based on the general formula for measuring the uncertainty (or, conversely, the structure) in a set of communication links. Uncertainty measures assume as a baseline that the phenomena of interest—in our case, the communication links in a group—are equally distributed. In other words, the assumption is that each person receives and/or sends an equal amount of communication.

To the extent that this assumption of equi-probability is not met, then there is a predictability or pattern in the observed relationships. Dominance is a measure of how much structure or inequality in communication links exists in a group. The more that communication is directed to one or a few members, rather than being equally spread among all members, the more dominated the group is. Dominance is obviously a desirable feature in task-oriented groups, where coordination and leadership are needed. If "brainstorming" and creativity are group goals, however, then lower dominance is probably functional since it reflects a more equal opportunity to communicate on the part of the group's members.

The fourth measure, openness, reflects the degree to which the group has linkages with its environment. A highly open group has many links to many other groups, while a closed group has few or no links outside of itself.

In a study using several of the descriptors mentioned above, Danowski (1974) used four network variables to predict connectedness at the group level. The four descriptors were group size, the zonal integration of each group, the size of each group's zone, and the group's openness. Using an N of 58 groups derived from the network study based on an N of 960 members noted above, he was able to predict 70 percent of the variability in group connectedness by the four other descriptors. Of this 70 percent, all but 20 percent was accounted for by group size alone. However, the remaining three descriptors each accounted for a statistically significant additional increment in the prediction.

In another related study, Danowski and Farace (1974) examined the linkages among the groups connected to a given focal group to determine the relationship between these linkages and the internal homogeneity of knowledge and attitudes among the group's members. The results suggest that as a focal group's zone members (other groups, in this case) become more interconnected, there is a greater homogeneity among the knowledge and attitudes of the members (individuals) of that focal group. This arises because one consequence of high interconnectedness among a group's zone members is that they communicate among each other. Thus, the messages reaching the group from any zone member are likely to be more homogeneous than will be found among groups whose zone members are relatively less connected to each other. The input of messages of greater similarity results in greater similarity of knowledge and attitudes within the group itself; in contrast, when the message inputs are more variable, intragroup similarity is less.

SUMMARY

In this chapter, the basic mechanism for organizational control and coordination—the communication networks through which messages move among the members—is described. These networks emerge from the repetitive communicative events that take place among organizational members. In contrast to Chapter 7, where the small-group micro-network studies were discussed, this chapter is devoted to the assumptions, procedures, and outcomes involved in analyzing networks at the organizational level.

Rather than dealing with the predetermined networks found in small-group studies, the initial problem in organizational-network analysis is one of detecting the networks—of locating communication groups, inter-group linkers, and isolates. Once these steps are outlined, a series of descriptors to be used in evaluating different characteristics of the networks is presented, and some examples of research using them are given.

III

Diagnosing and Managing Communication

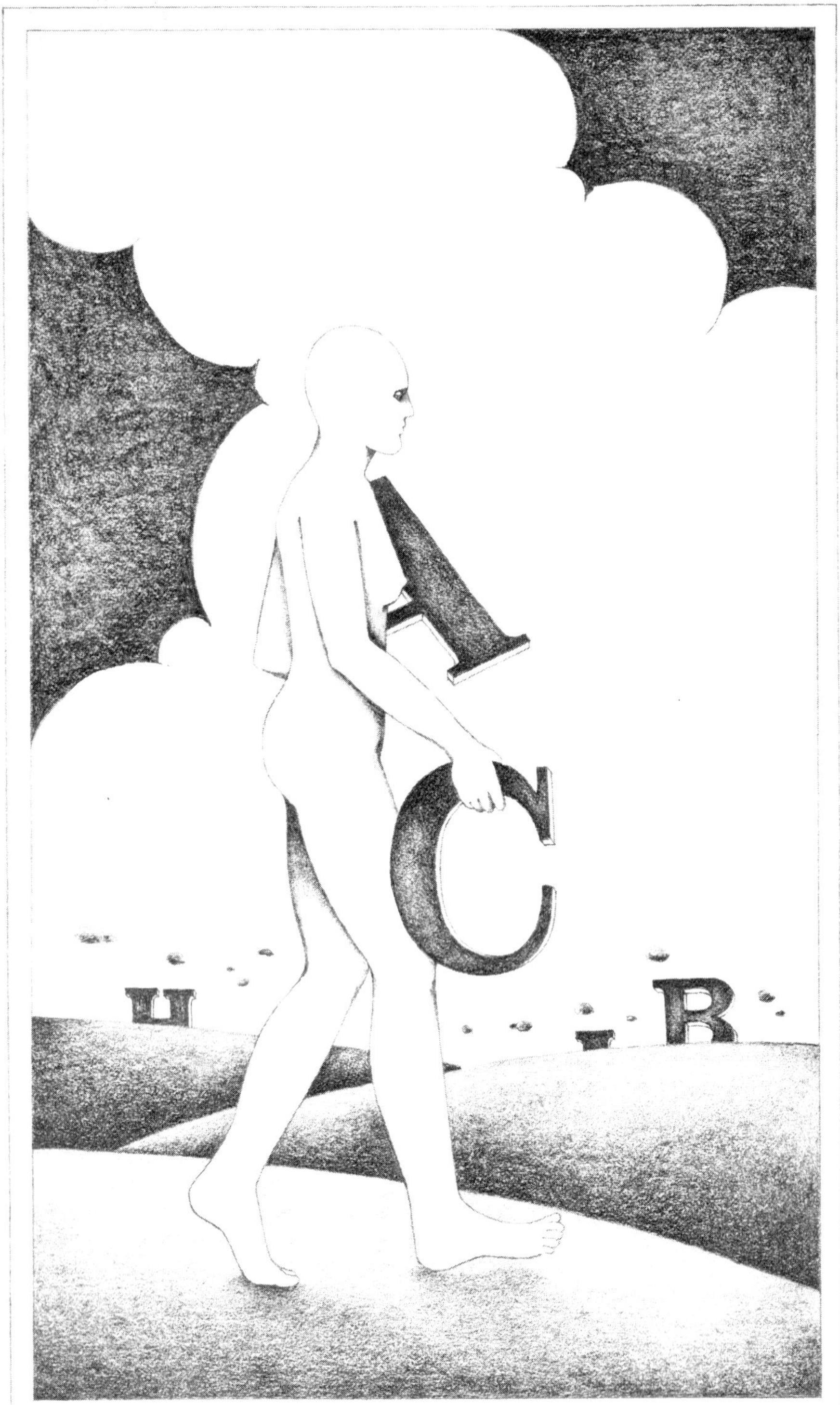

9
"Tools" for Diagnosing Communication Problems

Says Gardner (1963): "Most organizations have a structure that was designed to solve problems that no longer exist." Adds Toffler (1970), while describing the challenging future facing "organization man": "His position will be constantly changing, fluid, varied. And his organizational ties, like his ties with things, places, and people, will turn over at a frenetic and ever-accelerating pace."

Whether one subscribes to this view of organizational future, or maintains the belief that organizations will remain relatively stable in the years to come, it seems inescapable that local, national, and world conditions will change. Daily, there are shifting political alliances, a continuing international redistribution of wealth, radical fluctuations in the availability and prices of goods and services, new social values, population shifts, and even some indications that basic climate conditions are changing.

These changes may indeed alter the environment in which organizations function, and may put increasing pressures on organizations to rework their communication practices and procedures to meet the changing environmental conditions. In many organizations, there are already obvious shifts away from strict bureaucratic relationships and formal, top-down communication to less restricted, freer patterns of communication that seek to fulfill current needs. More and more frequently, managers establish communication relationships among themselves, and with nonmanagerial staff, on a unique, "once-only" basis, constructing new relationships as needed.

The key to successful communication in an organization lies in developing and maintaining regular *evaluation* or *monitoring* of existing communication patterns and procedures. Routine monitoring can indicate how well the present system meets the needs of the organization at a particular point in time. When environmental forces impinge on organizational structures, pressuring for change, it becomes increasingly important to know that the right communication is getting to the right people at the right time. The dangers in the "old" organizational structure of losing communication or cluttering up the minds and desks of those who do not need it, are very real.

The terms "evaluation" or "monitoring" of organizational communication are used to refer to the regular, extensive, problem-oriented analysis of communication behaviors of the organization's members. The purpose of this chapter is to outline some of the communication "tools" that are available to carry out different types of evaluations. In addition, some of the factors they can be used to measure are suggested, and some of the problems they can help resolve are described. This is not a technical chapter, dealing with communication-research methods as such. Instead, it should provide the reader with a basic conceptual understanding of several communication-research procedures so that it becomes clearer how they might be applied in the organizational setting.

The overall process for evaluating the state of an organization's communication system can be divided into four steps:

1. Select concepts to describe current communication practices and procedures—the "patterns" of communication.

2. Implement techniques for the rapid and economical description of these patterns, of reporting on the "state of the system."

3. Develop criterion measures (policies) for the evaluation of the degree to which current patterns meet current needs in the organization.

4. Implement programs to correct deficiencies in communication patterns, and repeat the three previous steps.

The first step in this process has been the subject of all of the preceding chapters, beginning with the initial discussion of the concepts of information and communication. The preceding chapters are thus one source of potential concepts for describing communication patterns. The present chapter concentrates on the main features of some of the communication-research techniques that affect the rapid and economical reporting on the "state of the system" as noted in step two above.

First, several methods for studying message structure and flow are compared and contrasted. Then, the procedures for analyzing communication "rules" are described. Finally, some comments on the analysis of other aspects of communication in organizations will be made. The reader should note that this chapter is very selective in the evaluative techniques to be discussed; no attempt is made to cover exhaustively the full spectrum of these techniques.

STUDYING COMMUNICATIVE NETWORKS AND FLOW

In earlier chapters it is argued that communication networks are a critical element in the operation of any organization. Thus, perhaps the most central aspect of any communication evaluation is the analysis of who is linked into different communication networks, what kinds of messages move along these networks, and how the networks meet the needs of the organization. Five different approaches to analyzing communication networks and the movement of messages within them will be reviewed and compared. To monitor the message flow in a communication system, the following concepts appear to be important traits whose behavior directly influences the organization's functioning:

1. Communication *structure*—the repetitive patterns or networks of communication exchange. As we have noted, this may or may not reflect the formalized organizational chart.

2. Communication *load*—the amount of time and effort (resources) members of the organization spend in communicating and/or processing information. Both communication overload and underload may occur, depending on an individual's linkages into the communication networks. Some optimum level of load needs to be established for individuals, units in the organization, and the organization itself.

3. *Rates* at which messages flow through the system—with rate expressed as the time messages take to diffuse through the system, especially to reach key destinations. The rate will be affected by such factors as the number of messages in the system, and the speed with which they are processed and transmitted.

4. Amount of *redundancy* built into the system—where redundancy is based on the receipt by an individual of essentially the same message, through different channels or sources. As with load, and the concepts below, there will be some optimum level required for satisfactory system performance.

5. *Efficiency* of the pathways used by messages as they diffuse through the network—it is possible to compare the actual pathways with the formal organization chart, or with theoretical pathways, to assess the efficiency of the networks that have developed. This comparison can be made in terms of various system costs that arise when too many links are required for a message to reach an individual, when unnecessary redundancy is present, etc.

6. Extent of messages' *distortion* as they move through the system—leveling, sharpening, and assimilation may occur to change the meaning or content of the messages, and dramatically affect their final impact. Leveling refers to the decrease in number of distinct points contained in a message; sharpening refers to the possible highlighting of certain parts of a message; and assimilation refers to the tendency of communicators to rephrase parts of a message into expressions that are closer to their own feelings than were present in the message when received.

7. Alternative networks or pathways followed by messages serving different *functions*—there are many different functional classifications that can be applied to messages, as discussed in Chapter 3. Three such functions will continue to be used:

- production—getting the job done
- innovation—exploring new alternatives
- maintenance—keeping the system and its components operating

Given these concepts, each of which is an indicator of the communication system's performance, five research techniques will be compared in terms of how well they are adapted to the measurement of these concepts, and how costly they are to implement. This review should enable the selection of the most appropriate technique for evaluating a particular concept.

Of the diversity of research techniques that are available, five distinct approaches have been applied to monitoring communication networks and message diffusion in organizations. These approaches are:

1. The *duty study*—using this approach, key respondents are furnished with a means of recording their communication behavior, and either continuously or periodically record the nature of their communication and the personnel with whom they interact.

2. The use of *observers*—trained observers accompany key respondents and record their communication behavior. This is essentially similar to the duty study, but does not require the respondents to take responsibility for recording their interaction.

3. The *cross-sectional* interview or questionnaire—perhaps the "standard" social science research technique, where all (or a sample of) members are asked to report their overall patterns of interaction. The emphasis here is on establishing general behavioral tendencies, from which specific message-handling activities can be inferred.

4. The *"small-world"* technique—this approach is based on following a message destined for a specified receiver, and tracing the steps that the message follows to reach this person. A specific message (usually in print form) is introduced into an organization and traced from person to person.

5. The study of the *diffusion* of selected messages—in contrast to the establishment of general patterns of message handling (as in approach 3), or the path to a specified receiver (as in approach 4), the diffusion approach focuses on the actual pathways many types of messages follow in their movement through the organization. By following a variety of messages (typically ones that occur "naturally," i.e., are not specifically created for a research study), this approach allows the measurement of the effects of the system on the message itself.

Each of these five approaches has its strengths and weaknesses, its advantages and disadvantages, in terms of measuring the seven concepts presented above. In the section below, the approaches are described in greater detail, and an assessment of each one is made.

The duty study. The duty study has been used by several researchers, including Burns (1954), Hinrichs (1964), Farace and Morris (1969), Conrath (1973) and others, to elicit information on the communication activities either of a random sample, or (more commonly) of purposively selected key individuals. These might be important managers, persons designated as liaisons, or other individuals from whom detailed reporting of communication activities is required. The technique requires respondents to record their communication activities, often throughout the entire day. In some cases, fixed or random time periods are sampled, with the appropriate time period indicated by a device that they carry. For example, randomly initiated time frames can be established by using a device which randomly emits an audible tone (Martin, 1967).

The duty study can potentially provide very detailed reports about the communication load that these individuals carry, and the communication network that they are linked into. It can also be used to determine the relative amount of time the respondents spend on communication that serves different functions. Because of the demands on respondent's time and the mass of "raw" data that is generated in a study of this kind, however, it is impractical as a way to determine the network or communication structure of all organizational members. This method is suited to assessing message distortion only in terms of the input and output differences in messages by that one individual. The duty study is not appropriate for defining actual message pathways, the rates of message flow, or the redundancy of the network.

The duty study also obviously demands a high degree of respondent cooperation and involvement over a considerable period of time. The technique is thus very costly to the system, and offers precise data only about limited numbers of individuals in most cases. Also, as noted by Farace and Morris (1969), the fact that the respondent is continually aware of this recording activity may make him (and his contacts as well) deviate from normal patterns of interaction and behavior.

The chief advantages of this technique lie in the avoidance of observer bias, and in the avoidance of reliance on memory about communication contacts. It would thus appear particularly appropriate for getting at the communication load carried by key personnel—but not particularly suited to measuring the other concepts.

Observers. The use of observers has long been a traditional technique for obtaining data on organizational communication. As noted by Davis (1953b), such observation was used in the Hawthorne studies of Roethlisberger and Dickson (1946). With this technique, trained observers stay with respondents and record their communication behavior.

Like the duty study, this technique suffers from a major risk of affecting and changing the interaction from its "normal" pattern. Similarly, its greatest use is in describing the communication behaviors of a relatively limited number of key respondents in great detail. Through the careful training of coders and their continuous monitoring of respondents, the technique is well suited to the measurement of the communication load of key personnel. To a lesser degree, this approach could also be used to describe the immediate contacts, or communication environments, of these individuals and their communication-processing behaviors. Similarly, the observer may be able to infer the functions that the communication appears to serve.

However, this approach loses some attractiveness because it is very costly, in terms of the time required by skilled personnel in data collection. Due to its focus on only certain key personnel, the use of observers is also not well suited to the measurement of rates of flow, distortion, and efficiency.

The cross-sectional survey. The cross-sectional survey has been the major research technique used by social scientists for obtaining data about a wide range of concepts, including studies of communication networks and message diffusion. The technique requires interviewing all (or a sample of) the study population about their overall communication patterns. Jacobson and Seashore (1951) reported one of the classic studies of communication structure in an organization in a study based on this approach. Schwartz (1968), MacDonald (1970), and others have also used this basic approach. Typically, respondents are asked to identify the persons with whom they talk, the various functions of the interaction, and its importance. From these data, the communication networks are then mapped out, using hand or computer-based techniques such as those described in Chapter 8.

As a result of this approach, the cross-sectional study is particularly suited to the description of relatively stable and enduring networks as they operate "on the average." The technique allows the identification of crucial communicators and the incumbents of key roles (such as liaisons and bridges), and also permits gross measurement of load and redundancy.

While being well suited to the description of general patterns of communication, however, the approach is based on general perceptions and extended recall. Thus it is not a very precise means for getting at the efficiency or redundancy of pathways for particular, specific messages. Also, due to the problems of extended recall, the survey is not well suited for measuring distortion and rates of flow. As noted by Farace and Morris (1969), direct interviewing is best suited to the measurement of highly salient or important aspects of a respondent's communication, but not to the recall of detailed aspects of his interaction.

The "small-world" approach. The "small-world" studies conducted by Milgram (1969), Shotland (1969), and others have focused on the linkages that respondents choose when asked to transmit a message to a specified person whom they do not know personally, using only those intermediates they know. The technique has many similarities to "chain" letters, where one person writes another, asks for something (say a recipe) and also requests that others be contacted for the same item. In this way a "pyramid" of results builds up and supposedly accrues to the participants in the chain. The essential feature of the small-world approach is that it describes *potential* networks, not necessarily those that are usually (or even ever) in use. In the same way that chain letters can lead to relatively infrequent or unusual contacts, small-world studies can activate highly unlikely linkages.

In the small-world studies, each person in the chain only passes the message on to one person, an approach which reduces the likelihood of measurement of contact redundancy. Similarly, because only one route taken by a message is documented, it is not suited to general descriptions of communication load, or to the actual networks that would normally be activated.

However, a relatively minor change to the standard technique, such as asking each person in the chain individually to encode the message, would allow some assessment of distortion. While primarily focusing on the number of links, and therefore efficiency, the technique also offers a way to distinguish the networks developed for different types of communication.

A major drawback to this approach is its high degree of artificiality. It is based on an introduced message and a relatively unreal task—forwarding the message, via persons who are personally known, to an unfamiliar target. Therefore, it is unlikely to reflect the actual communication patterns that would occur in the day-to-day activities of most organizations, except perhaps in the activity of the "grapevine." Where a researcher wants to focus on the operation of the informal communication network, or grapevine, then this approach may offer useful advantages.

The message-diffusion approach. A major research thrust by social scientists with diverse backgrounds has been in the study of the diffusion of news, the diffusion of innovations, and the flow of influence. Deutschmann and Danielson (1960) is a classic study of news diffusion; Rogers and Shoemaker (1972) present a major synthesis of the diffusion of innovations literature; and the classical study of influence was the Erie County study by Lazarsfeld, Berelson, and Gaudet (1948). The major thrusts of this vast body of research are summarized by Tannenbaum and Greenberg (1968) and by Rogers and Shoemaker (1972). In all of this research the focus has been essentially on the diffusion of one message (or innovation) through some specified social system. In general, the diffusion of innovations research has been characterized by a heavy dependence on long-term recall, while the social-influence and news-diffusion studies have focused on recent, high-salience messages.

Davis (1953 a, b) was one of the first persons to advocate this type of approach to the study of organizational communication. His approach, described as ECCO analysis (episodic communication channels in organizations), usually focuses on an internally generated message (e.g., a new organizational policy) and traces its diffusion through the organization. By following one message in its movement through the organization, this approach is readily suited to measuring rates of flow, distortion of messages, redundancy, efficiency of the activated linkages, the patterns of diffusion for messages seen as serving different functions, and to a lesser degree, the structure or network.

As Davis (1953b) notes, this approach offers the major advantage of dealing with actual concrete messages, rather than gathering information about general perceptions or predispositions. Also, there are major advantages that accrue from being able to build up the temporal sequence of the actual flow of the message. Finally, by collecting data immediately after the message has diffused, this approach does not suffer from the disadvantages of contamination, reactivity or long-term recall that are inherent in some of the other approaches.

The disadvantages of the approach include the apparent need to make a complete census of the study population in order to complete the description of the diffusion. Another problem, one that confronts all diffusion research, is the *time* dimension. The complete diffusion of any given message (or innovation) may take a very long period of time, and thus the effort to obtain a complete diffusion pattern must be weighed against the rapid loss of recall for many messages as the collection of data is delayed. Also, in common with the small-world approach, each message describes a unique diffusion pattern that may or may not approximate a somewhat stable and generalized communication network. Finally, this approach also introduces the problem of having to select a research vehicle (message) on short notice in order to follow its diffusion. This short period for data collection will be particularly acute if more routine and less salient messages are selected.

Despite these problems, the summary of each technique in Table 9-1 indicates that this approach does appear to be particularly well suited to the collection of data relating to the concepts or measures that were noted earlier in the chapter. Given the predicted transitory nature of many future work groups, it

Table 9-1. The suitability of differing research techniques to the measurement of selected indicators of communication network performance.

	\multicolumn{7}{c}{Network-performance measures}
Research technique	Structure	Load	Rates of flow	Distortion	Redundancy	Efficiency	Functions
Duty study	0*	2	0	0	0	0	1
Observers	1	2	0	0	1	0	1
Cross-section	2	1	0	0	1	1	2
"Small-world"	1	1	1	1	0	2	1
Diffusion	1	1	2	2	2	2	2

*2 = Very suitable technique
1 = Moderately suitable technique
0 = Basically unsuitable technique

may frequently be unnecessary to census the whole organization. Instead, the research can concentrate on whether newly organized groups have formed active linkages to crucial message sources, and whether these linkages are of the desired degree of efficiency, and so on. Similarly, by using such techniques as group interviewing or telephone interviews, it may be possible to collect the data very rapidly and with a minimum of contamination. The major advantages of this approach—the following of "real" messages and the description of the current pattern, not a prior generalized pattern—clearly fit into the important need to determine whether the right materials are getting to the right people at the right time.

Further development of this approach will hopefully answer some of the methodological questions that do not appear to have definite answers at this time. Some of these are:

1. How stable are the patterns of message diffusion within a particular system or subsystem—how many messages have to be traced in order to obtain a "true" picture of the network?

2. How frequently will these patterns change, and what factors will encourage or suppress these changes?

3. How can data be obtained with a minimum of delay, without contamination of the subsequent continued diffusion of the message?

Given that this method requires only a simple and short questionnaire or interview, Davis (1953b) notes that it has significant advantages of being relatively low in cost, having a short response period, being simple to administer and respond to, and being adaptable to many different situations. To these advantages can be added the further one that this approach is closely tied to the large body of diffusion literature, which offers a number of propositions and generalizations that relate to temporal and spatial message flow.

THE ANALYSIS OF COMMUNICATION "RULES"

As described in Chapter 6, communication "rules" are the norms or guidelines that regulate the interaction among pairs of organizational members. Most commonly, the manager-subordinate dyads are of major interest, since these dyads comprise the primary linkages for authority and compliance. However, much of the discussion that follows is applicable to coworkers as well, who often must also have well-functioning communication norms if they are to work cooperatively on a committee, project, or other assignment.

In this section, a set of questions is presented that deals with some of the most commonly encountered communication-rule areas. Their use to generate knowledge about the communication relationship in dyadic situations will be demonstrated; this knowledge can then be used in a diagnostic review and appraisal process that generates conclusions about the state of the organization's communication system, or about the communication performance of groups or individuals within the system.

The initial condition for carrying out a hierarchical communication "rules" analysis is that each person's immediate manager (and subordinates) be clearly identified. This would seem like a rather straightforward task—all employees should at least know who their immediate manager is, and managers are assumed to know whom they manage. This turns out not always to be the case, however. Some subordinates, even when given a common definition of "immediate manager" (for example: "the person who tells you what work to do and who evaluates that work") cannot report who the person is. This may be due to confusion resulting from the arrival of a new manager, a refusal to acknowledge someone as the manager, or the fact that no one in the organization is actually performing in the capacity of manager for the individual. It is also possible that the person may have more than one person performing this function.

Similarly, for designating subordinates, managers may not know that a new arrival is a subordinate, may decline to acknowledge the individual as a subordinate, or may erroneously consider someone a subordinate who in fact is another individual's subordinate.

All of this may seem unnecessarily detailed, but it is important to keep in mind that the foundation of a communication-rules analysis rests on the proper *pairing* of known individuals so that the elements of their relationship can be elaborated. Consequently, in most rules studies the initial task is to generate a hierarchical list or "map" of manager-subordinate relationships in which each person is clearly and unambiguously placed in the overall hierarchy. For a given individual, the manager must be identified; and if the individual is also a manager, the subordinates must be identified. Each person has only one immediate manager; each manager has one unique relationship with each subordinate. See Fig. 9-1 for an example of this point.

There are some instances, however, where the managerial structure is so unclear as to make this step impossible to achieve. In one particular situation, several levels of management were simply vacant—unfilled—and two levels did not have "acting" managers. In addition, nonmanagerial subordinates could have as many as four separate managers, depending on the time of day they worked and the overlap time between their work shift and that of the managerial personnel. There were professionals (psychologists, social workers, psychiatrists) who had implicit managerial control over the individual.

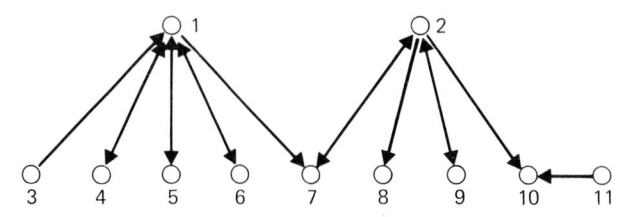

216   "Tools" for Diagnosing Communication Problems

Initial supervisory hierarchy: Dyads 1-4, 1-5, 1-6, 2-7, 2-9 agree on who is manager and who is subordinate. Problems of disagreement are 3-1 (not acknowledged by 1); 1-7 (not acknowledged by 7, but 2-7 agree); 2-8 and 2-10 (8 and 10 don't acknowledge); 10 and 11 are on same organizational level and should not be hierarchically related.

Fig. 9-1. Agreement and nonagreement in a manager-subordinate reporting hierarchy.

The person who completed the individual's job-evaluation form was in a central administration office that had no direct contact or control over the person's work. Needless to say, in this extreme situation, the concept of a "rules" analysis had to be abandoned until the basic managerial hierarchy was sufficiently straightened out to reduce the ambiguities and uncertainties of the existing structure.

However, in most situations, a relatively small percentage of manager-subordinate relations fall into this confused situation. In these cases, a systematic procedure must be adopted to resolve any discrepancy. Typically, *subordinates* should identify their managers, since it is the subordinate's perceptions of who provides supervision that presumably affect the subordinate's actions. Once subordinates indicate who their manager is, that person can provide an evaluation of the communication relationship with each subordinate.

The outcome of this first step is a "map" of the organizational hierarchy, as perceived by the members in it, and this map is often of considerable diagnostic value. Where areas of important disagreement over manager-subordinate relations exist, these will be identified. It is also possible to discover those individuals who subordinates designate as managers, but who are not "officially" considered as such by top management.

Once the organizational hierarchy is determined, the next step in the analysis is to define the communication-rule topics that are considered important in the investigation. As noted earlier, these rules will differ from situation to situation. An example of such rules, however, is given in the list below, where some 13 questions covering different aspects of the manager-subordinate interaction are presented.

Some of these questions deal with the content dimensions of interaction, while others deal with procedural matters. In addition—and this is often important as a diagnostic device—a number of these questions have a supplement which asks respondents to indicate their level of *satisfaction* with the other person on that aspect of their interaction. By adding satisfaction to the initial question (which asks for a description of the relationship), an important dimension of evaluation has been built into the questioning procedure.

Communication "Rules" Between You and Your Immediate Supervisor*

1. When two people begin to communicate, one of them has to ask for it to happen. Over time, when you and your supervisor communicate, who usually asks for the meeting to occur? Does he usually suggest...do you usually suggest...or do you suggest it about equally?

    ____I usually suggest the meeting.
    ____He usually suggests the meeting.
    ____We suggest it about equally.

2. Of course, it takes two to communicate. Sometimes one person suggests a meeting, but the other one delays it, or puts it off, or says he can't get together. Between you and your supervisor, who is more likely to put off getting together?

    ____He is more likely to put it off.
    ____I'm more likely to put it off.
    ____We do it about equally.
    ____Neither one of us puts off or delays a meeting.

3. When two people get together, one of them has to decide what they'll talk about. Generally, when you and your immediate supervisor talk, who usually decides on the topics to be discussed?

    ____He usually decides.
    ____I usually decide.
    ____It's split about evenly between us.

---

*These questions were developed in a research project in which all three authors participated. The project's over-all director was David K. Berlo, then chairman, Department of Communication, Michigan State University.

3a. How satisfied are you with this arrangement?

____I'd like more to say about what we talk about.
____I'm satisfied.

4. When you and your immediate supervisor talk, whose problems do you talk about for the most part...his problems or your problems?

____We talk more about his problems.
____We talk more about my problems.
____It's split about evenly between his and my problems.

4a. How dissatisfied are you with this arrangement?

____I'd like to talk more about problems I have.
____I'd like to talk more about problems he has.
____I'd like to talk more about both his problems and my problems.
____I'm satisfied the way it is now.

5. When you and your immediate supervisor talk about *work* problems (getting the job done, scheduling, etc.), who usually brings them up?

____He does.
____I do.
____It's split about evenly between us.
____We don't talk about work problems.

5a. How satisfied are you with the amount of talk you and he have about work problems?

____I'd like to talk more about work problems.
____I'd like to talk less about them.
____I'm satisfied now.

6. When you and your immediate supervisor talk about *people* problems (interpersonal relations, counseling people, solving personal problems, etc.), who usually brings them up?

____He does.
____I do.
____It's split about evenly between us.
____We don't talk about people problems.

6a. How satisfied are you with the amount of talk you and he have about people problems?

____I'd like to talk more about people problems.
____I'd like to talk less about them.
____I'm satisfied now.

7. When you and your immediate supervisor talk about *new ideas* or *new ways of doing things*, who usually brings the subject up?

____He does.
____I do.
____It's split about evenly between us.
____We don't talk about new ideas or new ways of doing things.

7a. How satisfied are you with the amount of talk you and he have about new ideas?

____I'd like to talk more about it.
____I'd like to talk less about it.
____I'm satisfied.

8. When two people talk, one or the other sometimes interrupts to change the subject. When you and your immediate supervisor talk, who usually interrupts to change the subject?

____He does.
____I do.
____It's split about evenly between us.
____Neither one of us interrupts to change the subject.

8a. How dissatisfied are you with having your immediate supervisor interrupt you?

____I wish he'd let me finish things without having him interrupt me.
____I'm satisfied.

9. Sometimes communication is interrupted by outside interference, e.g., phone calls, someone breaking into the conversation, etc. When this happens while you and your immediate supervisor are talking, who are the outsiders looking for usually?

____They are usually looking for him.
____They are usually looking for me.
____It's split about evenly.
____We aren't interrupted when we're talking with each other.

9a. How satisfied are you with the amount of these outside interruptions?

___I wish there were fewer of them.
___I'm satisfied.

10. When two people are talking, somebody has to decide to end the conversation. Over time, when you and your immediate supervisor communicate, who usually ends the conversation...who decides when it is time to stop?

___I usually end the conversation.
___He usually ends it.
___We do it about equally.

11. Overall, who would you say does most of the talking in your conversations with your immediate supervisor?

___He talks a lot more than I do.
___He talks a little more than I do.
___We talk about the same amount of time.
___I talk a little more than he does.
___I talk a lot more than he does.

11a. How satisfied are you with this?

___I'd like to do more of the talking.
___I'd like to do less of the talking.
___I'm satisfied.

12. On the average, aside from brief greetings, how often do you and your immediate supervisor communicate (face-to-face or telephone)?

___Several times a day.
___Once a day.
___Once or twice a week.
___Once or twice a month.

12a. How satisfied are you with the frequency with which you and your supervisor communicate?

___I'd like to get together more often.
___I'd like to get together less often.
___I'm satisfied.

13. When you and your immediate supervisor talk face-to-face, how long do your talks together usually last?

　　____5 minutes or less.
　　____6–10 minutes.
　　____11–20 minutes.
　　____21–30 minutes.
　　____More than 30 minutes.

13a. How satisfied are you with the length of these conversations between you and your immediate supervisor?

　　____I'd like to get together for longer periods of time.
　　____I'd like to get together for shorter periods of time.
　　____I'm satisfied.

Given this fairly broad sampling of "rules" questions, let us look now at the way this information can be assembled in order to provide us with information about a manager's interaction with subordinates. Two questions will be used. Question 12, dealing with frequency of interactions, and 12a, dealing with satisfaction with frequency.

In Chapter 6, *agreement* in a communication relationship was shown by comparing the similarity of viewpoints held by both manager and subordinate. In this example, the manager could have selected one of four responses to indicate the general frequency of contact with the subordinate—several times a day, once a day, once or twice a week, or once or twice a month. The subordinate had the same four options. They agree on this aspect of their relationship to the extent that they select the same response option, regardless of which option they select. If both report that they talk several times a day, there is perfect agreement; if both say they talk once or twice a month, there is still perfect agreement.

If, however, the subordinate reports that they talk once or twice a month, while the manager says they talk once or twice a day, then they do not agree. They have revealed a discrepancy in their perception of the communication relationship. By itself, it may mean nothing; on the other hand, it may be the beginning of a series of findings that reveal that there is a fundamental communication problem between the two. Furthermore, it may eventually lead to the finding that the manager has communication difficulties with many of his subordinates, or that certain subordinates have particularly frequent problems with their supervisors.

Let's move on to Question 12a, concerning their satisfaction with the frequency of their interaction. Do they both agree on that issue, or not? Both individuals may agree, or disagree to varying extents. Notice that their agreement on this question is independent of what they may have said on Question 12 concerning the actual frequency of their interaction.

By now the possibilities on agreement regarding frequency and satisfaction with frequency should be apparent. Each combination leads to a somewhat different conclusion and potential course of action. For example, both may agree that they seldom communicate, and both may be dissatisfied. In this case, the appropriate steps may be to facilitate more frequent interaction between them (perhaps give the manager additional support so that individual meetings with subordinates can be held). Both persons may agree about the frequency of their interaction, yet differ in satisfaction. In this case, the source of dissatisfaction would have to be determined, as well as the cause (and remedy) for it. Other combinations of agreement on frequency and satisfaction can be traced out, and decisions made as to whether any changes are needed in this aspect of the manager-subordinate communication relationship.

It should be apparent that this type of analysis can be systematically extended to cover the combined response of all subordinates for a given manager on this item. The manager can obtain a detailed picture of how frequently his or her subordinates perceive their contacts to be, and how satisfied they are with these frequencies. At the same time, the manager can learn about the degree of agreement that exists with subordinates on interaction frequency and the associated satisfaction.

Furthermore, this analysis can be extended in the same fashion to each of the other rule areas that are studied. If handling of the interruptions in interactions is the rule under study, it can be analyzed in the same fashion as frequency. Or if the question of who dominates the interaction is important, it can also be summarized and studied. In each case, it is important to note that the rules deal with specific behavioral aspects of communication, and where disagreement exists and communication problems are detected, it should be possible to develop specific behavioral solutions to the problems.

In addition to the concept of agreement, the concept of *accuracy* was discussed in Chapter 6. Accuracy, as noted earlier, reflects how clearly or fully one member of the managerial pair knows the position of the other on the rule in question. Does the manager know what the subordinates consider their frequency of interaction to be? Does the manager know how satisfied they are with the interaction frequency? The answer to this question comes by having each person rate the communication rule in terms of how the *other* person will describe it. For example, the manager states what the subordinate will probably specify as the frequency of their interaction. To the extent that the manager's rating of the frequency corresponds with the way the subordinate actually rates it, then we conclude that the manager's view of this portion of their overall communication relationship is accurate.

Accuracy, then, serves as yet another mechanism by which the communication relationship can be searched for problem areas. Perhaps the manager thinks that the interaction is as frequent as the subordinate desires, and that the subordinate is satisfied with the situation. Yet, when one examines the actual response of the subordinate, it turns out that communication frequency is much different and satisfaction is much lower. By informing a manager about the accuracy with which communication relationships with subordinates are perceived, a definite beginning can be made to identify and alleviate specific communication problems.

Accuracy can also be extended to more than one subordinate by pooling the accuracy levels for a manager across all his or her subordinates. Similarly, the accuracy concept can be systematically applied to each of the communication-rule areas that are under scrutiny. By summarizing these results, across subordinates and across rule areas, it is possible to develop a very detailed portrait of the communication relationship between a given manager and subordinates. This portrait can then serve as a starting point for an analysis and corrective feedback program for improving managerial communication.

For example, in one situation, the authors obtained this type of response from some 150 first-line supervisors and managers, and summarized it for each of them in an individualized letter. This letter was sent to their homes, in order to protect the confidentiality of the results. The letter indicated what communication rules had been studied, how the manager stood in absolute terms and in relation to ratings given the other supervisors, and where the individual's specific strong and weak points were.

Then, in the organization, a series of small-group discussions were held where the highlights of the results for all managers were reviewed, although no individuals were singled out. Problems that occurred frequently across the group were identified, and potential solutions to the problem areas were discussed. The advantages and disadvantages of the problem solutions, and the feasibility of implementing them, were also discussed. The managers returned to their work groups with, presumably, a clearer understanding of communication behaviors as seen by their subordinates. Furthermore, they possessed a set of suggestions for clearing up some of the more common problems. (Steps were taken to ensure that managers could not attribute a specific rating or set of ratings to any subset of their subordinates.)

OTHER DIAGNOSTIC COMMUNICATION TOOLS

One of the frequently studied aspects of organizational functioning is "climate," a term that generally refers to the overall "environmental quality" of the organization in which an individual participates. While there are numerous definitions of climate, it typically includes such factors as the kind and type of supervision, morale of organizational members, their attitude profiles on a variety of organizationally related topics, the general physical conditions under which they exist in the organization—in short, any and all factors that have an appreciable influence on the performance of organizational members.

The general term "organizational climate" is often refined into specific categories, of which "communication climate" is most centrally related to our view of communication and its role in the organization. Communication climate can encompass a variety of dimensions of its own, including openness, trust, quality of message flow, availability and usefulness of feedback channels, and other concepts that reflect one or another of communication activities in an organization.

A thorough and critical review of organizational climate in general, and managerial climate in particular, is found in Redding (1972, pp. 111-138; 139-422). Under the heading of managerial climate (which includes a strong component of communication), Redding singles out five subtopics for extended discussion: (1) supportiveness, (2) participative decision-making, (3) trust, confidence, and credibility, (4) openness and candor (with special attention to "upward" and "downward" communication), and (5) emphasis upon high performance goals.

Research instruments are available for measuring different facets of the organizational climate, or communication climate in particular, and these can be used to pinpoint "trouble" areas among employees and among a larger set of topics. Often, organizations maintain a system for routinely monitoring climate in order to establish, initially, a baseline for management, and then to track changes in climate as different programs are introduced, reorganization takes place, environmental factors intrude on the organization, or other forces for change are at work.

One other frequently used diagnostic tool is the "readership study," which is an analytic procedure for determining the amount and type of employee use of print and electronic messages distributed internally. Surveys are often conducted to determine how much (or how many) messages are consumed by employees, what the retention of their content is, and what features of the messages are most (or least) attractive. These results are used in the subsequent design and dissemination of additional in-house messages, and can prove useful in making cost-effectiveness decisions when alternative media or message "packages" are available for selection.

SUMMARY

This chapter has been primarily focused on the conceptual aspects of diagnostic tools for studying message flow and communication rules in organizational settings. Some of the main steps and procedures involved in using these techniques are indicated, and some of the uses to which they can be put are described. Their implementation can readily prove very informative to the organization.

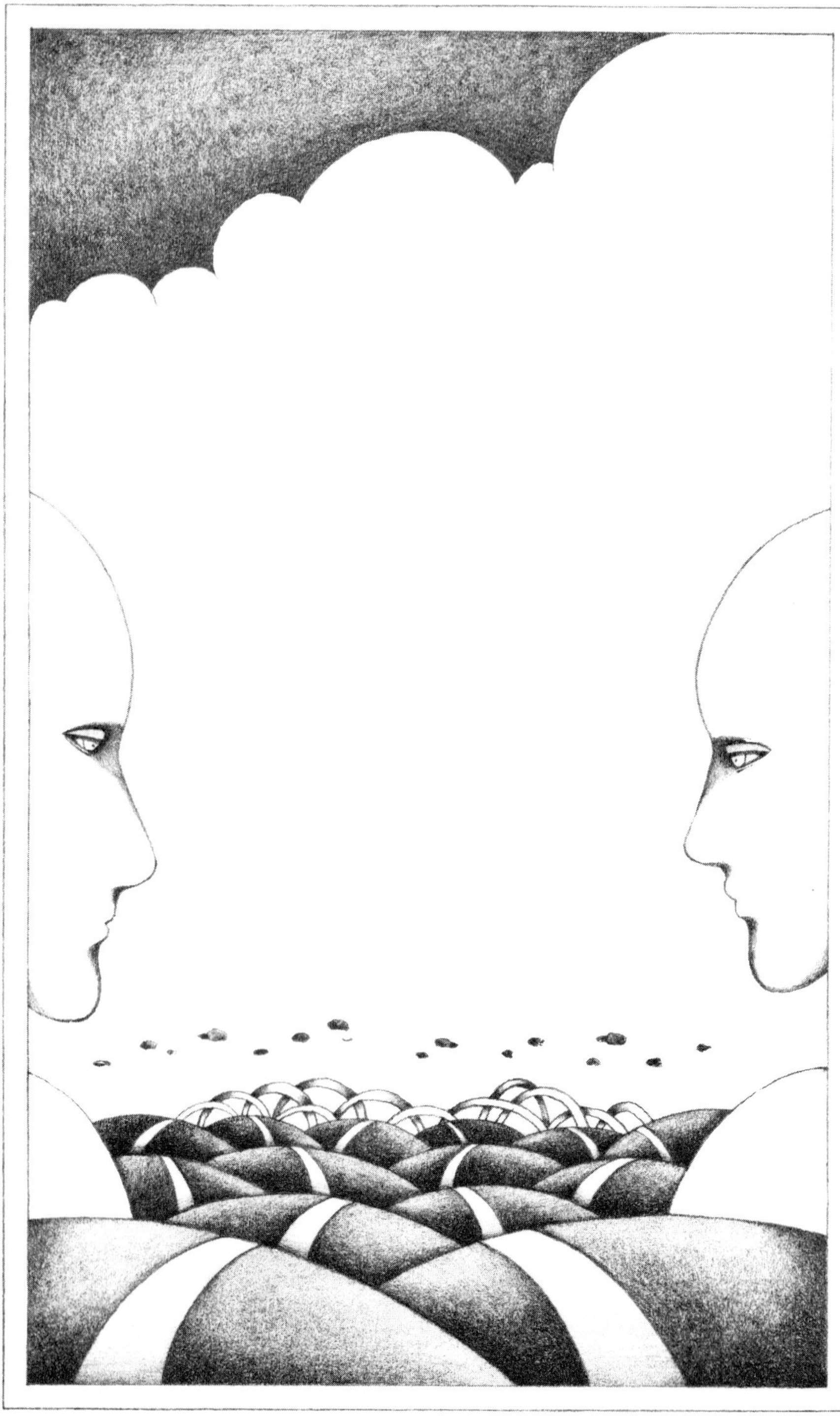

Macro-network Analysis— Procedures and Uses

10

The hypothetical organization, Company X, that we introduced in Chapter 8 to provide a setting for the discussions of network analysis, will be used here to provide a practical illustration of the Work Communication Network and the Innovation Communication Network in the organization. The purpose of this section is to show how some of the concepts in Chapter 8 can be specifically applied to an evaluation of the structure of an organization's communication networks.

ASSESSING THE WORK NETWORK

One of the most useful ways of arranging network data is to superimpose the communication network's groups on the organizational hierarchy of the company. Coded charts are often very useful for this purpose. Figure 10-1 presents the organizational hierarchy (identical to Fig. 8-1 in Chapter 8), with the addition of distinctive codes to represent the four communication groups in the Work Network.

The four groups are derived from an analysis of the communication links reported by members of the organization, in response to a question asking for the names of persons they communicate with about work-related matters. These links are symmetric because they are based on the relation "communi-

228   Macro-network Analysis—Procedures and Uses

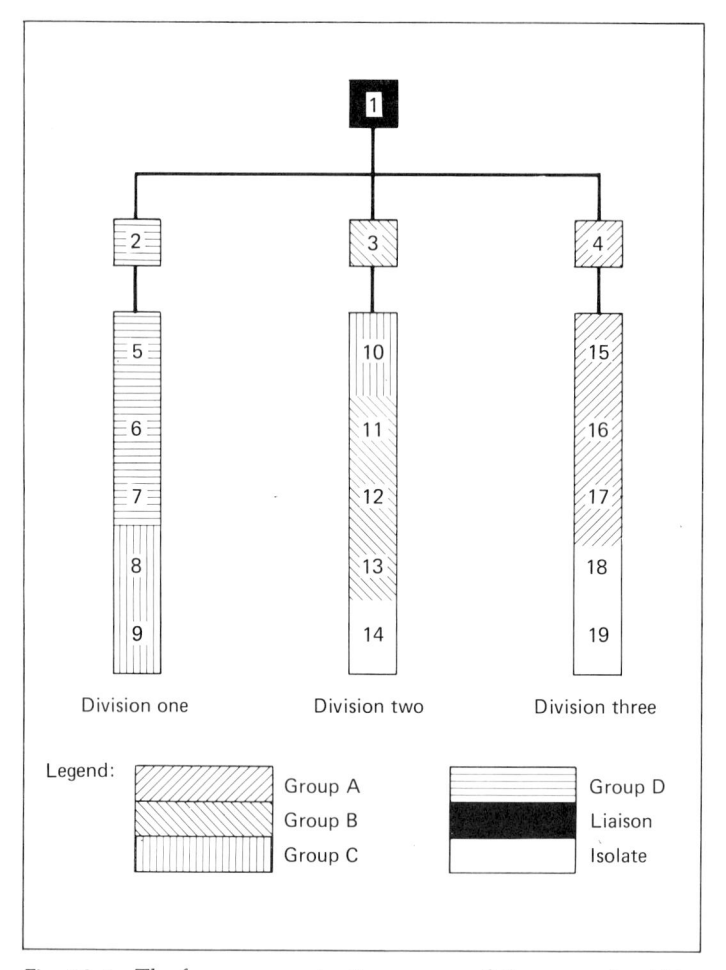

Fig. 10-1. The four communication groups of the network within the organizational hierarchy. The legend shows the codes that distinguish each communication group, liaisons, and isolates.

cates with"; they are equal in strength, because a link is either present or absent; and they are reciprocal, because both persons were required to report the link before it was officially counted. The groups are derived by applying the criteria outlined under the section headed *Communication Network Roles* in Chapter 8 to the data provided by the members. The other roles are developed in the same fashion. Person 10, for instance, is a member of Group C, and Group C's hierarchical location in Company X can be easily located in Fig. 10-1. With this simple graphic representation, a network analysis begins to provide some useful information, e.g., the location of each individual group in the overall hierarchy.

Group A of the Work Network has four members (4, 15, 16, 17), all of whom are in Division 3. But what of Division 3's other two members, Persons 18 and 19? They are both isolates (blank code). Thus, Division 3 has two individuals who appear to be isolated from (i.e., not communicating with) others in their division. Obviously, this finding might be used by management to institute changes for improving the performance of Division 3; at the least, the reasons why the two are isolates need to be determined.

Communication Group B contains members 3, 11, 12, and 13. All of them are in Division 2, and, therefore, seem to be a logical grouping. However, of the two remaining members of Division 2, one is an isolate (14) and the other (10) is a member of an entirely different communication group—Group C.

Group C has members from Division 1 (8, 9) and from Division 2 (10). C does not fit "neatly" into the corporate hierarchy. A finding such as this may indicate that a reevaluation of the corporate hierarchy may be in order. Since these three persons function together as a group, would a better corporate structure result if they were placed under the same supervisor? Would a breakdown in communication within this division be dysfunctional to the organizational hierarchy? Or does a high need for coordination normally cause members of one division to interact more with members of another division than they do with members of their own division?

Network analysis cannot give definitive answers to questions of this type; instead, it functions as a *diagnostic device* to locate such problems and to provide initial suggestions for solutions that are logical from a communication-flow viewpoint. These issues should become clearer later in the chapter, on examination of the bridge and liaison patterns of these groups.

Communication Group D (Persons 2, 5, 6, 7) appears quite consistent with the organizational hierarchy, since all members are found in Division 1.

Thus far, merely by "fitting" the communication groups into the corporate structure of Company X, some interesting patterns have begun to emerge, e.g., isolated persons, unexpected groupings. Additional important observations can be made by examining Figs. 10-2 and 10-3, which show the bridge and liaison links between the groups.

Figure 10-2 shows the bridge links between the four groups. Note that Group A has two links to the other three groups, while Group B, on the other hand, has bridge links to all three of the other communication groups. Also note that Group C (the "problem" group) appears to be reasonably connected to the other groups since it has two bridge links.

In Fig. 10-3, Person 1 emerges as the only liaison in the organization. This would seem plausible since Person 1 is hierarchically located above all the groups. Also, it is not surprising that each of Person 1's links are to the division managers, Persons 2, 3, and 4. This is worthy of note, since Group C,

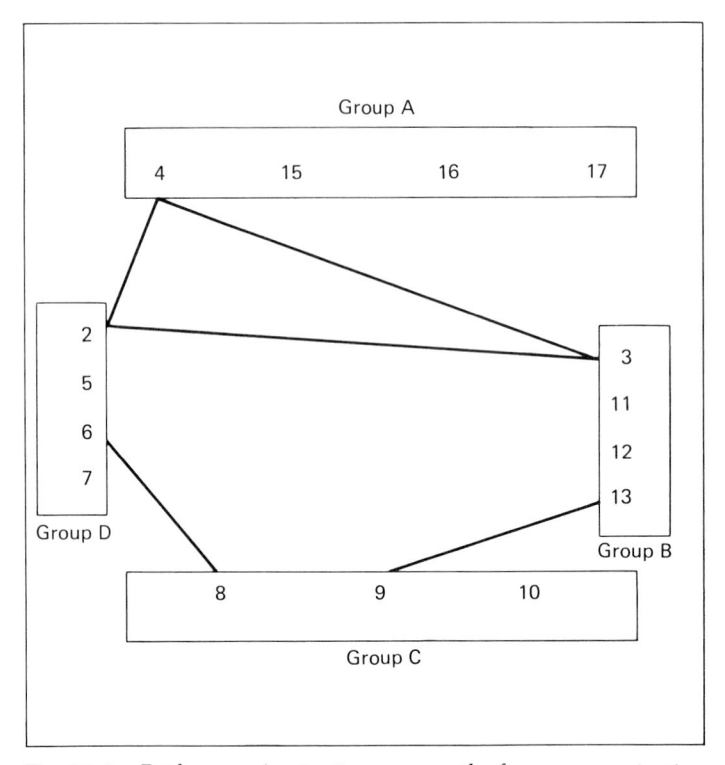

Fig. 10-2. Bridge communications among the four communication groups of the Work Network.

which is not an organizationally recognized grouping, is thereby cut off from direct communication with Person 1. Not all liaisons, however, are "higher-level" people; liaisons may—and frequently do—function at other levels in the organizational hierarchy. The placement of liaisons is an important point for management attention.

As a result of the analysis, Company X might want to consider a reevaluation of its hierarchy to create a more functional environment for Group C. Also, the fact that three of the 19 individuals within the organization are isolated might well indicate a need to improve the communication channels to these persons. A repeat of the network analysis after restructuring has taken place should indicate whether these problems have been cleared up (or new ones created).

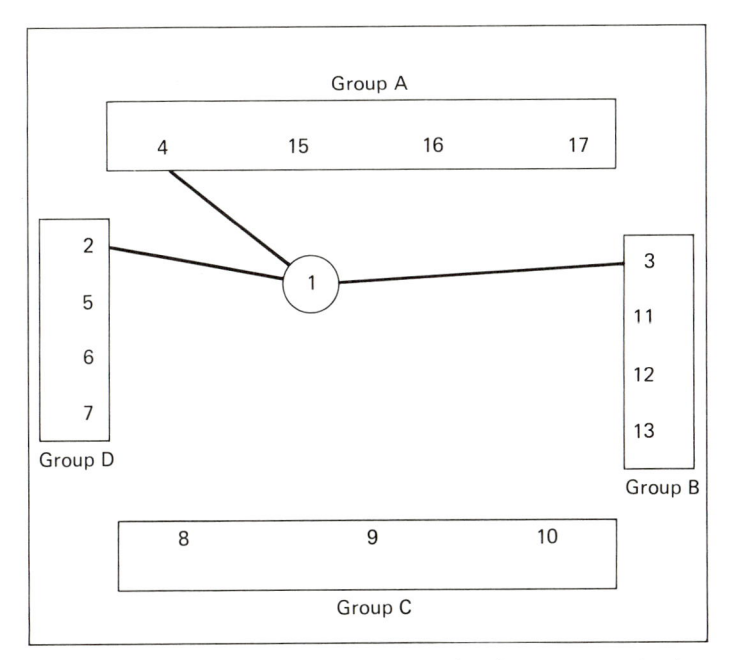

Fig. 10-3. Liaison connections among the four communication groups of the Work Network.

ASSESSING THE INNOVATION NETWORK

The preceding discussion has revealed some things about the Work Network. It is often useful, however, to consider more than one kind of network within an organization; in fact, many different networks can be considered, as we noted earlier. Next the diffusion of new ideas through Company X via the Innovation Network is discussed.

Figure 10-4 shows three isolated communication groups in the Innovation Network; these groups are quite different from those in the Work Network. It is interesting to note how these groups fit into the formal organizational structure: Group P, with nine persons, is found in Divisions 1 and 2 of Company X. This innovation-communication group does not extend to higher managerial levels.

232 Macro-network Analysis—Procedures and Uses

Group Q, however, has membership in all three divisions of Company X. It is obvious from Fig. 10-4 that this is not an ordinary set of persons. Indeed, it is composed of *only* higher managerial personnel. Communication about new ideas, then, seems to be shared only with other managers at this level.

Communication Group R contains three persons and is found in Division 3 of Company X. Note also from Fig. 10-4 that there are two isolates in this network (15 and 16) and one liaison (14).

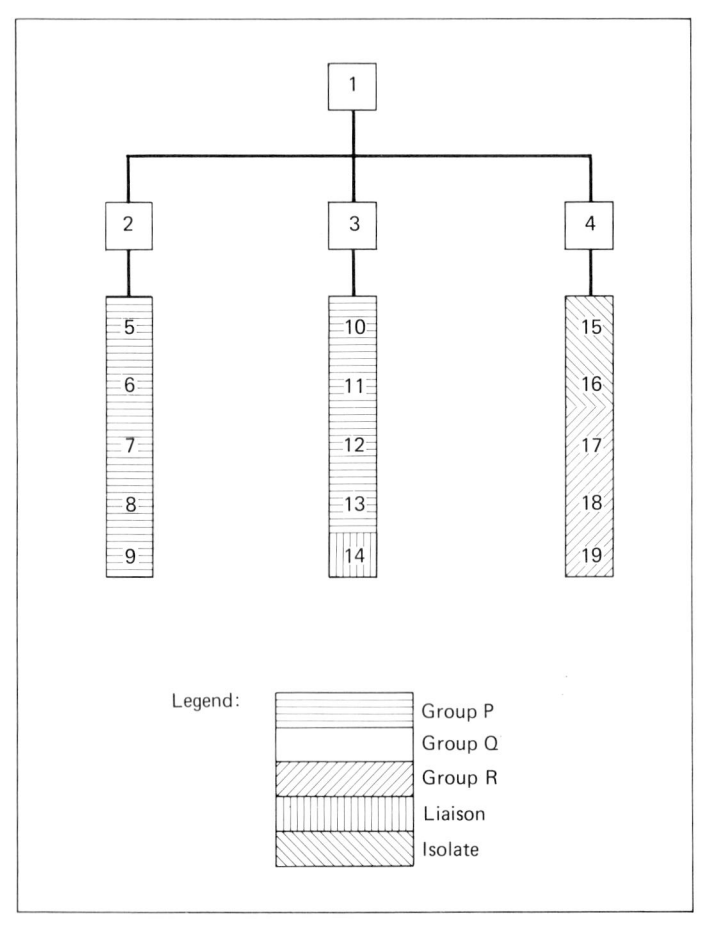

Fig. 10-4. The three communication groups of the Innovation Network within the organizational hierarchy. The legend shows codes distinguishing the communication groups, liaisons, and isolates.

Before additional evaluation of the network is undertaken the relationships among the communication groups should be considered. To do this, reexamine the intergroup connections, i.e., the bridge and liaison linkages. Figure 10-5 shows the bridge connections in the same manner as was done in Fig. 10-2 for the Work Network. None of the groups is isolated; in fact, all of them have a good number of links. Group P, for example, has the most links (7), which is due in part to the fact that it has the most members.

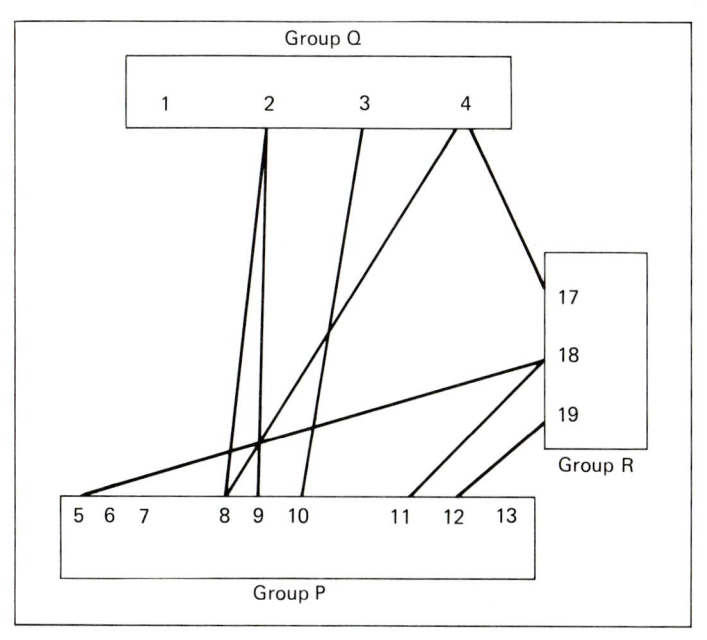

Fig. 10-5. Bridge connections among the three communication groups of the Innovation Network.

The other type of intergroup connections, the liaison links, is depicted in Fig. 10-6. There is also a large number of liaison links here, with one liaison (14) connecting all three groups.

COMPARISON BETWEEN NETWORKS

Additional insight into the functioning of the organization is often provided by comparing the networks to one another. Often, findings in one network may uncover (or explain) problem areas in another. For instance, according to Fig. 10-1, Persons 14, 18 and 19 were all isolates. When the Innovation Network is examined, a possible explanation for their behavior in the Work Network is found—they seem to be persons who are very active innovators and perhaps less important (communicationally) as workers.

Person 14 was an isolate in the Work Network, but Fig. 10-6 shows that Person 14 is an important liaison in the Innovation Network. Similarly, Persons 18 and 19 are in a well-functioning communication group in the Innovation Network (Fig. 10-6).

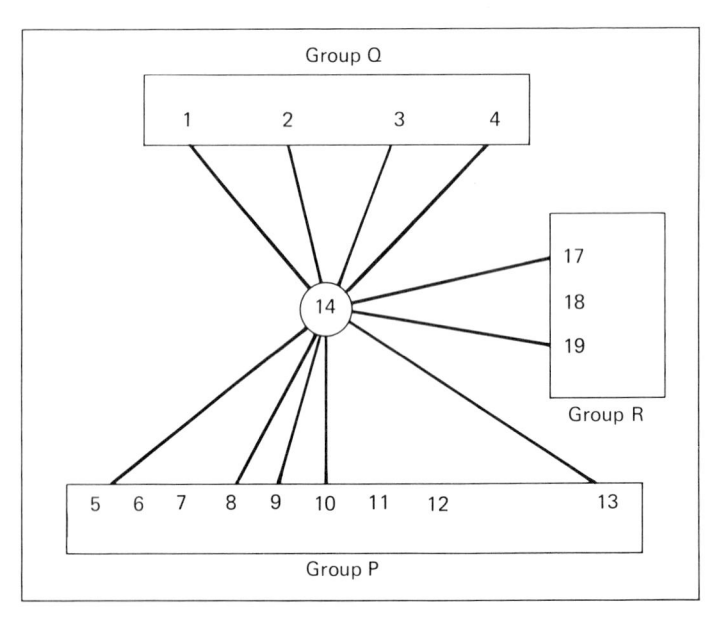

Fig. 10-6. Liaison connections among the three communication groups of the Innovation Network.

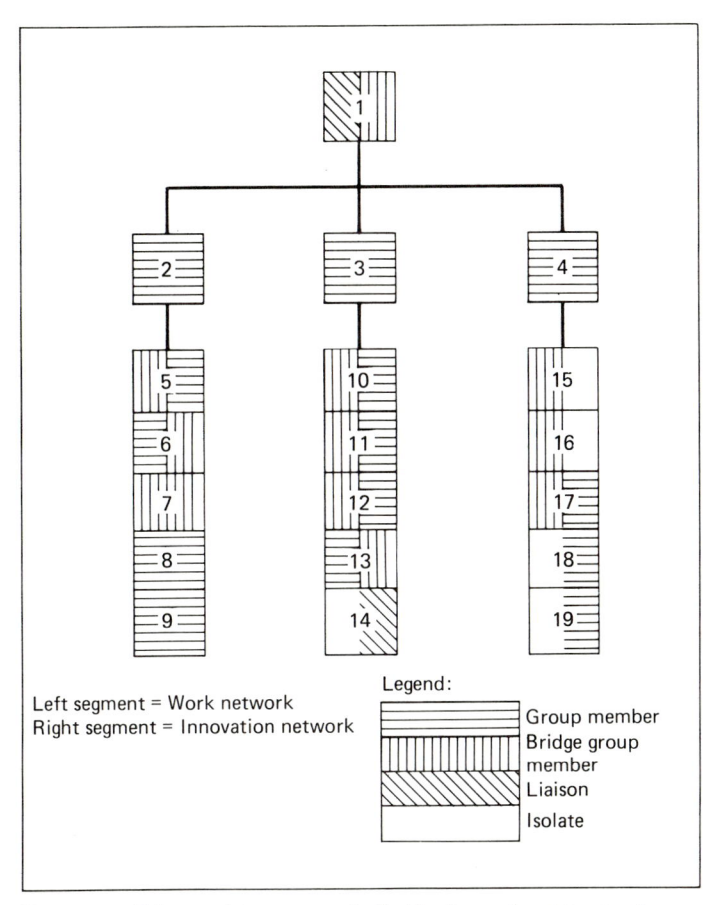

Fig. 10-7. Relationships among individual memberships in the Work and Innovation Networks. Left segment of each person's box shows role in Work Network, and right shows Innovation role. Legend specifies which of four roles a person occupies in each network.

Also interesting is Person 1, who was the liaison of the Work Network. In the Innovation Network, however, Person 1 is not a liaison, and does not have any bridge contacts. Person 1's only inter-group link is a liaison contact. This might be interpreted to mean that "the boss" is more concerned with getting the job done than with dealing with new ideas.

A useful technique for comparing various network roles is illustrated in Fig. 10-7. Much of the information in Figs. 10-1 to 10-6 is combined here. Each person's hierarchical position has been divided into two segments (since there are two networks), and each segment has been coded according to the person's role in the network. The accompanying legend explains the coding scheme.

Examining Person 1's position shows that Person 1 is a liaison in the Work Network and a group member in the Innovation Network. Person 14, on the other hand, is an isolate in the Work Network and a liaison in the Innovation Network.

Comparing networks in this manner calls attention to individuals who fulfill broadbased communication roles or who are more limited in their network participation. A person who is an isolate in *all* networks, for instance, may have significant communication problems. Similarly, Persons 2, 3, 4, 8 and 9 "stand out" since they are bridges in both networks.

The network-analysis techniques described so far provide data on two levels: first, the general adequacy of the overall organizational hierarchy; and second, an evaluation of specific groups within the hierarchy. A third level of details, to be discussed in the following section, deals with individuals.

SOME DESCRIPTORS FOR COMPANY X: GROUP AND INDIVIDUAL

In this section various aspects of the networks are quantified as ratios or percentages. This allows greater precision in describing communication groups and individuals within the networks. It also permits communication networks to be studied in relation to other important organizational dimensions, such as productivity, climate, error rate, and employee satisfaction, since these numerical measures can be related to other measures. First, descriptors are presented which may be used to assess the communication groups. Then, ways of evaluating individual network members are shown. Since the Work Network of Company X contained only a few bridge and liaison links, the Innovation Network will be used to show group descriptors. In developing individual indicators, data and examples from both the Work and the Innovation Networks will be used.

One of the first evaluations that can be made of a communication group is its *connectedness*. This measure uses the number of links that exist among the members of a group, and is expressed as a proportion of the total possible number of links in the group. If a group has only a few of its possible "within-group" links it is said to be "loosely" connected. If everyone in a group had a link with everyone else, its group connectedness would be 100 percent. This measure is influenced by group size, since members of larger groups may find

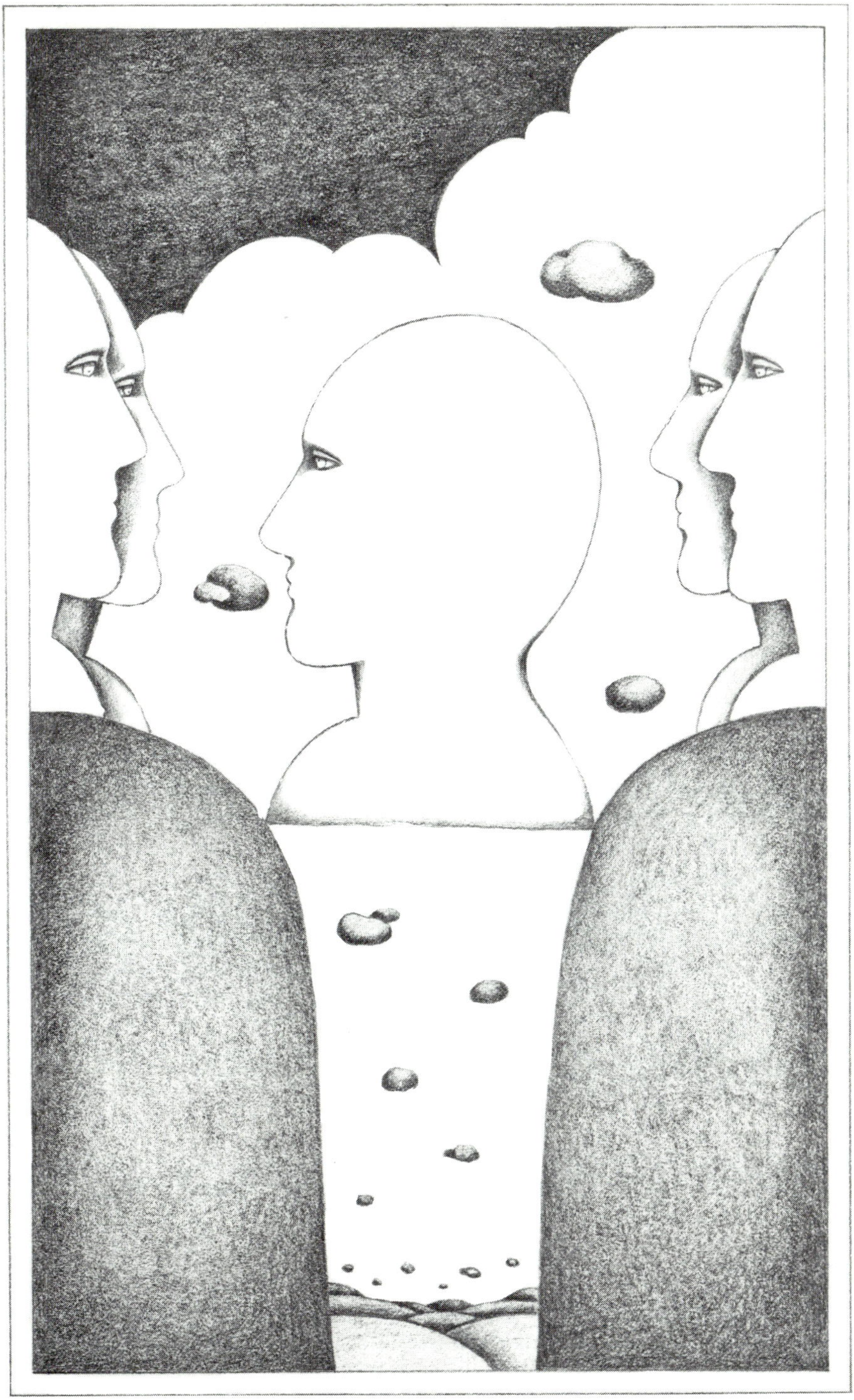

that it is more difficult to communicate with everyone else. Thus, as shown in Table 10-1, the largest group also has the lowest group connectedness, i.e., Group P has a value of 63 percent. Similarly, Group R has a 100 percent connectedness; however, since it only had three members, this is not a surprising result.

Table 10-1. Summary values for the three communication groups of the Innovation Network.

Group	Number in group	Connectedness	Group bridge linkage	Group liaison linkage
P	9	63%	44%	46%
Q	4	75%	31%	36%
R	3	100%	25%	18%
			100%	100%

Group *bridge linkage* and group *liaison linkage* are both straightforward quantifications of Figs. 10-5 and 10-6, respectively. These measures indicate the percentage of total bridge or liaison contacts that exist in a group. In Fig. 10-5 there are a total of 16 bridge links. Group P has seven of these 16, which accounts for 44 percent of the total. Group Q has five (31 percent), and Group R, four (25 percent).

Calculations for group liaison linkage are made just like those for bridge linkages. There are 11 liaison links; Group P has five links or 46 percent of the total, Group R, 18 percent, and Group Q, 36 percent. The format of Table 10-1 is very useful for "ranking" different groups, especially when a large number of groups is present.

There are, of course, many ways by which a communication group may be described; the descriptors presented here are both straightforward and useful. At this point two concepts should be briefly reintroduced, however—*indirect links* and *dominance*.

The concept of "distance" is based on direct and indirect links, as noted before. For instance, suppose an individual (like Person 1) does not have a link with another person (say, Person 2). However, Person 1 does have a communication link to someone else (say, Person 3) who is linked to Person 2. Thus for communication to flow from Person 1 to Person 2, it would have to pass through Person 3. The link from Person 1 to 2 is called an indirect link, a two-step link. Similarly, indirect links may be three-step, four-step, or n-step in length. In a communication group, the maximum "distance" can be examined between any pair of group members, or methods of quantifying "average distance" could be developed.

"Dominance" describes the degree to which communication in a group is centered around only one (or a few) of the persons in the group. A group with low dominance would be one in which a large proportion of members communicate directly with each other; therefore the ratio of direct to indirect links is quite high. In a group with high dominance, communication is centered around one (or a few) person(s), yielding a low ratio of direct to indirect links, i.e., information in the group flows to others only through these dominant individuals.

Normally, the choice of how many and what types of measures to use when undertaking the analysis of a large organization remains up to the particular investigator. There are many measures to choose among, so the primary criterion for selecting a particular measure must involve careful consideration of the purpose of the investigation.

As has been pointed out earlier, if a network is large and/or richly connected, a hand-drawn graphical display of every single link for every person in the network is both cumbersome and impractical. It is possible, however, to present data for each individual in tabular form, thus providing a basis for evaluation of individual communicators. Table 10-2 illustrates a typical but abbreviated tabular summary for the Work Network of Company X.

Data in this table are arranged by communication group, and then by person-identification number, in ascending order. This number is entered in the first column. In the "Role" column the designation "M" is used for group member, "B" is used for bridge-group member, "L" indicates liaison, and "I" represents an isolate. The column entitled "Group" designates a person's group affiliation. Naturally, liaisons and isolates are not group members and will thus have no entry for "Group."

The next seven columns give two breakdowns for the type of communication links possessed by an individual. The first column indicates a person's total links. The next three, "Within," "Bridge," and "Liaison," describe the individual's internal and external links.

The "Liaison" column, for example, shows the number of links a person has with liaisons. Person 4, for instance, has one liaison contact. If one wanted to locate this liaison contact, he might refer to Fig. 10-3, where it can be seen that the person is Liaison 1 (often, though not in this example, there are several liaisons in an organization). Similarly, if one wanted to know who Person 4's two bridge contacts were, by consulting Fig. 10-2 it would be seen that Per-

Table 10-2. Summary of individual communicators in the Work Network of Company X.

Network member	Role	Group	Total	Within	Bridge	Liaison	Reciprocated	Unreciprocated	Unacknowledged	% Reciprocity	% Individual connectedness	% Individual bridge linkage	% Individual liaison linkage	% Contribution to group-bridge linkage	% Contribution to group-liaison linkage	% Contribution to between-group linkage
						Links										
4	B	A	6	3	2	1	1	2	3	33	100	67	33	100	100	100
15	M	A	2	2	0	0	0	1	1	0	67	0	0	0	0	0
16	M	A	3	3	0	0	0	1	2	0	100	0	0	0	0	0
17	M	A	2	2	0	0	0	2	0	0	67	0	0	0	0	0
3	B	B	6	3	2	1	2	1	3	67	100	67	33	67	100	75
11	M	B	2	2	0	0	0	2	0	0	67	0	0	0	0	0
12	M	B	3	3	0	0	1	0	2	100	100	0	0	0	0	0
13	B	B	3	2	1	0	0	2	1	0	67	67	0	33	0	25
8	B	C	3	2	1	0	1	2	0	33	100	67	0	50	0	50
9	B	C	3	2	1	0	1	0	2	100	100	67	0	50	0	50
10	M	C	2	2	0	0	1	0	1	100	100	0	0	0	0	0
2	B	D	6	3	2	1	2	4	0	33	100	67	33	67	100	75
5	M	D	3	3	0	0	1	1	1	50	100	0	0	0	0	0
6	B	D	4	3	1	0	3	0	1	100	100	50	0	33	0	25
7	M	D	3	3	0	0	2	0	1	100	100	0	0	0	0	0
Liaison(s)																
1	L	–	3	–	–	–	3	0	0	100	–	–	–	–	–	–
Isolates																
14	I	–	1	–	–	–	1	0	0	100	–	–	–	–	–	–
18	I	–	1	–	–	–	1	0	0	100	–	–	–	–	–	–
19	I	–	1	–	–	–	0	1	0	0	–	–	–	–	–	–

sons 2 and 3 were involved. Also, the number of within-group (internal) links, plus the number of bridge and liaison (external) links, equal the total number of links.

The last three columns under the "Links" section of Table 10-2 present the number of reciprocated, unreciprocated, and unacknowledged links for a person. These should also add to equal the total number of links. It is sometimes useful to know which person in an unreciprocated link reported the relationship (assuming symmetry). To do so, the unreciprocated category is subdivided into: (1) unreciprocated links—those people who list a relationship that the other person does not also list, and (2) unacknowledged links—those people who are listed in a relationship which they themselves do not list.

A measure has also been developed by which to identify a person's perception of his or her communication contacts. *Reciprocity* is determined by calculating the percentage of the contacts a person mentions who also mention that person. That is, reciprocity represents the percent of the links a person indicates which are responded to "in kind" by those who are mentioned. For Person 4 it can be seen that one-third of the people mentioned by 4 also respond; Person 4's reciprocity index is therefore 33 percent.

The *Individual-connectedness* measure signifies how many links a person has within the group. If there were 15 members in a group and one member had links with all of them, the connectedness score would be 100 percent. This becomes clearer by examining Person 4, who has three within-group links. Since there are only three people in this group (besides Person 4), connectedness must be 100 percent since communication with all three takes place.

Two other individual measures are *individual-bridge* and *liaison linkages*, which are distinct from the group-level measures presented earlier. Individual-bridge linkage indicates the percentage of a person's total contacts which are bridge contacts. There is a necessary qualification, however; the individual-bridge linkage measure represents the percentage of bridge contacts a person possesses of the total he or she could possess and *still qualify* as a group member. In the previous example, Person 4 had a total of six contacts. If all six were bridge links to other groups, Person 4 would certainly not qualify as a member of Group 1 (since at least half of a person's contacts must be with people in a group in order to be a member of that group). Thus, a person with a bridge-linkage measure of 100 percent would have half of his or her contacts within a group and the remaining contacts would have to be with persons in one other group. In other words, the person would have the highest percentage possible of contacts to other groups and still remain a group member. On the other hand, a person without bridge linkages would have all contacts within his or her own group (or with liaisons and others).

Another measure of an individual's linkage to other groups is individual-liaison linkage, which is obtained in a manner identical to individual-bridge linkage. The individual-liaison linkage measure indicates the proportion of a person's links that are to liaisons. Again, since a person could not have *all* links to liaisons and still be a group member, this quantity has been expressed as a percentage of the *possible* number of liaison links a person could have and still belong to a group. Thus, individual-liaison linkage, like individual-bridge linkage, can range from zero percent to 100 percent.

A measure that signifies the percentage of bridge links which an individual provides to his or her communication group is *contribution to group-bridge linkage*. If a person's communication group has ten bridge links, one involving the person, the contribution to group-bridge linkage would be one-tenth, or ten percent.

The *contribution to group-liaison linkage* provides a measure of the proportion of the group's liaison contacts which are supplied by each person. Thus, if a person's contribution to group-liaison linkage were 50 percent, then one-half of all the liaison contacts to the group would involve this person.

Contribution to between-group linkage—for this measure, the bridge and liaison links have been combined for a group and a determination has been made of the proportion of the total between-group linkage which is contributed by each individual. For example, if a group had five liaison links and five bridge links, then the total number of links for that group would be ten. If a person within this group provided three of the bridge links and two liaison links, the total contribution would amount to five of the group's ten contacts, or 50 percent. This measure, then, combines contribution to group-bridge linkage and contribution to group-liaison linkage.

So far, Table 10-2 has been discussed as a means of analyzing and evaluating the total network characteristics of individuals. To do so, the row of figures for any given individual is examined. A second useful set of results in the table is found in the columns, which should be examined for distinctively high or low values. For instance, considering the "contribution to between-group linkage" column, Person 4 of Group A provides 100 percent (note also that Person 4 is the manager of this group). Interesting observations may be made when this value is highest for a person other than the designated supervisor.

The discussion so far has centered on the Work Network. To complete our set of metrics for Company X, it is necessary to provide a Summary of Individual Communicators table for the Innovation Network. Thus, a separate table is needed for each network unless the data are presented in a combined format such as in Table 10-3.

In Table 10-3, data are arranged by person, not by communication group. The table shows how a person performs in both communication networks. For instance, Person 1 is a liaison in the Work Network with a reciprocity of 100 percent. In the Innovation Network, however, Person 1 is a group member with a reciprocity of 50 percent. Person 18, on the other hand, is an isolate in the Work Network. In the Innovation Network, however, Person 18 is a group member with fairly high individual values.

The advantages of comparing several networks were discussed earlier (increased perspective, confirming trouble areas, etc.). One drawback, how-

Table 10-3. Combined individual profiles for both networks of Company X.

Network	Role	Group	Total	Within	Bridge	Liaison	Reciprocated	Unreciprocated	Unacknowledged	% Reciprocity	% Individual connectedness	% Individual bridge linkage	% Individual liaison linkage	% Contribution to group-bridge linkage	% Contribution to group-liaison linkage	% Contribution to between-group linkage
Person 1																
W	L	–	3	–	–	–	3	0	0	100	–	–	–	–	–	–
IN	M	Q	4	3	0	1	2	2	0	50	100	0	50	0	25	10
Person 2																
W	B	D	6	3	2	1	2	4	0	33	100	67	33	67	100	75
IN	B	Q	6	3	2	1	3	0	3	100	100	67	33	33	25	30
•																
•																
•																
Person 14																
W	I	–	1	–	–	–	1	0	0	100	–	–	–	–	–	–
IN	L	–	10	–	–	–	7	1	2	88	–	–	–	–	–	–
•																
•																
•																
Person 18																
W	I	–	1	–	–	–	1	0	0	100	–	–	–	–	–	–
IN	B	R	4	2	2	0	3	1	0	75	100	100	0	50	0	33
Person 19																
W	I	–	1	–	–	–	0	1	0	0	–	–	–	–	–	–
IN	B	R	4	2	1	1	1	2	1	25	100	50	50	25	50	33

ever, is loss of the ability to locate high values within groups easily, since the order by groups has been removed. The decision to use one form or another to display results depends on whether group or individual results are most important. The format of Table 10-3 is more useful for individual findings, while Table 10-2 is more helpful in showing relationships within groups.

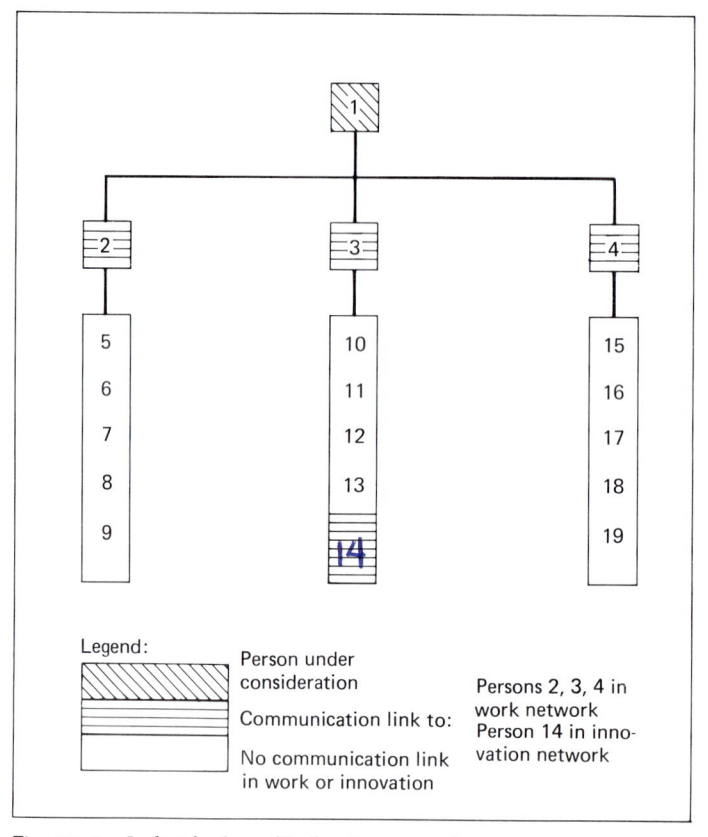

Fig. 10-8. Individual profile for Person 1 showing communication links in the Work and Innovation Networks.

In certain instances, highly specific information about specific individuals in an organizational hierarchy may be desirable, e.g., the organization may wish to consider the communication performance of its high-level supervisors. It would be additionally desirable to compare the performance of individuals within different communication networks. To make such specific evaluations, it is necessary to examine explicitly who communicates with whom; this information is readily available. To merely examine, however, with whom each person communicates would be to examine a tremendous amount of raw data. Therefore, a method which summarizes the results and provides the desired "between network" comparison is needed. To do this, a drawing is made for each person being considered; these drawings are merely the organizational hierarchy with certain codings provided. These drawings are compiled for all network members to create an "individual communicator's portfolio." An example of one such drawing is shown in Fig. 10-8.

FURTHER COMMENTS ON APPLICATIONS OF NETWORK ANALYSIS

There are several general problem areas where network techniques can prove especially useful in the organizational setting. If organizations are viewed as sets of interdependent individuals, linked through communication, then the lengthy example just given shows how certain functional traits related to the "health" of the communication network can be monitored. The examples focus on the location of different types of groups, their inter-group linkages, the presence of isolates, and their relationship to the authority hierarchy or to other network-content dimensions.

Networks can also be viewed from the perspective of each individual member, and close attention given to his or her needs for communication, and sources of communication. By analyzing the communication requirements of the individual, the existing sources of this communication (i.e., the network through which it reaches the person), and the communication outputs of the individual, the adequacy of the person's communication flow can be evaluated. As this overall flow is better understood, it is then possible to improve the organization's *policies* for communication distribution and collection.

Network analysis need not be viewed as a "one-shot" solution to organizational communication-flow problems. In fact, if organizations are considered to be continuing processors of communication, then the performance of the networks is a topic requiring continued monitoring. Hence repeated, unobtrusive monitoring of the overall networks is needed. This will provide such information as whether: (a) needed liaison roles are being filled, (b) individuals or groups are receiving and distributing messages properly, (c) new members of the organization are being integrated adequately into the basic network, and (d) group meetings, memo-distribution systems, telephone networks, and other communication modes are operating. To keep in touch with key network traits, then, routine monitoring of the communication networks is needed.

Implicit in the comments made about network analytic techniques is their use in organizational design or restructuring of personnel work space—such matters as the location and functions of work space. Communication networks are only one of the bases for linkage in an organization (with authority another obvious one), yet the processes of organizing require communication networks to function. Consequently, designing communication networks should receive the same kind of attention on an explicit basis as other aspects of organizational structuring typically do.

There are at least three examples in the organizational world where network techniques are used in varying ways explicitly to augment the design of organizing structures. One of these is the so-called "office-landscape" school of design. Basically, in this procedure, communication data are gathered reflecting the task-related and other types of interactions that occur in an office setting.

Then, in the simplest case, an entire physical layout of work stations and offices is designed around the resulting patterns of communication. Often, a simple principle is followed: those individuals (or groups) whose work requires the most direct interaction are placed closest to one another. Sometimes, unalterable physical constraints in the form of existing office structures (such as walls and floors) will dictate a placement of work stations that is less than optimal. And, of course, the prerequisites of top-level management often lead to network arrangements at variance with other criteria.

The second example is in the same industry that provides communication technology. Firms in this industry develop telephone networks that are designed to replace the need for direct face-to-face interaction, and/or to facilitate it. The major telephone industries, as well as smaller competitive firms, offer services to clients that can include an analysis of the intra-organizational electronic communication patterns among members. Given these results, hardware systems are then designed and installed to handle the internal flow of a portion of the organization's total information-handling activities.

The third example is the emergence of so-called "word-processing" systems, which are generally oriented towards automated production of print messages, whether by typewriters, copying machines, or other similar devices. Some firms in this industry also provide network analytic services analogous to those we have been describing.

SUMMARY

The communication structure of an organization is composed of one or more networks enabling the movement of communication among its members. It is this communication movement, along with the movement of materials and energy, that allows basic organizing processes to occur, and that provides the "grist" for control and coordination of the organizing processes. The proper functioning of these networks is vital to any success that is achieved in attaining goals or objectives at the individual, group, or whole-organization level.

This chapter was devoted to a detailed example of the application of network analysis to a hypothetical organization, with emphasis on the kinds of results and evaluation of networks that can be gleaned from such an analysis for the possible improvement of the functioning of the networks. The use of network analysis to evaluate the communication flows of an organization, including repeated monitoring of these flows over time, was described. Finally, some broader applications of network analysis to organization design and restructuring in specific industries were described.

11 Managing Communication

All organizational members "manage" their communication activities, in the sense that they follow procedures for gathering messages, processing messages in different ways, storing and retrieving messages, and even disseminating some of them. This is not to say that all members are equally effective or efficient in their use of communication. Nor does it imply that all organization members are involved in an equal amount of communication activity —clearly, some types of organizational roles contain far more communication responsibility than others. But the important point here is that organizing processes require parallel communicating processes so that goals and objectives can be met.

Consequently, the appropriate uses of communication should be the responsibility of all organizational members. There have been many instances mentioned in previous chapters where communication breakdowns have the potential for creating havoc in the organization. These included basic misunderstandings in the meaning assigned to symbols, failure to identify key communication mechanisms influencing other aspects of organizational behavior, inequity in distribution of communication load, failure to deal with the subtleties of communication rules, inadequate group communication processes, deficiencies in the organizational communication networks, and many other topics. Clearly, the resolution of such a broad spectrum of potential problems cannot be left unattended by organizational members. Since communication problems can be created by almost any organizational member, all members should share in the responsibility for avoiding or limiting these problems.

The recognition of shared responsibility for managing communication is a crucial beginning towards grappling with the problem. However, it is only the first of several such steps; it is easy to pay "lip service" to it, and is quite unproductive unless further definite steps are carried out. Earlier, four major steps in the evaluation of an organization's communication system were presented; they bear repeating here:

1. Select concepts to describe current communication practices and procedures—the "patterns" of communication.

2. Implement techniques for the rapid and economical description of these patterns, for reporting on the "state of the system."

3. Develop criterion measures (policies) to evaluate the degree to which current patterns meet current needs in the organization.

4. Implement programs to correct deficiencies in communication patterns, and repeat the three previous steps.

The present chapter is based on the premise that, while effective organizational communication is based on the composite performance of its members, mere acknowledgement of the premise is insufficient. More specifically, what is required is that the communication responsibilities of each organizational member be clarified, be conveyed to the member, and become part of the person's overall performance assessment. In other words, communication activities should become as explicit a part of job-performance appraisal as many other activities, such as output, attendance, and quality now are.

In order to carry out the four-step diagnostic improvement procedures noted above, it is not realistic to assume that organizational members with primary responsibility beyond communication can adequately do the job. Instead, individuals whose primary function is managing the communication aspects of the organization are needed. And, of course, in many organizations, such individuals (or units) already exist. They are found in such diverse areas as personnel, training, public relations, corporate communication, human resources, internal publications, marketing communication, and manpower development. The remainder of this chapter presents a discussion of some of the *job responsibilities* of a communication manager, drawn both from the activities that are frequently performed by individuals in these job areas and from our own suggestions about what should be done by these "commu-

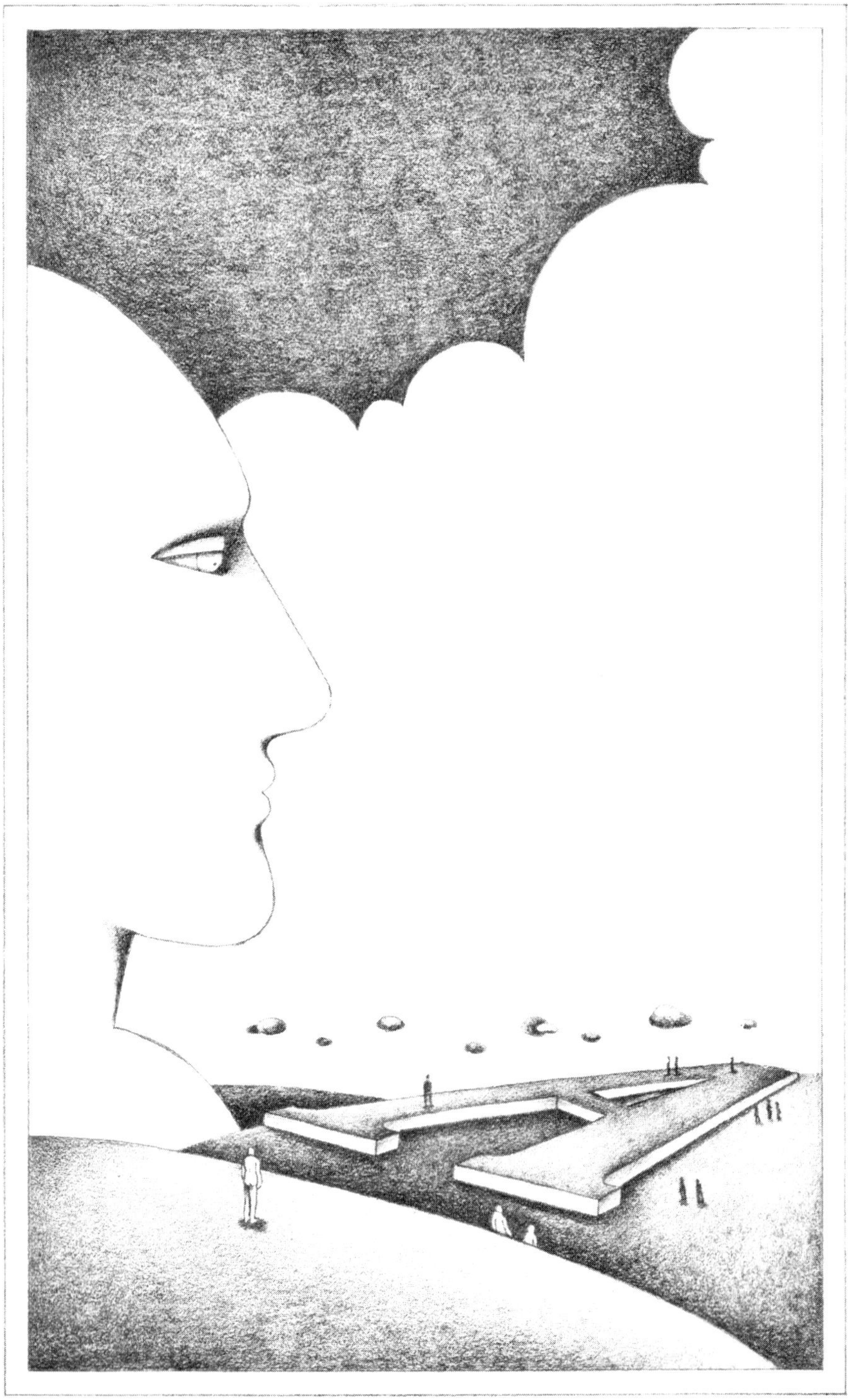

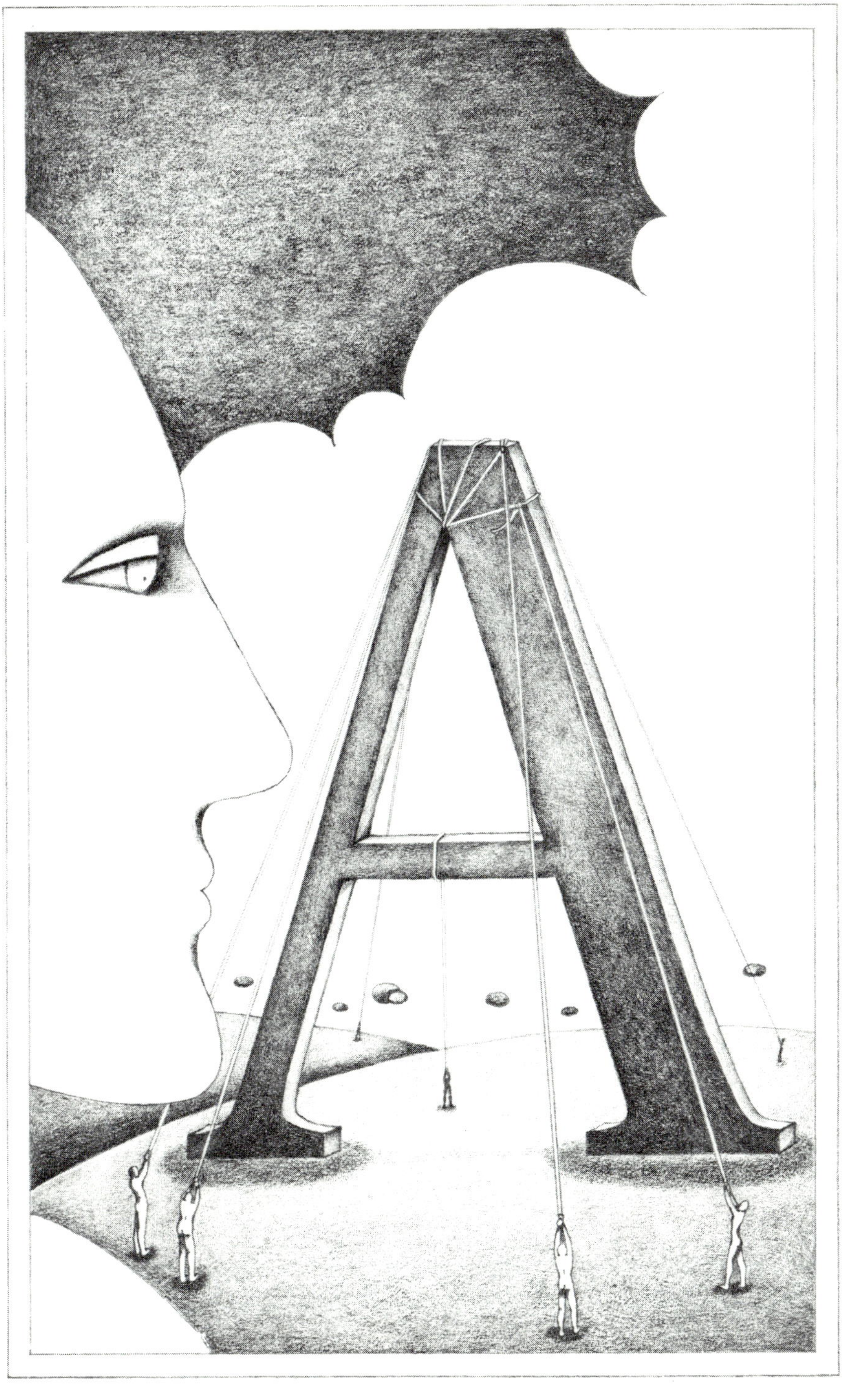

nication managers." In effect, this chapter contains an illustration of the major skills and types of knowledge required of a communication manager.

WHAT DOES A COMMUNICATION MANAGER DO?

A person whose job responsibilities encompass a broad array of communication management is a very busy individual. In general, the communication manager should be located at the center of message flow in the organization. This means that the manager has knowledge of all important types of message flow (although the amount of direct control over that flow depends on the willingness of top management to delegate this authority). By operating in or near the center of the organization's message flow, the manager is able to serve as a bridge or liaison to the other units in the organization, and hence directly affect such characteristics as the quality, quantity, timing, and form of the messages these units receive and send.

The communication manager participates in meetings with other managers in at least two capacities. First, as other managers make decisions that will have to be conveyed to organizational members, it is the communication manager's task to determine the optimum procedures for doing this. Such decisions obviously require a considerable amount of knowledge about communication and about the specific organizational setting as well. The second way in which the communication manager interacts with other managers is in making the basic decisions of communication policy: What will be the organization's general way of dealing with the different types of communication problems it faces (for example, how much emphasis—if any—to place on the encouragement of new ideas about improving internal efficiency)? These two activities are very important influences on the long-run performance of the communication manager, because these decisions set the limits or constraints on what the communication manager can and cannot do. In general, the remaining relevant managerial actions can be grouped into the basic communication processes—acquisition, processing, storage and retrieval, and dissemination.

In terms of acquisition, for example, when a decision is made to improve the organization's fund of knowledge about changing economic conditions, the communication manager designs a procedure to make acquisition of the needed materials a routine. As messages flow in the organization, managers need efficient ways of categorizing and filing them, of converting them into summary form, and of routinely seeing that they are sent out to others who need them. The communication manager helps design and implement ways of processing these messages.

Storage and retrieval problems can be as simple as establishing a usable filing system, or as frighteningly complex as a large-scale management-information system containing full records on sales, production, forecasts, etc., for a lengthy time period. Communication managers are particularly involved in dissemination problems, for here there are many choices to be made about which channels to use (print, audio, face-to-face), who the audiences are, how to structure the content, and how to have timely dissemination.

With this brief overview of the job responsibilities in communication management, next we turn to a somewhat more extensive discussion of selected job responsibilities.

COMMUNICATION MANAGEMENT: SOME SPECIFIC EXAMPLES

1. *Interact with other managers to develop communication strategies and policies.* This activity is perhaps the most crucial of all that the communication manager engages in, because it is through these interactions that the scope and authority of the position becomes determined. There are two commonly held views about the role of the manager. The first is that the manager is primarily a technician who waits at the fringes of key management decision-making activities and, when told the outcome, goes off and prepares a message for release to the proper audience. The communication manager has no voice in the actual decision, and very little voice in its implementation.

The second view is one that takes communication processes into greater consideration by realizing that the impact of a management decision and the way it is communicated are in fact very closely tied together. Good management decisions are made with a detailed knowledge of the attitudes and probable reactions of the persons affected by the decision; the communication manager should be able to convey information about these persons as the decision is being formulated. Issues that might arise when people attempt to interpret a decision can be considered and planned for in advance. The timing of a new message in relation to others that are taking place can be considered—are there other important communication campaigns underway that might seriously influence how this new message will be interpreted?

The communication manager should be able to indicate the proper sequencing of the message—which individuals should learn about it first, which second, and so on. The question of redundancy is important, from both an impact point of view (how many different messages or channels should be used) and a cost point of view (how much money needs to be spent). The communication manager should be especially helpful in determining the wording of the message in such a way that the intent of the decision-makers is carried out as precisely as possible. Obviously, this kind of activity requires close collaboration between the managers involved in the decision and the communication manager as well.

From the perspective of policy development, the communication manager today operates in relatively fertile areas in most organizations—fertile areas because it is only within the past few decades that top management has developed increasing concern with the communication policies that exist in the organization. There are many examples where communication policy needs to be formulated. And, of course, as the manager becomes successful in this task, then concrete suggestions about what types of policies should be considered become an important "resource base."

There are many areas where policy can be developed. A crucial one is job-performance appraisal—what kinds of communication should take place between manager and subordinate about the work being done, or the topics which should be covered, how "open" the manager should be to disagreement over any subordinate evaluations that are made, how frequently these appraisals should take place, and what kinds of records and substantiation of the discussions should be kept.

Another area for policy development is the whole problem of "How do I find out what's going on around here?" In other words, what kinds of questions should members of the organization expect to find answers to, how should they go about getting answers, and what should they do if the answers they obtain are incomplete or otherwise unsatisfactory? A third example centers on the communication skills of managers—how capable should they be of learning about the work problems or personal problems of their subordinates, how effective should they be at running group meetings intended to inform subordinates about changes in the organization and/or to get questions and reactions from subordinates about various organizational activities? Fourth, how standardized should the rules and procedures for communication be across the different component parts of the organization; under what conditions should different procedures (e.g., different rules for access to managers) be encouraged?

These examples are only four of many that fall under the purview of the communication manager. And, like most policy questions, there is no "right answer" that is independent of the actual situation. What they do suggest, however, is that the communication manager should be responsible for identifying these areas, developing preliminary policy recommendations about them, determining where in higher management to go to get the recommendations considered, and proceeding from there.

2. *Supervise the planning and production of internal and external communication programs.* This heading covers a wide variety of activities, ranging from internal newsletters, newspapers, or "house organs," to mass distribution of memoranda, preparation of speeches for top executives, recruiting new employees, and advertising programs. Depending on the way these tasks are delimited, then, the communication manager can be involved in a very wide range of activities involving message production and message distribution.

Consequently there are many things a manager needs to know in order to perform this task effectively. These include effective writing, alternative costs and effectiveness of different media, the nature of the distribution systems for each medium, and some indication of the kinds of probable outcomes or effects from messages sent along the various media channels. One of the most crucial aspects of this set of tasks is a knowledge of the nature of the audiences for each of the media. For example, an important internal problem for a communication manager is the question of which individuals are reached by the various distribution systems. Only as this knowledge is obtained is it reasonably possible to predict who will actually receive a key message.

An important consideration from the communication manager's viewpoint here is *load*, i.e., the amount and frequency of messages that are being sent to individuals along different distribution systems. Are some systems being used so heavily that people do not always pay much attention to the messages that come along them? Do any of the systems have special "importance" attached to them so that, if used, organizational members are likely to pay close attention to the message (personally typed letters from top organizational managers may fall in this category)?

A policy area requiring the communication manager's attention is found in the question of access rights to the distribution system. What persons, under what conditions, are allowed to introduce messages into the system? Are there prior clearance procedures that are needed to avoid embarrassment if the systems are used improperly? At what level can access take place? Who has the responsibility? How should access be encouraged, discouraged, or generally regulated?

3. *Devise communication programs for organizational units to facilitate production.* For many organizational units, a key to their level of quality output is the flow of work-related messages they need to operate efficiently. The communication manager should be able to examine a work-flow process, identify the pieces of knowledge that members need in order to do their work, and then develop improved systems for providing them with those pieces of knowledge.

For example, consider the case of salesmen in the field, selling a product that requires interaction not only with the main office but with other salespersons as well. What are the things they need to know? Where do they find them out? What problems do they have in getting what they want when they want it? These are the types of questions that a communication manager would address while in the process of evaluating and improving the system for providing work-related messages to some part of the organization.

This idea can be readily moved into the actual organization, where the flow of messages within units or between units can be examined in the same fashion. Basically, the problem is one of identifying the particular networks involved, specifying their major problem areas, and then determining ways to alleviate the problems. The initial task in this activity is a conceptual one on the part of the manager. It need not involve any acquisition of communications hardware, computer facilities, or other items until their need has been fully justified. The greatest problems to be overcome in designing such systems are, initially, conceptual—and only subsequently do issues of technology become important.

4. *Modify and expand the job-performance appraisal system to reflect communication skills.* This topic area is one where the communication manager has an especially sensitive and important role to play in bringing the organization's general philosophy and its communication practices into alignment. An organization's performance-appraisal system represents the central communication linkage between the individual member and the larger organization. Through the appraisal process, the employee is supposed to learn about the strengths and weaknesses of his or her performance as seen by managers, and to recognize the relationship between performance and rewards (pay increases and promotions).

For all employees, but especially for managers, the performance-appraisal process offers an excellent opportunity to tie specific desired communication behaviors and organizational rewards and sanctions together. In other words, as manager-subordinate communication policy is developed and introduced throughout the organization, the appraisal process becomes the appropriate point at which to bring success with communication into the overall reward mechanism. To the extent that managers show they are using the communication policy, then they should be rewarded.

In our experience, when significantly new communication behaviors are expected of managers (e.g., more group meetings, more openness, more concern for work and personal problems, and more searching for answers to subordinate questions), there is often a series of genuine obstacles confronting the managers. Initially, if their work flow is heavy enough and the production demands on them are sufficiently severe, they simply do not have the added energy to adopt the new communication behaviors. The two usual solutions to this are to reduce their work flow or to provide them with some additional administrative support in areas other than communication with subordinates. Of course, it is always possible simply to order them to increase their interaction with subordinates.

When the initial problem is overcome, a second, formidable one arises. Many managers, even with very sincere intentions, do not possess the communication skills they are being urged to adopt. So even if they had the additional energy, they lack the specific skills needed actually to implement the new behaviors. Consequently, a significant amount of time needs to be set aside for training in the desired communication skills. Often, this training can be done within the organization, and typically it should be under the direction of the communication manager.

Given the additional energy, and given proper training, there still remains an extra barrier to overcome. Since communication as a label is often used in organizations, most managers have the problem of deciding how serious top management is when a new "communication program" is introduced. To underscore the concern for improving communication, it is important to make the adoption of these behaviors a part of the larger performance-appraisal process, thus tying together the reasons for increased energy, extra training, and communication emphasis. By incorporating communication skills into the appraisal process, management's full commitment is emphasized far more than if it is kept separate.

5. *Prepare manuals outlining policies and procedures.* This task presents an opportunity to formalize many different aspects of organizational performance in general and communication within the organization in particular. A policy and procedure manual can indicate the desired or preferred communication rules across levels of the managerial hierarchy. It can contain specific directions on where to find out about such topics as benefits, attendance policies, changing jobs within the organization, examinations for promotions, and other issues. The manual can contain statements of the communication responsibilities of all employees, both managers and subordinates. The preparation of this document requires close collaboration with top management to ensure that it is both accurate and complete.

6. *Develop and implement communication training programs.* Two general kinds of communication training programs can prove especially valuable. The

first is a program or set of programs aimed at introducing new employees to all facets of the organization. The content of these programs can cover many topics about the organization—its purpose, the types of work to be done, its values—and can be structured around a variety of media. Besides the traditional lecture or small-group discussion, there are many other possibilities, such as slide shows, audio or video cassettes, brochures, etc. The introductory materials for new employees can be broken down into many units which can be used throughout the early months of the employee's stay with the organization, thus avoiding the frequent "overload" that can occur if too much material is presented too quickly at the outset of the employee's career.

The other type of program which the communication manager can develop focuses specifically on the communication itself. Training programs can be directed toward various levels of employees to provide them with the specific requisite communication skills. These can range from techniques of writing, the conduct of group meetings, managerial communication, and performance appraisal, to fundamental techniques for designing systems to provide a work unit with the desired materials it needs to accomplish its work.

SUMMARY

The role of communication manager is emerging more frequently in organizations as attempts are made on a more formal basis to deal directly with the processes of organizational communication. The task of communication management represents an opportunity to blend practical experience, research, and theory, and bring them to bear on one of the main leverage points in modern organizations—their communication activities.

Top management is beginning to view a communication manager as a person who manages a wide variety of human resources and who is expected to be accountable and assume responsibility for cost effectiveness. Thus it is imperative that communication managers develop and implement a systematic program for improving the communication performance of personnel throughout the organization.

Three actions are required to develop such a program. First, it is necessary to _know how things are_ in the organization's communication system. This implies that the communication system be carefully defined and that procedures be implemented for message flow to all points in the organization, assessment of quality of messages (including such things as timeliness, believability, and relevance), delineation of communication networks, specification of information load, and careful attention to communication relations. Monitoring these various aspects of the system can be accomplished with tools and techniques that are readily available today, and that have been discussed earlier in the book.

The second aspect of the program to improve communication performance is to *decide how the system should operate*. This means that criteria should be established for each aspect of the communication system that is being monitored. For example, levels should be determined and varied according to the people who will read various documents. Network liaisons should be identified and utilized as key information sources. Tolerable amounts of message distortion should be specified for different types of messages.

The third and final aspect of the program is *knowing how to change the communication system*. The key to success in this phase is *institutionalization*. One way to accomplish this is to analyze each job for its communication requirements and incorporate these as a part of the job description. Another approach is to include communication objectives as a part of each person's overall annual objectives and annual performance review. A final way to institutionalize communication change is to include a set of communication objectives as a part of each person's career development.

Taken together, these three steps—monitoring the communication system, establishing criteria for adequate performance, and institutionalizing change—should create a program that will allow a communication manager to improve the communication performance of members of the organization. In so doing, he or she will begin to meet the changing expectations of top management by giving an adequate accounting for management of human resources and by assuming responsibility for cost effectiveness.

Bibliography

ACKOFF, R. (1957). Towards a behavioral theory of communication. *Management Science* 4: 218-234.

ACKOFF, R., and F. EMERY (1972). *On Purposeful Systems.* Chicago: Aldine-Atherton.

AMEND, E. (1971). Liaison communication roles of professionals in a research dissemination organization. Unpublished doctoral dissertation, Department of Communication, Michigan State University.

AMIDON, E. J., and N. FLANDERS (1967). Interaction analysis as a feedback system. In E. J. Amidon and J. B. Hough (eds.), *Interaction Analysis: Theory, Research, and Application,* pp. 121-140. Reading, Mass.: Addison-Wesley.

AMIDON, E. J., and J. B. HOUGH (eds.) (1967). *Interaction Analysis: Theory, Research, and Application.* Reading, Mass.: Addison-Wesley.

ARGYRIS, C. (1957). *Personality and Organization.* New York: Harper.

―――― (1964). *Integrating the Individual and the Organization.* New York: Wiley.

BALES, R. F. (1950). *Interaction Process Analysis.* Cambridge, Mass.: Addison-Wesley.

―――― (1953). The equilibrium problem in small groups. In T. Parsons, R.F. Bales, and E.A. Shils (eds.), *Working Papers in the Theory of Action,* pp. 111-161. Glencoe, Ill.: Free Press.

BARNARD, C. I. (1938). *The Functions of the Executive.* Cambridge, Mass.: Harvard University Press.

BARNES, J. A. (1969a). Graph theory and social networks: A technical comment on connectedness and connectivity. *Sociology* 3: 215-232.

―――― (1969b). Networks and political process. In J.C. Mitchell (ed.), *Social Networks in Urban Situations.* Manchester: Manchester University Press.

BARNLUND, D. C., and C. HARLAND (1963). Propinquity and prestige as determinants of communication networks. *Sociometry* 26: 467-479.

BARRETT, J. H. (1970). *Individual Goals and Organizational Objectives.* Ann Arbor, Mich.: CRUSK/ISR.

BAVELAS, A. (1948). A mathematical model for group structures. *Applied Anthropology* 7: 16-30.

_____ (1950). Communication patterns in task-oriented groups. *Accoustical Society of America Journal* 22: 725-730.

BERLO, D.K. (1969) Human communication: The basic proposition. Unpublished paper, Department of Communication, Michigan State University.

BERRIEN, F.K. (1968). *General and Social Systems.* New Brunswick, N.J.: Rutgers University Press.

BEUM, C. O.,Jr., and E. G. BRUNDAGE (1950). A method for analyzing the sociomatrix. *Sociometry* 13: 141-145.

BLAKE, R.R., and J.S. MOUTON (1964). *The Managerial Grid.* Houston: Gulf.

BORGATTA, E. F., and W. STOLZ (1963). A note on a computer program for rearrangement of matrices. *Sociometry* 26: 391-392.

BOTT, E. (1965). *Family and Social Networks.* London: Tavistock Publications.

BOYD, B., and J. M. JENSEN (1972). Perceptions of the first-line supervisor's authority: a study in superior-subordinate communication. *Academy of Management Journal* 15(3), 331-342.

BRILLOUIN, L. (1962). *Science and Information Theory.* New York: Academic.

BUCKLEY, W. (1967). *Sociology and Modern Systems Theory.* Englewood Cliffs, N. J.: Prentice-Hall.

BURKE, R. J., and D. S. WILCOX (1969). Effects of different patterns and degrees of openness in superior-subordinate communication on subordinate job satisfaction. *Academy of Management Journal* 12(3): 319-326.

BURNS, T. (1954). The directions of activity and communication in a departmental executive group. *Human Relations* 7: 73-97.

CAMPBELL, D. T. (1958). Systematic error on the part of human links in communication systems. *Information and Control* 1: 334-369.

CHAFFEE, S., J. McLEOD, and J. GUERRERO (1969). Origins and implications of the coorientational approach in communication research. Paper presented to the Association for Education in Journalism, Berkeley, California.

COHEN, A. M., E. L. ROBINSON and J. L. EDWARDS(1969). Experiments in organizational embeddedness. *Administrative Science Quarterly* 14: 208-221.

COLEMAN, J. S. (1958). Relational analysis: The study of social organizations with survey methods. *Human Organization* 17: 28-36.

_____ (1964). *Introduction to Mathematical Sociology.* London: Free Press.

COLEMAN, J. S., E. KATZ, and H. MENZEL (1957). The diffusion of an innovation among physicians. *Sociometry* 20: 253-270.

COLEMAN, J. S., and D. MacRAE, JR. (1960). Electronic data processing of sociometric data for groups up to 1,000 in size. *American Sociological Review* 25 (5): 722-727.

COLLINS, B. E., and H. GUETZKOW (1964). *A Social Psychology of Group Processes for Decision-Making*. New York: Wiley. Quote from pp. 214-215, reprinted by permission.

COLLINS, B. E., and B. H. RAVEN (1969). Group structure: Attraction, coalitions, communication, and power. In G. Lindzey and E. Aronson (eds.), *The Handbook of Social Psychology*, Vol. IV (2nd ed.), pp. 102-214. Reading, Mass.: Addison-Wesley.

CONRATH, D. W. (1973). Communications environment and its relationship to organizational structure. *Management Science* 20: 586-603.

CUSHMAN, D., and G. WHITING (1972). An approach to communication theory: Toward consensus on rules. *Journal of Communication* 22: 217-238. Quote reprinted by permission.

DANOWSKI, J. A. (1974). Environmental uncertainty, group communication structure, and stress. Unpublished master's thesis, Department of Communication, Michigan State University.

DANOWSKI, J., and R. FARACE (1975). Communication network integration and group uniformity in a complex organization. Unpublished paper. Department of Communication, Michigan State University.

DAVIS, J. H. (1969). *Group Performance*. Reading, Mass.: Addison-Wesley.

DAVIS, K. (1953a). Management communication and the grapevine. *Harvard Business Review* 31 (5): 43-49.

──── (1953b). A method of studying communication patterns in organizations. *Personnel Psychology* 6: 301-312.

DEARDEN, J., F. W. McFARLAN, and W. ZANI (1971). *Managing Computer-Based Information Systems*. Homewood, Ill.: Irwin.

DeCHARDIN, PIERRE (1961). *The Phenomenon of Man*. New York: Harper.

DEUTSCHMANN, P., and W. DANIELSON (1960). Diffusion of knowledge of the major news story. *Journalism Quarterly* 37: 345-355.

DOWNS, A. (1964). *Inside Bureaucracy*. Santa Monica, Calif.: Rand Corporation.

EMERY, F., and E.L. TRIST (1965). The causal texture of organizational environments. *Human Relations* 18: 21-32.

ETZIONI, A. (1961). *A Comparative Analysis of Complex Organizations*. New York: Free Press.

──── (1964). *Modern Organization*. Englewood Cliffs, N. J.: Prentice-Hall.

FARACE, R., and C. MORRIS (1969). The communication system of Justin Morrill College. Unpublished paper, Department of Communication, Michigan State University.

FARACE, R., and M. PACANOWSKY (1974). Organizational communication role, hierarchical level and relative status. Paper presented to the Academy of Management Association, Seattle, Wash.

FESTINGER, L. (1949). The analysis of sociograms using matrix algebra. *Human Relations* 2: 153-158.

FESTINGER, L., S. SCHACHTER, and K. BACK (1950). *Social Pressures in Informal Groups.* New York: Harper.

FISHER, B. A. (1974). *Small Group Decision Making: Communication and the Group Process.* New York: McGraw-Hill.

FORSYTH, E., and L. KATZ (1946). A matrix approach to the analysis of sociometric data. *Sociometry* **9**: 340–347.

GALBRAITH, J. (1973). *Designing Complex Organizations.* Reading, Mass.: Addison-Wesley.

GARDNER, J. W. (1963). *Self-Renewal: The Individual and the Innovative Society.* New York: Harper Colophon.

GIBB, C. A. (1969). Leadership. In G. Lindzey and E. Aronson (eds.), *The Handbook of Social Psychology,* Vol. II (2nd. ed.). pp. 205–282. Reading, Mass.: Addison-Wesley.

GLANZER, M., and R. GLASER (1959). Techniques for the study of group structure and behavior: I. Analysis of structure. *Psychological Bulletin* **56**: 317–332.

_____ (1961). Techniques for the study of group structure and behavior: II. Empirical studies of the effects of structure in small groups. *Psychological Bulletin* **58**: 1–27.

GOODING, J. (1972). *The Job Revolution.* New York: Walker.

GUETZKOW, H. (1965). Communication in organizations. In J. G. March (ed.), *Handbook of Organizations,* pp. 354–413. Chicago: Rand McNally.

GUETZKOW, H., and H. A. SIMON (1955). The impact of certain communication nets upon organization and performance in task-oriented groups. *Management Science* **1**: 233–250.

GUIMARAES, L. L. (1970). Network analysis: An approach to the study of communication systems. *Technical Report,* No. 2, Project of the Diffusion of Innovations in Rural Societies, Michigan State University.

GULLAHORN, J. T. (1952). Distance and friendship as factors in the gross interaction matrix. *Sociometry* **15**: 123–134.

HABERSTROH, C. J. (1965). Organization design and systems analysis. In J. G. March (ed.), *Handbook of Organizations,* pp. 1171–1211. Chicago: Rand McNally.

HAGE, G. R. (1975). *Organizational Communication and Control.* New York: Interscience-Wiley.

HARARY, F., R. Z. NORMAN, and D. CARTWRIGHT (1965). *Structural Models: An Introduction to the Theory of Directed Graphs.* New York: Wiley.

HAWES, L. C. (1972a). Can a seeker of a process methodology find happiness with a Markov model? Paper presented to the University of Minnesota Symposium on Communication Theory and Practice, Minneapolis, Minn.

_____ (1972b). The effects of interviewer style on patterns of dyadic communication. *Speech Monographs* **39**: 114–123.

HEMPHILL, J. K. (1952). Theory of leadership. Unpublished staff report, Personnel Research Board, Ohio State University.

HERZBERG, F. (1966). *Work and the Nature of Man.* New York: World.

HINRICHS, J. R. (1964). Communications activity of industrial research personnel. *Personnel Psychology* 17: 193-204.

HUNT, R. G., and C. LICHTMAN (1970). Role clarity, communication and conflict. *Management of Personnel Quarterly* 9 (3): 26-36.

JACOB, M. A. (1972). The structure and functions of internal communication in three religious communities. Unpublished doctoral dissertation, Department of Communication, Michigan State University.

JACOBSON, E. W., and S. E. SEASHORE (1951). Communication practices in complex organizations. *Journal of Social Issues* 7: 28-40. Quote reprinted by permission.

JAY, A. (1971). *Corporation Man*. New York: Random House.

JOHNSON, H. M. (1960). *Sociology: A Systematic Introduction*. New York: Harcourt, Brace.

KATZ, D., and R. L. KAHN (1966). *The Social Psychology of Organizations*. New York: Wiley.

KATZ, E., and P. LAZARSFELD (1955). *Personal Influence*. New York: Free Press.

KRIPPENDORF, K. (1970). On generating data in communication research. *Journal of Communication* 20 (3): 241-269.

LAZARSFELD, P., B. BERELSON, and E. GAUDET (1948). *The People's Choice*. New York: Columbia University Press.

LEAVITT, H. J. (1951). Some effects of certain communication patterns on group performance. *Journal of Abnormal and Social Psychology* 46: 38-50.

LIKERT, R. (1961). *New Patterns of Management*. New York: McGraw-Hill.

_____ (1967). *The Human Organization: Its Management and Value*. New York: McGraw-Hill.

LINDZEY, G., and D. BYRNE (1969). Measurement of social choice and interpersonal attractiveness. In G. Lindzey and E. Aronson (eds.), *The Handbook of Social Psychology*, Vol. II (2nd ed.). pp. 452-525. Reading, Mass.: Addison-Wesley.

LITTERER, J. A. (ed.) (1969). *Organizations: Structure and Behavior*, Vol. I (2nd ed.). New York: Wiley.

LONGABAUGH, R. (1963). A category system for coding interpersonal behavior as social exchange. *Sociometry* 26: 319-344.

LOOMIS, C. P., and J. A. BEEGLE (1950). *Rural Social Systems*. New York: Prentice-Hall.

LORRAIN, F., and H. C. WHITE (1971). Structural equivalence of individuals in social networks. *Journal of Mathematical Sociology* 1: 49-80.

LUCE, D. R., and A. D. PERRY (1949). A method of matrix analysis of group structure. *Psychometrika* 14: 95-116.

MACHLUP, F. (1962). *The Production and Distribution of Knowledge in the United States*. Princeton, N. J.: Princeton University Press.

MACDONALD, D. (1970). Communication roles and communication content in a bureaucratic organization. Unpublished doctoral dissertation, Department of Communication, Michigan State University.

MACKENZIE, R. (1972). *The Time Trap.* New York: American Management Association.

MARTIN, M. W. (1967). A new approach to the analysis of random alarm generated data. Paper presented to the Operations Research Society of America, Philadelphia.

MAYO, E. (1949). *The Social Problems of an Industrial Civilization.* London: Routledge, Kegan & Paul.

MCGREGOR, D. (1960). *The Human Side of Enterprise.* New York: McGraw-Hill.

_____ (1968). Theory X and theory Y. In D. R. Hampton, C. E. Summer, and R. A. Webber, *Organizational Behavior and the Practice of Management.* Glenview, Ill.: Scott, Foresman.

MEIER, R. L. (1962). Communications overload; proposals from the study of a university library. *Administrative Science Quarterly* 7: 521–544.

_____ (1972). Communications stress. *Annual Review of Ecology and Systematics* 3: 314–389.

MERTON, R. (1957). Patterns of influence: Local and cosmopolitan influentials. In R. Merton, *Social Theory and Social Structure.* New York: Free Press.

MILGRAM, S. (1969). The small world problem. *Psychology Today*, May, pp. 61–67.

MILLER, G. A. (1956). The magical number seven plus or minus two: Some limits on our capacity for information processing. *The Psychological Review* 63: 81–97.

MILLER, G., E. GALANTER, and K. PRIBRAM (1960). Plans and the structure of behavior. New York: Holt.

MILLER, J. G. (1960). Information input overload and psychopathology. *American Journal of Psychiatry* 116: 695–704.

_____ (1964). Psychological aspects of communication overload. In R. W. Waggoner and D. J. Carek, *International Psychiatry Clinics: Communication in Clinical Practice*, Vol. 1. Boston: Little, Brown.

_____ (1971). Living systems: The group. *Behavioral Science* 16: 277–398.

_____ (1972). Living systems: The organization. *Behavioral Science* 17: 1–182.

MITCHELL, J. C. (ed.) (1969). The concept and use of social networks. In *Social Networks in Urban Situations.* Manchester: Manchester University Press.

MONGE, P. R. (1972). The conceptualization of human communication from three system paradigms. Unpublished doctoral dissertation, Department of Communication, Michigan State University.

MORENO, J. L. (1934). *Who Shall Survive?* Washington, D. C.: Nervous and Mental Disease Monograph, No. 58.

MOUZELIS, N. P. (1967). *Organization and Bureaucracy: An Analysis of Modern Theories.* Chicago: Aldine.

NEWCOMB, T. M. (1953). An approach to the study of communicative acts. *Psychological Review* 60: 393–404.

OESER, O. A., and F. HARARY (1962). A mathematical model for structural role theory: I. *Human Relations* 15: 89–109.

_____ (1964). A mathematical model for structural role theory: II. *Human Relations* 17: 3–17.

PARSONS, T. (1951). *The Social System.* New York: Free Press.

PORAT, M. (1975). The information economy. Unpublished paper, Institute for Communication Research, Stanford, Calif.

PORTER, L. W., and K. H. ROBERTS (1972). *Communication in Organizations.* Technical Report No. 12. Irvine, Calif.: University of California.

PRINCE, T. R. (1970). *Information Systems for Management Planning and Control* (rev. ed.). Homewood, Ill.: Irwin.

PROCTOR, C. H., and C. P. LOOMIS (1951). Analysis of sociometric data. In M. Jahoda, M. Deutsch, and S. W. Cook (eds.), *Research Methods in Social Relations,* Vol. II. pp. 561-586. New York: Dryden.

RAVEN, B. H. (1965). Social influence and power. In I. D. Steiner and M. Fishbein (eds.), *Current Studies in Social Psychology.* New York: Holt.

REDDING, W. C. (1972). *Communication Within the Organization: An Interpretive Review of Theory and Research.* New York: Industrial Communication Council.

REINDL, M. (1970). Propositions on information management of innovation processes in organizations. Unpublished doctoral dissertation, Department of Communication, Michigan State University.

RICHARDS, W. D. (1971). A conceptually based method for the analysis of communication networks in large complex organizations. Paper presented to International Communication Association.

RICHARDS, W., R. FARACE, and J. A. DANOWSKI (1974). "NEGOPY" program description. Unpublished paper, Department of Communication, Michigan State University.

ROETHLISBERGER, F. J., and W. J. DICKSON (1946). *Management and the Worker.* Cambridge, Mass.: Harvard University Press.

ROGERS, E. M., and F. SHOEMAKER (1972). *The Comunication of Innovations: A Cross-Cultural Approach.* Glencoe, Ill.: Free Press.

ROGERS, L., and R. FARACE (1975). Analysis of relational communication in dyads: New measurement procedures. *Human Communication Research* 1 (3): 222-239.

RUSSELL, B. (1948). *Human Knowledge: Its Scope and Limits.* New York: Simon and Schuster.

RUSSELL, H. M. (1972). Coorientational similarity toward procedural aspects of communication: A study of communication between extension agents and their supervisors. Unpublished doctoral dissertation, Department of Communication, Michigan State University.

SCHACHTER, S. (1951). Deviation, rejection and communication. *Journal of Abnormal and Social Psychology* 46: 190-207.

SCHEFF, T. (1967). Toward a sociological model of consensus. *American Sociological Review* 32: 32-46.

SCHEIN, E. H. (1970). *Organizational Psychology,* 2nd ed. Englewood Cliffs, N.J.: Prentice-Hall.

SCHROEDER, H., M. DRIVER, and S. STRUFERT (1967). *Human Information Processing.* New York: Holt.

SCHWARTZ, D. F. (1968). Liaison-communication roles in a formal organization. *Communimetrics Report*, No. 1. Fargo: North Dakota State University.

SCOTT, W. G. (1969). Organizational theory: An overview and an appraisal. In J. A. Litterer (ed.), *Organizations: Structure and Behavior*, Vol. I. (2nd ed.). New York: Wiley.

SHANNON, C., and W. WEAVER (1949). *The Mathematical Theory of Communication.* Urbana: University of Illinois Press.

SHAW, M. E. (1964). Communication networks. In L. Berkowitz (ed.), *Advances in Experimental Social Psychology*, Vol. I, pp. 111-147. New York: Academic.

SHAW, M. E. (1971). *Group Dynamics: The Psychology of Small Group Behavior.* New York: McGraw-Hill.

SHEPERD, C.R. (1964). *Small Groups: Some Sociological Perspectives.* Scranton, Pa.: Chandler.

SHOTLAND, R. (1969). The structure of social relationships at Michigan State University: A communication study. Project Report No. 302, Educational Development Programs, Michigan State University.

SIMON, H. A. (1957). *Administrative Behavior* (2nd ed.). New York: Macmillan.

TANNENBAUM, P., and B. GREENBERG (1968). Mass communication. *Annual Review of Psychology* 19: 351-385.

TAYLOR, F. W. (1947). *Scientific Management.* New York: Harper.

TERKEL, S. (1974). *Working: People Talk about What They Do all Day and How They Feel about What They Do.* New York: Pantheon (Random House).

THAYER, L. (1968). *Communication and Communication Systems.* Homewood, Ill.: Irwin.

TOFFLER, A. (1970). *Future Shock.* New York: Random House.

TOSI, H.L., and W.C. HAMNER (1974). *Organizational Behavior and Management: A Contingency Approach.* Chicago: St. Clair Press.

TRYON, R. C., and D. E. BAILEY (1970). *Cluster Analysis.* New York: McGraw-Hill.

VALENTINE, K. B. (1972). The analysis of verbal innovation deviance in small group interaction. Paper presented to the Convention of the Speech Communication Association, Chicago.

WALTON, E. (1963). *A Magnetic Theory of Communication*, NOTS publication III. China Lake, Calif.: Naval Ordinance Test Station.

WATZLAWICK, P., J. BEAVIN, and D. JACKSON (1967). *Pragmatics of Human Communication.* New York: W. W. Norton.

WEBER, M. (1947). *The Theory of Social and Economic Organization.* Edited by T. Parsons, translated by M. Henderson and T. Parsons. New York: Free Press.

WEICK, K. (1969). *The Social Psychology of Organizing.* Reading, Mass.: Addison-Wesley. Quote from p. 33, reprinted by permission.

―――― (1970). The twigging of overload. In H. B. Pepinsky (ed.), *People and Information*, pp. 67-129. New York: Pergamon.

WEISS, R. S. (1956). *Processes of Organization*. Ann Arbor: Institute for Social Research, University of Michigan.

WEISS, R., and E. JACOBSON (1955). A method for the analysis of the structure of complex organizations. *American Sociological Review* 20: 661–668.

WICKESBERG, A. K. (1968). Communication networks in the business organization structure. *Academy of Management Journal* 11: 253–262.

ZUBEK, J. P. (ed.). (1969). *Sensory Deprivation: Fifteen Years of Research*. New York: Appleton-Century-Crofts.

Indexes

Author Index

Ackoff, R., 30, 56
Ackoff, R., and Emery, F., 30
Amend, E., 190
Amidon, E.J., and Flanders, N., 174
Amidon, E.J., and Hough, J.B., 173
Argyris, C., 85, 78

Bales, R.F., 165, 173, 174
Barnard, C.I., 56, 71, 78
Barnes, J.A., 193, 200
Barnlund, D.C., and Harland, C., 193
Barrett, J.H., 77, 78
Bavelas, A., 159
Berlo, D., 56, 59, 217
Berrien, F.K., 91
Beum, C.O., and Brundage, E.G., 196
Blake, R.R., and Mouton, J.S., 78
Borgatta, E.F., and Stolz, W., 197
Bott, E., 193
Boyd, B., and Jensen, J.M., 147

Brillouin, L., 26
Buckley, W., 24, 91
Burke, R.J., and Wilcox, D.S., 148
Burns, T., 131, 138, 209

Campbell, D.T., 116
Chaffee, S., McLeod, J., and Guerrero, J., 142, 144
Cohen, A.M., Robinson, E.L., and Edwards, J.L., 161
Coleman, J.S., 52, 196
Coleman, J.S., Katz, E., and Menzel, H., 193
Coleman, J.S., and MacRae, D. Jr., 197
Collins, B.E., and Guetzkow, H., 167
Collins, B.E., and Raven, B.H., 161, 163
Conrath, D.W., 209
Cushman, D., and Whiting, G., 134, 135

273

Danowski, J.A., 49, 202
Danowski, J.A., and Farace, R.V., 203
Davis, J.H., 161, 162
Davis, K., 210, 212, 214
Dearden, J., McFarlan, F.W., and Zani, W., 116, 124
de Chardin, P., 36
Deutschmann, P., and Danielson, W., 212
Downs, A., 50

Emery, F., 30
Emery, F., and Trist, E.L., 36, 58
Etzioni, A., 56

Farace, R.V., and Morris, C., 209, 210, 211
Farace, R.V., and Pacanowsky, M., 185, 198
Festinger, L., 196
Festinger, L., Schachter, S., and Back, K., 193
Fisher, B.A., 173, 174
Forsyth, E., and Katz, L., 196

Galbraith, J., 116
Gardner, J.W., 205
Gibb, C.A., 165, 166, 167, 168
Glanzer, M., and Glaser, R., 161, 194
Gooding, J., 101
Guetzkow, H., 50
Guetzkow, H., and Simon, H.A., 193
Guimaraes, L.L., 194, 196
Gullahorn, J.T., 107, 193

Haberstroh, C.J., 56
Hage, G.R., 69
Harary, F., Norman, R.Z., and Cartwright, D., 197, 202
Hawes, L.C., 174

Hemphill, J.K., 165
Herzberg, F., 78, 85
Hinrichs, J.R., 209
Hunt, R.G., and Lichtman, C., 149

Jacob, M.A., 56, 57, 185
Jacobson, E.W., and Seashore, S.E., 188, 197, 211
Jay, A., 54, 114
Johnson, H.M., 56

Katz, D., and Kahn, R.L., 50, 55, 56
Katz, E., and Lazarsfeld, P., 188
Krippendorf, K., 52

Lazarsfeld, P., Berelson, B., and Gaudet, E., 212
Leavitt, H.J., 159
Likert, R., 56, 78, 87, 88, 90, 91, 92, 188
Lindzey, G., and Byrne, D., 193
Litterer, J.A., 77
Longabaugh, R., 173
Loomis, C.P., and Beegle, J.A., 193
Lorrain, F., and White, H.C., 196
Luce, D.R., and Perry, A.D., 196

Machlup, F., 75
MacDonald, D., 190, 211
MacKenzie, R., 107
Martin, M.W., 209
Mayo, E., 78, 81, 82
McGregor, D., 72, 78, 85, 86, 91
Meier, R.L., 115, 116
Merton, R., 188
Milgram, S., 211
Miller, G.A., 104
Miller, J.G., 104, 107, 110, 116
Miller, G., Galanter, E., and Pribram, K., 107
Mitchell, J.C., 193, 194
Monge, P.R., 61, 93
Moreno, J.L., 194

Author Index

Mouzelis, N.P., 77

Newcomb, T.M., 142

Oeser, O.A., and Harary, F., 158

Parsons, T., 56
Porat, M., 74, 75
Porter, L.W., and Roberts, K.H., 50
Prince, T.R., 116, 124
Procter, C.H., and Loomis, C.P., 194, 195

Raven, B.H., 163
Redding, W.C., 50, 56, 224
Reindl, M., 39
Richards, W., 185
Roethlisberger, F.J., and Dickson, W.J., 78, 81, 82, 210
Rogers, E.M., and Shoemaker, F., 59, 107, 212
Rogers, L.E., and Farace, R., 137
Russell, B., 158
Russell, H.M., 149, 151

Schachter, S., 169
Scheff, T., 145
Schein, E.H., 81
Schroeder, H., Driver, M., and Strufert, S., 107

Schwartz, D.F., 188, 211
Shannon, C., and Weaver, W., 24
Shaw, M.E., 157, 159, 161, 170
Sheperd, C.R., 168, 169, 170
Shotland, R., 211
Simon, H.A., 78, 83, 84, 90, 92

Tannenbaum, P., and Greenberg, B.S., 212
Taylor, F.W., 78
Terkel, S., 110
Thayer, L., 56
Toffler, A., 5, 93, 205
Tosi, H.L., and Hamner, W.C., 92
Tryon, R.C., and Bailey, D.E., 197

Valentine, 174

Walton, E., 188
Watzlawick, P., Beavin, J., and Jackson, D., 53, 135
Weber, M., 78, 79, 80, 82, 83, 84, 90, 91, 92
Weick, K., 19, 36, 52, 116, 164, 174
Weiss, R.S., 197
Weiss, R., and Jacobson, E., 197
Wickesberg, A.K., 56

Zubek, J.P., 108

Subject Index

Communication. *See also* Function; Structure
  concept of, 41–45
  definition of, 26
  downward, 149, 179. *See also* Communication rules
  effective, 206, 251
  environmental, 30–31, 33–35
  evaluation of, 206, 251
  horizontal, 79
  instructional, 31, 33–35
  meaning, 133
  motivational, 30–33
  role of, 5, 71
  upward, 149, 179. *See also* Communication rules
Communication links. *See also* Network roles
  group-bridge linkage, 240, 242–243
  group-group linkage, 240, 242–243
  group-liaison linkage, 240, 242–243
  individual linkage, 241
  reciprocity, 181–182, 185, 240–241, 243
  strength, 181–182
  symmetry, 181–182, 227
Communication load, 51, 97–127, 156. *See also* Overload; Underload
  definition of, 110, 207
  determinates of, 105–108
  examples of, 97–102
  measurement of, 103–105
Communication management, 249–259
  examples of, 253–258
  manager's role, 252–253
Communication problems, accuracy. *See* Coorientation model
  agreement. *See* Coorientation model
  attentiveness, 12
  breakdown, 9, 178

277

distortion, 16, 42
examples of, 9
information distribution, 28
listening, 12
misconception of, 7
networks, 12
noise, 42
sharing of, 249-251
techniques for minimization of, 42
Communication processing, amount of, 75-76
capabilities, 115-116
channel capacity for, 104-105
chunking, 120
definition of, 4-5
diffusion of. See Message and Network
gathering of information, 4
information storage, 4, 40-41
retrieval, 40
skills, 6
statistics on, 75
system levels, 113-115
Communication rules, 127-153
accuracy, 141-152, 221-222. See also Coorientation model
acquisition of, 133
agreement, 141-152, 222-223. See also Coorientation model
amount of communication, 140
content vs. procedural, 134-135
definition of, 11, 131-132
dyadic interaction, 54, 156, 214-217
examples of, 129-132
formal vs. informal, 130, 132
initiation of communication, 138-139
interruption, 139
openness, 148
questionnaire, 217-221
satisfaction with, 140-141

supervisor-subordinate, 150, 214-223
termination of communication, 140
topic of communication, 139
Coorientation model. See also Communication rules
accuracy, 11, 54, 141-152, 221-222
agreement, 11, 54, 141-152, 221-223
agreement vs. accuracy, 142-144
agreement vs. understanding, 142
application of, 150-153
dyad, 141-142
explanation of, 142
levels within, 144-147

Diffusion of messages/information. See Message and network
Dyad, authority relationships, 28
communication properties of, 128-129
communication rules, 214-217
coorientation, 141-142. See also Coorientation model
formation of, 127-128
fundamental unit, 127
overlapping, 128
satisfaction, 217-221
Function, innovation, 6, 58-59, 66-68, 77, 80, 83, 85, 88, 90-91, 208
maintenance, 55, 58-59, 67-68, 77, 80, 83, 85, 88, 90-91, 208
production, 55, 58-59, 62, 64, 76, 80, 83, 85, 88, 90-91, 208
small groups, 156
Hawthorne Studies, 81, 210
Information, absolute, 26-28, 32-34
communication, 25
distributed, 26-28, 32-34
matter/energy, 21-22, 39
pattern, 22-23

randomness, 23
theory, 103
Information load. *See*
    Communication load
Information processing. *See*
    Communication processing
Leadership, definitions of, 165
    interaction theory, 166–168
Message, content vs. control, 53
    diffusion of, 4, 41, 65, 208–209, 212–214
    directionality of flow, 75–76
    distortion of, 16, 42
    flow, 49, 207–208
    initiation of, 75–76
    storing of, 4
    timeliness of receipt, 65

Network, anchorage, 194
    centrality, 160–161, 194, 236–238
    channel, 193
    choice status, 194
    communication flow, 49, 207–208
    connectedness, 194, 238, 240–241, 243
    content of, 182
    definition of, 5, 158, 178–180
    density, 194
    diffusion techniques, 208–214
    dominance, 239
    flexibility, 75–76
    formal vs. informal, 179. *See also*
        Communication rules
    individual connectedness, 240–241
    links. *See* Communication links
    macro-network, 158, 177–203
    micro-network, 158–162
    mode of communication in, 182–183
    monitoring techniques, 208–214
    nervous system analogy, 178
    organization functions, 97

problems, 5–6
range, 194
reachability, 194
relative status, 198–199
use of, 12
Network analysis, application of, 245–246
    criteria for, 180
    descriptors, 197–203
    example of, 227–245
    function of, 229
    historical basis of, 192–193
    individual interaction, 194
    links. *See* Communication links
    methodologies, 194–197
    network comparison, advantages, 234–236
        disadvantages, 242–245
        examples of, 234–236
Network roles, bridge, 186, 192, 229, 233, 235, 236, 238–240, 243
    determination of, 184–185. *See also*
        Network analysis
    group composition criteria, 185–186
    group members, 157–158, 185–186, 192, 228–229, 231–233, 239–240, 243
    isolates, 185–186, 190, 192, 229, 234, 240, 243
    liaison, 8, 186–192, 229–230, 232, 234–236, 238–240, 243
    linking pin, 88, 188
    opinion leaders, 188
Organization, central processes in, 18
    coordination, 18
    definition of, 15–16
    dynamic aspect of, 20
    organizing vs. organization, 19–20
    size, 52. *See also* Systems
    view of, 8
Organizational environment,

climate, 224
disturbed-reactive, 37
enacted, 36, 38
placid-clustered, 37-38
placid-randomized, 36
space, 35-38
structural-functional framework, 62-68
turbulent, 37-38
uncertainty, 23, 74, 103
view of, 66
Organizational models,
accommodation, 78, 90-91
McGregor's theory Y, 72-73, 85-86, 91
contingency, 78, 90-91
systems model, 90-93
exchange, 78, 90-91
Harvard Human Relations, 81-82, 90
Simon's Administrative Behavior, 83-84, 90, 92
Weker's Bureaucratic, 79-80, 90
goals integration, 77
role of communication in, 72-73
socialization, 78, 90-91
Likert's System IV, 87-88, 91
Organize, definition of, 3
Overload, consequences of, 108-112
definition of, 10, 21, 101
example of, 97-98, 101-102
strategies for coping with, 115-124

Power, communication, 164
definition of, 162-163
Raven classification, 163

Relational control, definition of, 53-54, 135-136
example of, 137-138

measurement of, 136-137
Research techniques. *See also* Network analysis
cross-sectional interview, 209-213
duty study, 208-210
observer technique, 208, 210, 213
"small-world" approach, 209, 211-213

Small groups, 155-175
existence of, 168-172
function of, 156, 175
generalizability of research, 161-162
interaction, 156, 172-175
interaction theory, 166-168
structure of, 156-158, 168, 175
Structural-functionalism, communication, 75
communication load, 105-106
framework, 8
functional analysis example, 62-68, 108
groups, 156, 175
perspective, 65-66, 93, 172
procedures for analysis, 61
Structure. *See also* Organizational models
communication concepts, 75-76
communication processing, 75-76
definition of, 207
directionality of message flow, 75-76
message initiation, 75-76
network, 60-62, 75-76
Systems. *See also* Function; Structure
boundary, 17-18, 48-49
closed, 48
components, 48
criticism of research on, 51
definition of, 48

input, 16, 18, 98–99, 110
interdependence, 16–17, 49, 51, 74, 150
levels, 50, 52, 54, 55, 77
    open, 48–49
    output, 16, 18, 64, 110
    size, 16, 17, 49, 50–55, 77
    subsystems, 49–50
    suprasystems, 49–50
throughput, 16, 18

Underload, consequences of, 108–111
    definition of, 21, 101
    example of, 99, 101–102